QUEEN VICTORIA'S DESCENDANTS

by Marlene A. Eilers

Baltimore
GENEALOGICAL PUBLISHING CO., INC.
1987

Published by Genealogical Publishing Co., Inc.
1001 N. Calvert St., Baltimore, MD 21202
In cooperation with Atlantic International Publications
Library of Congress Catalogue Card Number 87-81272
International Standard Book Number 0-8063-1202-5
Made in the United States of America

Edited, Layout, and Jacket Design
By Paul Nikolaos

DEDICATION

This book is dedicated to my parents, Gertrude Last and Thomas Eilers, but especially for my mother because she provided the inspiration and the interest in things royal, and because she didn't live to see the book's completion.

ABBREVIATIONS

*	Indicates a descendant of Queen Victoria when the descendant marries another descendant
Div.	Divorced
HH	His or Her Highness
H Ill H	His or Her Illustrious Highness
HIH	His or Her Imperial Highness
HI & RH	His or Her Imperial and Royal Highness
HIM	His or Her Imperial Majesty
Hon.	The Honourable
HRH	His or Her Royal Highness
HSH	His or Her Serene Highness

TABLE OF CONTENTS

GENEALOGY

The Descendants of:

ORDER OF SUCCESSION TO THE BRITISH THRONE

1. HRH The Prince of Wales
2. HRH Prince William of Wales
3. HRH Prince Henry of Wales
4. HRH The Duke of York
5. HRH The Prince Edward
6. HRH The Princess Royal
7. Peter Phillips
8. Zara Phillips
9. HRH The Princess Margaret, Countess of Snowdon
10. Viscount Linley
11. Lady Sarah Armstrong-Jones
12. HRH The Duke of Gloucester
13. The Earl of Ulster
14. Lady Davina Windsor
15. Lady Rose Windsor
16. HRH The Duke of Kent
17. The Earl of St. Andrews[1]
18. Lord Nicholas Windsor
19. Lady Helen Windsor
20. Lord Frederick Windsor[2]
21. Lady Gabriella Windsor
22. HRH Princess Alexandra, the Hon. Mrs. Angus Ogilvy
23. James Ogilvy
24. Marina Ogilvy
25. The Earl of Harewood[3]
26. Viscount Lascelles[4]
27. Hon. Alexander Lascelles
28. Hon. Edward Lascelles
29. Hon. James Lascelles[5]
30. Rowan Lascelles
31. Tewit Lascelles
32. Sophie Lascelles
33. Hon. Jeremy Lascelles
34. Thomas Lascelles
35. Ellen Lascelles
36. Amy Lascelles
37. Hon. Gerald Lascelles[6]
38. Henry Lascelles
39. The Duke of Fife
40. The Earl of Macduff
41. Lady Alexandra Carnegie
42. King Olav V of Norway
43. HRH Crown Prince Harald of Norway
44. HRH Prince Haakon Magnus of Norway
45. HRH Princess Märtha Louise of Norway
46. Princess Ragnhild of Norway, Mrs. Lorentzen
47. Olav Lorentzen[7]
48. Ragnhild Lorentzen
49. Princess Astrid, Mrs. Ferner
50. Alexander Ferner
51. Carl Christian Ferner
52. Cathrine Ferner
53. Benedikte Ferner
54. Elisabeth Ferner
55. HRH Princess Margarita of Roumania[8]
56. HRH Princess Helen of Roumania, Mrs. Medford Mills
57. Nicholas Medforth-Mills
58. HRH Princess Irina of Roumania, Mrs. Krueger
59. Michael Krueger
60. Angelica Krueger

1. In June 1987, the Duke and Duchess of Kent announced the engagement of their elder son, the Earl of St. Andrews, to Miss Sylvana Tomaselli. Because Miss Tomaselli is a Roman Catholic, Lord St. Andrews will automatically be excluded from the succession when they marry.
2. Lord Frederick and Lady Gabriella Windsor are the children of HRH Prince and Princess Michael of Kent. Prince Michael is no longer in succession because of his marriage to a Roman Catholic. The two children were baptised Anglicans.
3. The Earl of Harewood's fourth son, the Hon. Mark Lascelles, is not listed because he was born prior to his parents' marriage.
4. Lord Lascelles' eldest son, Hon. Benjamin Lascelles, and daughter, Hon. Emily Lascelles, are not listed because they were born prior to their parents' marriage.
5. James Lascelles' younger daughter, Tanit, is not listed because she was born prior to her parents' marriage.
6. Gerald Lascelles' younger son, Martin, is not listed because he was born prior to his parents' marriage.
7. Olav is the son of Haakon Lorentzen, son of Princess Ragnhild. Haakon is married to a Roman Catholic and is no longer listed in the Succession. Olav was christened Luthern. Princess Ragnhild's elder duaghter, Ingeborg, also is no longer listed because she is married to a Catholic.
8. Princess Margarita of Roumania is the eldest of five daughters of King Michael of Roumania. Michael no longer is listed in the Succession because of his marriage to a Roman Catholic. His five daughters, however, are Roumanian Orthodox.

PREFACE

Why another Royal genealogy? Do royal enthusiasts or professional genealogists, historians, and librarians really need another one? There are a number of excellent royal genealogies including *Burke's Royal Families of the World*, Arthur Addington's *The Royal House of Stuart*, and the *Genealogische Handbuch des Adels* series, to say nothing of the forerunner of all royal genealogies, the *Almanach de Gotha*, which was regularly thumbed by royal parents seeking the 'right' royal bride or groom for their sons and daughters, until it ceased publication in 1944.

My goal in compiling *Queen Victoria's Descendants* was to produce a genealogy that is usable for both the amateur and professional genealogist, and to provide a totally accurate record. Where data was unavailable or questionable, that fact is made clear.

When I first began preparing my list of Victoria's descendants (which now number more than 650), I found many discrepancies and omissions among the various published genealogies as to dates of birth, places of death, and even parents' names.

Queen Victoria's Descendants has taken more than ten years of preparation - sending out letters and questionnaires to descendants, secretaries and archivists, as well as research in newspaper libraries around the world. I also had the benefit of working as a librarian in The Associated Press's News Library where I was able to verify dates by looking through AP's own index. Wire services provide same day coverage of an event, unlike newspapers, which carry the story the morning after.

The Court Circular in *The Times* (London) also provided confirmation of dates (although on one occasion the Court Circular was wrong!) Most royal genealogies list October 12, 1894 as the date of birth for Princess Elisabeth of Roumania. The date is correct. But Elisabeth's mother, Queen Marie, in her memoirs, gives October 11th as the date of birth. This date is corroborated by the Court Circular in *The Times* for October 12: "Princess Ferdinand of Roumania was safely delivered yesterday of a daughter at Sinaia." According to Elisabeth's former sister-in-law, Lady Katherine Brandram, Elisabeth was born on the 12th; the error in *The Times* was attributed to the fact that the telegram - sent to London by the Roumanian court- had arrived on the 12th, which lead to the mistake that the baby had been born the day before. The mistake in Queen Marie's autobiography can be attributed to a not-so-careful editor or typist.

A mistake in the Court Circular is rare; generally, newspapers provide genealogists with one of the best sources for genealogical information. Royal letters are an even better source; and Victoria's letters are exceptional in that respect. Her missives to family and friends fill many volumes.

My interest in Queen Victoria and her descendants began when I was 12 and I read Elizabeth Longford's *Queen Victoria: Born to Succeed*. I was intrigued by the genealogical tables at the end of the book. I also was impressed by this woman who reigned over an age of industrial and imperial expansion, but who was also Prince Albert's devoted and adoring wife.

Queen Victoria's Descendants is not merely a compilation of names, dates and places of birth, death and marriage. The data is arranged in a usable format - children are listed in order of birth, and not as is often in case of royal genealogies, males first.

Because of intermarriage, more than 120 persons are descended more than once from Victoria. With the exception of Prince Philip of Greece and Denmark (now the Duke of Edinburgh), these descendants are listed under their *first* male line of descent, e.g., the descendants of Prince Henry of Prussia and Princess Irene of Hesse and By Rhine - the first of Victoria's grandchildren to marry each other - will be found in Chapter II, the line of Prince Henry of Prussia, rather than Chapter V, because the primary line of descent is through the male line. Multiple entries are cross-referenced.

Titles have been anglicized, e.g. Baron rather than Freiherr, Prince instead of Fürst or Prinz; but names are not, except for Greek and Russian, where the different alphabets make it impractical to use any but the English versions.

I also use the traditional titles for members of German royal and noble families, even though present German law recognizes titles as only a part of the surname. For example, the present head of the Prussian Royal Family is legally named Louis Ferdinand Prinz von Preussen. In this genealogy, I use the royal style of HI & RH Prince Louis Ferdinand of Prussia.

Several members of the Prussian Royal Family have made what is commonly known as morganatic or unequal marriages (in nicht hausgesetzmässinger Ehe.) The children of these marriages are legally surnamed Prinz or Prinzessin von Preussen. Within the family, however, these children are denied the qualification of Royal Highness. Before 1918 (when the German republic was established), morganatic wives would have been given a title of lesser rank, and their children would have taken their titles and rank from their mother, not their father.

Therefore, the answer to the question of whether or not another royal genealogy is needed is 'yes' and 'no'. There is no complete and accurate current genealogy dedicated exclusively to the descendants of Queen Victoria. *Just* another Royal genealogy may not be needed. A current, accurate genealogy is needed, and will be a valuable tool for the historian, professional and amateur genealogists, and royalty watchers alike.

QUEEN VICTORIA
(Author's collection.)

CHAPTER I

QUEEN VICTORIA

The Duchess of Kent, objecting to the improprieties at the British court, kept the young Victoria at home, and discouraged her disreputable uncles and aunts from paying visits to Kensington Palace. On the other hand, the young princess was constantly encouraged to regard her Coburg relatives as living on a level altogether superior to that occupied by the English side of her family.

From 'dearest uncle Leopold' enthroned on the apex of the moral pyramid, down to 'poor Aunt Julie,' the Coburgs were viewed through rose-tinted glasses. The fact that her Coburg relatives lived at a distance, and were therefore largely unseen, merely added to their allure, while her English relatives were viewed as an ever-present menace. After eighteen years of her mother's partisan propaganda, it is not surprising that on her accession to the throne, Victoria knew little that was good of the British Royal Family, and nothing that was bad of the Coburgs.

It hardly mattered that for every dissolute Duke Ernest of Cumberland there was an equally dissolute Duke Ernst of Coburg; that if Princess Sophia of England had been wayward in her youth, Princess Julie of Coburg, if rumor is to be believed, remained wayward until late in life; if King George IV had taken mistresses, King Leopold I of the Belgians saw no reason why he too should not enjoy similar regal privileges: in short, for every libertine at the court of St. James, there was a counterpart at the Coburg court.

The pattern formed during her childhood was to remain with her throughout life, although she later discovered that her family cupboard also contained an unexpected number of Coburg skeletons. Nevertheless, her Continental relatives, however remote genealogically or geographically, occupied positions of special importance in her eyes, and this affected both her family and political decisions. As she grew older, she found herself, by no means unwillingly, involved not only in the lives of her uncles and aunts and cousins, but also with those of her nephews and nieces and, after the establishment of her own line, with those of her children, grandchildren and great-grandchildren.

'You don't tell me enough about the people you see,' she admonished to her oldest daughter in a letter in 1858. 'You had to dinner the other day . . . Countess Blankensee who is a very old friend of mine and whom I knew so well as a child; she was Aunt Feodore's bridesmaid [Victoria's half-sister] and a great friend of

1

dear Papa's mother. I am sure she talked to you about me . . . and say everything kind to her from me, and tell her, I hope to see her some day again.'

The obscure countess merited such attention because she was a cousin of King William IV's widow, Queen Adelaide.

The role of Queen Victoria as a mother is an aspect of her life to which biographers have given a great deal of attention. Her role as a grandmother and progenitor of an expanding web of royal dynasties has, however, been little explored, but is one to which she herself devoted considerable time and energy. It is difficult to say which interested her most: the proliferating family connections, or the use of these relationships to promote her foreign policy. Her own unhappy childhood, as well as her far-flung family, were a strong influence on Victoria as Queen.

It must not, however, be assumed that membership in the family ensured immunity from criticism. Another relative was Prince Ferdinand of Saxe-Coburg-Kohary, the son of her cousin Augustus and Princess Clementine of Orléans.

His election to the Bulgarian throne in 1887 provoked Queen Victoria to an epistolary broadside that a mortified ex-Tsar lived long enough to see published. 'He is totally unfit, delicate and effeminate,' Queen Victoria wrote.

Although she had absorbed eighteen years of Coburg influence, she nonetheless had her father's hot Hanoverian blood coursing through her veins. By 1839, there appeared a distinct possibility that England was to be ruled by a passionate and headstrong queen, every bit a fitting successor to her libertine uncles. During the first two years of her reign she more than once displayed sharp outbursts of temper like those of her father; she acquired a partiality for frivolous conversation; she danced the night away, climbing in the early hours of the morning to the roof of Buckingham Palace to watch the sun rise over London; once, in a fit of jealousy she had a sharp exchange of words with her cousin, Princess Augusta of Cambridge, over the handsome Tsarevitch Alexander.

Troubles mounted rapidly. In a short time her early popularity plummeted. Her inexperience, coupled with an over-eager willingness to listen to malicious gossip, led her into the Flora Hastings affair. As a result her name was dragged through the gutter by the press, and she was hissed at Ascot by no less a personage than the Duchess of Montrose. In London, the mob contemptuously called "Mrs. Melbourne" as her carriage passed, alluding to her close friendship with the Prime Minister. At this point she again met her cousin Prince Albert of Saxe-Coburg and Gotha. 'It was with some emotion that I beheld Albert,' she wrote in her journal that evening. Characteristically, she proposed, and the Victorian legend was born.

Queen Victoria had narrowly escaped disaster. Just as her childhood experiences were significant in shaping her attitude toward her family, her marriage to Prince Albert became equally important.

THE PRINCE CONSORT
(Author's collection)

She firmly believed it had saved her from disaster, and she never ceased to acknowledge a debt she thought she owed him. After all, it was an age of religious fervor, of the salvation of souls and missionary zeal. It is, therefore, appropriate to re-emphasize Prince Albert's importance in this story.

His marriage to Victoria had been envisioned before either of them reached their first birthday. In later life, Victoria liked to refer to herself rather dramatically as a 'fatherless child,' and in truth she was only exaggerating slightly. The Duke of Kent's death had left a void which she was perpetually attempting to fill: witness uncle Leopold, Lord Melbourne, John Brown, Prince Henry of Battenberg, and the Munshi - all male supports on whom the Queen-Empress of the British Isles and Empire leaned at various times.

Albert's place, of course, was at the apex of this edifice of father substitutes. Unfortunately for him, he was also cast in the role of father of their nine children, husband, secretary and political adviser. He endured all roles bravely for twenty years, but a constitution as basically weak as his was ill-suited to withstand such relentless demands and he succumbed at the early age of forty-two.

Like Victoria, Albert's childhood had been disrupted by marital strife. In his case by the sudden disappearance of his mother when he was six. He was to learn later that her unexpected departure had been due to scandal, adultery and divorce. This loss turned a sensitive, often tearful child, into a young man noted for being singularly immune to feminine attraction. He became a cold, calculating, old-before-his-time youth who knew nothing of ardor or temptation. He was dedicated to work, learning and self-restraint.

Albert's letters to his elder brother warning him of the dangers of riotous living are models of their kind. It is ironic that the rakish Ernst survived his moralistic brother by more than thirty years.

Although both Albert and Victoria had surviving parents, neither was of much comfort. His elder brother declared 'a more beautiful bond between a father and his sons it would be hard to find,' but his father's character left little to commend him and almost everything to be desired. When their father died in 1844, Albert and his brother had their mother brought back to Coburg to rest in the same mausoleum.

His latest biographer notes that one who knew him well subsequently wrote that the presence of evil 'depressed him, grieved him, horrified him. His tolerance allowed him to make excuses for the vices of individual man; but the evil itself he hated.'

Victoria's relations with her mother worsened with each year. Whether or not the young princess ever in fact witnessed some impropriety between the Duchess of Kent and Sir John Conroy is not certain: what is undeniable is the extent to which the young Queen distanced herself, politely but very firmly, from her mother.

Arranged and planned though their marriage was, for both Albert and Victoria it filled an emptiness they had felt since childhood. Above all, it gave them a feeling of 'belonging.' Marriage was more important for Victoria, whose temperament was more passionate and visible, but we must not suppose that Albert's feelings were any less strongly engaged, Though not demonstrative by nature, the young prince found in marriage a fulfillment that was both domestic and political. Biographers have long puzzled over the true nature of this marriage and almost always conclude that Victoria's commitment was far deeper than her husband's. The truth is probably that it was a perfect match, in which both partners complemented and enriched one another.

Her many critics have accused Victoria of being a dictatorial matchmaker, pairing off royalties regardless of suitability or sentiment. In fact, she realized that for royalty, failure to choose the right partner could be disastrous. Appearance, intelligence and background were all important. Family connections assumed magnified proportions, delicate enquiries had to be made into the health of the prospective partner; religion often precluded an otherwise perfectly suitable candidate; politics frequently intruded to make the whole business a royal nightmare. In the case of her three eldest children, most of the groundwork was done by the Prince Consort before his death; the remaining six marriages were her own handiwork.

The protracted negotiations (lasting over ten years) which preceded her second son's marriage demonstrate the lengths to which Victoria was prepared to go to obtain whom she considered the right partner for her children. Describing a prospective bride, Princess Marie of Saxe-Altenburg, she wrote, 'I have taken all the means to ascertain all about her health, and am anxiously awaiting the results. Affie says only one tooth is not good and she has not large feet and hands.' If at times the Queen's attitude seems impersonal and the atmosphere like that of a cattle auction, it simply serves to illustrate the importance she attached to the subject.

By the time her granddaughters were of marriageable age, Queen Victoria was the most experienced marriage negotiator in Europe. She was in the unique position of being both Queen Regnant and Empress, as well as head of her family. Moreover, she was a sovereign of over forty years' standing. Unrivaled by any other royal matriarch, she was perfectly placed to deal with all rivals, particularly those who might try to be 'difficult.'

When Prince Alfred's engagement to Tsar Alexander II's only daughter, Marie, was to be announced, the Tsarina proposed, through the Queen's daughter, Alice, a meeting with the Queen in Cologne. This had the effect of driving the Queen into a frenzy. Instead of speeding her august body in the direction of the Rhine, she fired off a warning letter to the luckless Alice. 'You have *entirely* taken the Russian side, and I do *not* think, dear child, that *you* should tell *me* who have been nearly *twenty years longer* on the throne than the Russian Emperor and am the doyenne of sovereigns and am a *reigning* sovereign which the Empress is *not* . . . *what I ought to do.* I think I know *that.* The proposal received for me to be at Cologne . . . tomorrow was one of the coolest things I ever heard.'

The Tsarina (a Hessian princess by birth), a comparative novice in these matters, cannot have known that the British Queen had penned a similar letter sixteen years before when it was suggested that her oldest daughter's wedding should take place in Berlin. 'The Queen would never consent to it. . . . Whatever the usual practices of Prussian princes it is not every day that one marries the eldest daughter of the Queen of England. The question, therefore, must be considered settled and closed.' Needless to say, the wedding took place in London.

5

If there is an appropriate monument to Queen Victoria, it must be both the failures and the successes of the marriages she arranged, and the descendants who survive her. Today, her descendants either reign or are pretenders to the thrones of Denmark, Norway, Sweden, Spain, Germany, Russia, Roumania, Greece, Yugoslavia and, of course, Great Britain.

CHAPTER II

PRINCESS VICTORIA

By 1914, Queen Victoria's descendants sat on the thrones of Britain, Germany, Spain, Russia, Norway, Greece, Roumania, Hesse and By Rhine, Saxe-Meiningen and Saxe-Coburg, either as sovereigns or their consorts. This year represented the climax of a journey which began in 1858, when her eldest daughter, Princess Victoria Mary Adelaide Louisa ("Vicky"), traveled with her new husband Prince Friedrich Wilhelm Nikolaus Karl of Prussia ("Fritz") to begin her married life in Germany. The channel crossing had been stormy, the train journey across the North German plain freezing, and the reception in Berlin icy. All proved symbolic, not only of Vicky's life in Germany, but for those of her descendants as well.

Eight children – the future Kaiser Wilhelm II, Charlotte, Henry, Waldemar, Victoria, Sigismund, Sophie, and Margarete – were born between 1859 and 1872.

Highly intelligent and well-educated, Vicky was intended by her father (the marriage of Vicky to Prince Friedrich had long been planned by the Prince Consort) to carry the seed of liberalism to the Continent to fulfill his vision of a Europe converted to constitutional monarchy, led by a united and liberal Germany with Prussia at the helm. It was not meant to be. Kaiser Wilhelm I lived for thirty more years, to within a fortnight of his ninety-first birthday. Under his and Bismarck's rule, Germany took a different path, and Vicky spent thirty years waiting in vain for her husband to ascend the throne. When he finally became Kaiser, as Friedrich III, he was already mortally ill from cancer, and after only 98 days as Kaiser, Friedrich followed his father to the grave. He was succeeded by their oldest son, Wilhelm II, who bestrode the European stage for the next thirty years, creating dislike and mistrust for himself and Germany in every quarter.

From his early youth, the future Kaiser Wilhelm II had grown apart from his parents. The circumstances of his difficult birth and withered left arm undoubtedly had their effect, but his basic nature was more in keeping with that of his grandfather and of Bismarck than with his 'liberal' parents. Wilhelm deeply loved his grandmother, Queen Victoria, but he developed a strong aversion to his Uncle Bertie. This family reift, along with his unpleasant nature, combined with the rivalry already existing between Germany and England, provided the fuel for eventual trouble. There is little doubt

7

PRINCESS VICTORIA and CROWN PRINCE FRIEDRICH
(Preussichen Königshauses, Haus Archiv.)

KAISER WILHELM II
(Preussichen Könighauses, Haus Archiv.)

that Kaiser Wilhelm allowed his pride and dislike of King Edward to lead him and Germany to the brink of war, from which he did not have the skill or ability to withdraw, but as soon as war came, little was heard of the Supreme War Lord. Events passed beyond Wilhelm's control. His last visit to Britain was in 1913 to attend the unveiling of the memorial to his grandmother outside Buckingham Palace.

Exiled in Holland after Germany's defeat, the Kaiser spent the rest of his life sawing wood and writing his memoirs, leading a life not unlike that of a country gentleman. The breach between the Prussian and British Royal Families was complete. Soon after the Armistice in 1918, King George V's son, Prince Albert, serving with the Royal Air Force in Germany, met the Kaiser's sister, Princess Victoria, who expressed the hope that the families could still be friends. King George confirmed his son's answer that it would not be possible for a great many years, noting, 'the sooner she knows the real feeling of bitterness which exists here against her country the better.'

The silence was not broken until January 27, 1939, when telegrams of congratulations were received by the Kaiser from King George VI and Queen Elizabeth on the occasion of his 80th birthday. Three months earlier, after the Munich crisis, Wilhelm had written to Queen Mary giving thanks that Europe had been spared from a most fearful catastrophe.

Two of his grandsons, however, had established warm bonds with the British Royal Family. Prince Ernst August of Hanover and Prince Friedrich of Prussia both walked in George V's funeral procession and attended the 1937 coronation. Ernst August was a favorite of Queen Mary who was a godmother to his first child. Friedrich of Prussia became a great friend of the late Duke and Duchess of Kent, and Princess Marina was godmother to his daughter, Victoria.

By a curious twist of fate, in 1940, as the Germans invaded Holland, the ex-Kaiser was offered refuge in England at Churchill's behest, 'with consideration and dignity,' but the offer was declined. 'Old bones,' Wilhelm said, 'cannot be transplanted.' The Jewish persecutions in 1938 made Wilhelm declare, 'I am ashamed to be a German,' and when he died in 1941, although the Nazis offered a state funeral in Berlin, he was buried at Doorn at his request.

Crown Prince Wilhelm, Kaiser Wilhelm's eldest son, was married to Princess Cecilie of Mecklenburg-Schwerin, and was the father of four sons and two daughters. Even so, looking more like Frederick the Great as each year passed, he spent the best part of his life in pursuit of women.

CROWN PRINCE WILHELM of GERMANY
(Author's collection.)

The christening of Princess Felicitas of Prussia, 1934 Front row, left to right: Crown Princess Cecilie of Prussia; Princess Dorothea of Prussia who is holding her daughter, Princess Felicitas; Crown Prince Wilhelm. Behind Princess Dorothea is Prince Wilhelm of Prussia, Princess Felicitas's father. (HRH Princess Felicitas, Frau von Nostitz-Wallwitz.)

Although the Crown Prince had commanded the 5th Army and counseled peace at the Battle of the Marne, his character and misspent life did not help the cause of restoration, and in December 1918, he renounced his rights to the throne. In 1931, there was a move that he should stand for the presidency in opposition to Hindenburg, but the Kaiser forbade it. In the following year, a financial agreement signed with Göring ensured the dynasty's abstention from politics.

German statesman Gustav Stresemann believed that, 'the world [has] received a distorted picture' of Crown Prince Wilhelm.

Prince Wilhelm, Crown Prince Wilhelm's eldest son, fell in love with Dorothea von Salviati while studying in Bonn. The Crown Prince welcomed the match but the Kaiser was implacably opposed to an unequal marriage, and Prince Wilhelm had to give up his rights in the line of succession when he married.

In the early months of World War II, fifteen princes of the House of Hohenzollern were at the front. Prince Wilhelm was severely injured in fighting at Valenciennes, and three days later died in an army hospital, leaving a widow and two young daughters, Felicitas and Christa, the younger of whom is now a noted Munich art dealer.

Prince Louis Ferdinand, Crown Prince Wilhelm's second son, became second in the line of succession. In 1929, he also risked losing his place in the line of succession to the German throne. While working at the Ford factory in Detroit he met and fell in love with the French film actress Lili Damita, who later married Errol Flynn. The romance attracted much publicity, but the combined efforts of his grandfather and Henry Ford saw that he was packed off to Buenos Aires. In 1938, he married his cousin, Princess Kira of Russia, a match that in Imperial days would have been considered brilliant, but which in 1938, despite a brave display of pomp, had an air of unreality.

Kira, whose father, Grand Duke Kirill, had proclaimed himself Tsar-in-exile, was realistic in her attitude toward life. 'The experience of our family has given me a great human understanding,' she said in an interview just before the wedding. 'I am more interested in people than I am in their calling or station in life. It isn't the social calendar that interests me, but the intrinsic worth of people.'

Louis Ferdinand is an intelligent pragmatist and in the 1930s made several visits to Britain, meeting the Prince of Wales and Lloyd George, and he was also befriended by Franklin D. Roosevelt. During World War II he kept a low profile, although he maintained contacts with friends in the German resistance movement. In early 1943, there was a suggestion by the plotters against Hitler that he should be put forward as the legitimate heir to the throne, but he insisted that his father, the Crown Prince, should not be passed over and another opportunity for a Hohenzollern restoration was lost. Following his father's death in 1951, Prince Louis Ferdinand succeeded as Head of the Royal House of Prussia.

Perhaps because of his brother's renunciation, Prince Louis Ferdinand, in his turn, has insisted that two of his sons renounce their rights because of unequal marriages. One may admire this strong adherence to principle, but it does leave Prince Louis Ferdinand (and his fellow pretenders) in a difficult position. None of them wish to be regarded as an anachronism. Yet, in this respect they insist on turning the clock back to pre-1914 days. The Queens of Denmark and the Netherlands, the Crown Prince of Norway, and the Kings of Sweden and Belgium have all married outside the royal caste. Where reigning monarchs tread, pretenders fear to follow.

Louis Ferdinand's third son, Prince Louis Ferdinand, made a suitable marriage in 1975 to Countess Donata zu Castell-Rüdenhausen. He died of injuries received while on military maneuvers a year after the birth of his son, Georg Friedrich, in 1976. It is on this young life that rests the continuation of the legitimate Prussian line. Most others, despite it being a prolific family, are debarred because of morganatic marriages.

PRINCE LOUIS FERDINAND of PRUSSIA
Celebrates his 75th birthday, November 1982
Front row: Princess Friedrich Wilhelm holding her daughter, Viktoria Luise; Prince Louis Ferdinand. Second row: Princess Kira; Prince Friedrich Wilhelm, holding his son, Friedrich Wilhelm; Nataly Prinzessin von Preussen; Duchess Rixa of Oldenburg; Duke Paul-Wladimir of Oldenburg; Duchess Marie-Cecilé of Oldenburg; Kira Harris Johnson. Back row: Duke Friedrich August of Oldenburg; Prince Michael of Prussia and his wife, Gitta; Princess Donata; Prince Christian-Sigismund (partially hidden); Mitchell Johnson. The children in front: Patrick Lithander, who is kissing his grandfather; Kira-Marina Liepsner; Prince Georg Friedrich of Prussia and Duchess Bibiane of Oldenburg (The Associated Press.)

14

THE FAMILY OF PRINCE FRIEDRICH OF PRUSSIA
Back: Prince William Andrew; the Marquess of Douro;
Prince Rupert; Philippe Achache; Major Anthony Ness;
Prince Nicholas; Lady Brigid Ness. Front: Princess
William Andrew with daughter, Tatiana; Princess
Victoria, Mrs. Achache with son, George; the Earl of
Mornington; the Marchioness of Douro with daughter,
Lady Honor Wellesley; and Princess Nicholas with her
daughter, Beatrice (Lady Brigid Ness.)

Prince Hubertus, Crown Prince Wilhelm's third son, took up farming in South West Africa (once a German colony) in 1950, where he died of appendicitis three months later. Of his children, the elder, Anastasia, is married to the Hereditary Prince of Lowenstein-Wertheim-Rosenberg, while the younger, Marie-Christine, died of head injuries following a car accident in 1966.

Prince Friedrich, Crown Prince Wilhelm's fourth and youngest son, settled in Britain just before war broke out in 1939. For a time interned in Canada, he was finally able to return to England where he too became a farmer. Married in 1945 to Lady Brigid Guinness, Friedrich adopted the name George Mansfield, but in the 1950s he resumed his German title. In April 1966, Prince Friedrich was reported missing from his home. Two weeks later his body was recovered from the Rhine. The autopsy concluded that he either committed suicide or had died accidentally.

*Prince and Princess Nicholas von Preussen with two
of their daughters, Florence and Beatrice, 1986
(HRH Prince Nicholas von Preussen.)*

Prince Friedrich's eldest son, Prince Nicholas, served in the British Army. He is now head of the British branch of the Prussian royal family. Nicholas is employed by the Guinness family's Iveagh Trust. He and his wife, the former Hon. Victoria Mancroft, live in London with their three daughters.

Nicholas's younger sister, Princess Antonia, also married into the British nobility. She is married to the Marquess of Douro, heir to the Duke of Wellington. Appropriately enough, as a future Prince of Waterloo in The Netherlands, Duke of Victoria in Portugal and Duke of Ciudad Rodrigo in Spain, he is a member of the European Parliament. Among the wedding guests were the Queen Mother, the Prince of Wales, and the bride's uncle, Prince Louis Ferdinand. Lord and Lady Douro have three children: one son and two daughters. The younger daughter, Lady Mary Wellesley, is a goddaughter of the Princess of Wales.

Princess Cecilie and husband, Clyde Harris, 1949
(Kira Harris Johnson)

Crown Prince Wilhelm's two youngest children were daughters. The eldest, Alexandrine (named for her maternal aunt who was queen consort of Denmark), died unmarried in 1980.

Princess Cecilie met her husband, Oklahoma-born Clyde Harris, an interior decorator, while he was serving in the U.S. Army Historic Monuments Division. One of his assignments took him to Schloss Wolfsgarten, near Darmstadt, the home of Prince and Princess Ludwig of Hesse and By Rhine, from which an estimated forty million dollars worth of paintings had been stolen, including a Holbein Madonna. Just before Christmas in 1945, Harris recovered half of Prince Ludwig's paintings, including the priceless Madonna. The paintings were found near Coburg, which was just outside the Russian zone. 'The Russians had cabbaged onto the other half of the treasure,' Harris said in a 1957 interview with the Saturday Evening Post.

A mutual attraction sprang up between the couple, and when Harris returned to the U.S.A. in 1946 they began to correspond. On his return to Europe in 1949, they decided to marry and sought Crown Prince Wilhelm's permission. Then living in a small house at the foot of Burg Hohenzollern, 'little Willie,' perhaps recalling his own association with the American singer Geraldine Farrar, happily gave his blessing and the couple were married in the family chapel in Burg Hohenzollern in 1949. Both died at an early age and are survived by a daughter Kira. Married to a film producer, Kira and her husband and young son live in Fort Worth, Texas.

*Kira Harris and husband, Mitchell Johnson, 1982
(Kira Harris Johnson.)*

Prince Eitel Friedrich of Prussia and his fiancée,
Duchess Sophie Charlotte of Oldenburg
(Author's collection)

Prince Eitel Friedrich, Kaiser Wilhelm's second son, bore no physical resemblance to Frederick the Great, but in his private life had tastes which were similar. Married to Duchess Sophie of Oldenburg, an heiress who was anxious to escape an uncongenial stepmother, he chased after young men with all the enthusiasm his elder brother, the Crown Prince, devoted to women. Like her sister-in-law, Crown Princess Cecilie, Sophie ran away from her husband, but both women were persuaded to return. Eitel Friedrich's marriage, which ended in divorce in 1922, was, not surprisingly, childless.

Victoria Marina Prinzessin v. Preussen
Tochter des Prinzen und der Prinzessin Adalbert

(Dohna Pearl.)

Prinz Adalbert von Preussen.

Kaiser Wilhelm's third son, Adalbert, once regarded as a possible husband for the Grand Duchess Olga of Russia, married instead a Princess of Saxe-Meiningen. Like his uncle Heinrich, he served in the German Imperial Navy, and like him again, Adalbert managed to make a reasonable adjustment to life after the revolution. He and his wife lived for many years in Switzerland where they used the titles Count and Countess von Lingen.

Prince Adalbert with twin sons, Christoph and
Philipp, 1986 (HRH Prince Adalbert of Prussia)

Prince Adalbert's daughter, Victoria Marina, added another American link to the Prussian royal family. In 1947 she married Kirby Patterson of Springfield, Missouri. They have three children: twins Berengar and Marina (now a nurse in Downey, California), and Dohna, a housewife in Taos, New Mexico, where her husband is employed at a ski resort. Princess Marie Louise, daughter of Adalbert's son, Wilhelm-Victor, lives in Spain. Her daughter, Sophie, born in 1979, is a goddaughter of her cousin Queen Sofia of Spain. Marie Louise's brother, Adalbert, lives in Munich with his wife and three sons, including twins Christian and Philipp.

PRINZ AUGUST WILHELM u. PRINZESSIN ALEXANDRA VICTORIA

Prince August Wilhelm, the Kaiser's fourth son, was the only member of his immediate family to embrace Nazism with enthusiasm. Known in the family as 'Auwi,' he joined the Nazi Party in March 1930, declaring, 'Adolf Hitler is God's gift to Germany.' He was convinced that Hitler intended to restore the Hohenzollerns. He was not alone among his relatives in making this mistake; another fervent supporter was his stepmother, the Empress Hermine, who was captured and imprisoned by the Russians at the end of the war, and died in their hands in 1947.

When Hitler turned on the Hohenzollerns, Auwi's early support did nothing to save him. Expelled from the SS and stripped of his uniform, he was placed under arrest. He survived the war only to face the further ignominy of trial before a denazification court. Sentenced in 1948 to two-and-a-half years' imprisonment, he died in 1949.

Gräfin Ina Marie von Ruppin

PRINCE OSKAR OF PRUSSIA AND HIS WIFE INA
(Preussischen Königshauses, Haus Archiv.)

Prince Oskar, Kaiser Wilhelm's fifth son, was reluctantly allowed to marry morganatically. Oskar fell in love with Countess Ina-Marie von Bassewitz, who was one of his mother's ladies-in-waiting. Permission for the marriage was finally obtained from the Kaiser by his daughter, Viktoria Luise, as a christening present for her son, Prince Ernst August of Hanover. In 1920, Kaiser Wilhelm created Ina-Marie a Princess of Prussia with the rank of Royal Highness.

Prince and Princess Oskar had five children. Their eldest son, Oskar, died in Poland only two days after Britain had declared war on Germany. Oscar's second son, Prince Burchard, studied law and sits on the board of numerous European companies. He is married to Countess Eleonore Fugger von Babenhausen whose daughter, Victoria Anne, from a previous marriage to American Robert Bee, is married to Prince Georg of Hanover, another descendant of Queen Victoria.

Princess Herzeleide-Ina-Marie of Prussia and her husband, Karl, Prince Biron von Curland, 1981. (HSH Karl, Prince Biron von Curland.)

Prince Oskar's youngest son, Wilhelm-Karl, is a businessman with international interests who lives with his family in Holzminden, and bears the title Herrenmeister der Ballei Brandenburg of the Johanniter Order.

Princess Herzeleide-Ina-Marie, Prince Oskar's only daughter, married Prince Karl Biron von Curland. Now widowed, the Princess lives in Munich, as do her three children and their families. The present Prince Biron von Curland is her eldest son, Prince Ernst Johann, who is a physicist. He has two adopted daughters, and therefore the eventual heir to the family title is his brother, Michael.

Prince Joachim, the youngest son of Wilhelm II, was wounded in World War I, where he served as a captain. He idolized his elder brother, the Crown Prince, and like Wilhelm, he was a womanizer. In addition, he gambled, and after his father's abdication in 1918 found it impossible to accept his new status. Separation from his wife, the former Princess Marie Auguste of Anhalt, followed soon after the end of the war. Prince Joachim also suffered from fits of depression that became increasingly difficult to throw off. In 1920, three weeks after visiting his parents at Doorn, Joachim committed suicide. His parents were shattered by his death, particularly since they were unable to attend his funeral. The Kaiserin never recovered from the shock, and she died a few months later.

The Weimar government permitted Auguste Victoria's burial at Potsdam, and thousands of German monarchists used her funeral to display their continued loyalty to the House of Hohenzollern.

Prince Karl Franz Joseph, Prince Joachim's only son, was named for the Austrian Emperor who died in 1916, the year of the young Prince's birth. Prince Karl Franz Joseph died in Chile in 1975, having married three times. His first wife was the daughter of the Kaiser's second wife by her previous marriage to Prince Johann-Georg of Schönaich-Carolath. By his third wife, Eva, he had two daughters, Alexandra and Désirée. Désirée lives in Montevideo, Uruguay, with her husband, a Peruvian diplomat, and their infant son. Both Alexandra and Désirée served as bridesmaids at the wedding of their half-brother, Prince Franz-Wilhelm, to Princess Maria Wladimirovna of Russia, another example of marriage between descendants of Queen Victoria.

Princess Viktoria Luise, who was Kaiser Wilhelm's only daughter, was married in May 1913 to Prince Ernst August of Hanover. Their marriage is considered the swan-song of European monarchy, as it was the last time that the three cousins, Wilhelm II, Nicholas II and George V were to meet.

The couple met under tragic circumstances. In 1912, Ernst August's elder brother, Prince Georg Wilhelm, driving through Prussia to Copenhagen for the funeral of his uncle Frederik VIII of Denmark, was killed in a car crash. Seizing on the drama of the event, Kaiser

Wilhelm dispatched two of his sons to stand as guards of honor at the coffin, and at the same time sent a telegram of sympathy to the dead prince's parents, the Duke and Duchess of Brunswick-Lüneburg. In due course, the Duke sent his surviving son, Prince Ernst August, to thank the Kaiser personally. While in Berlin, Prince Ernst August met Princess Viktoria Luise, and they fell in love.

Both families opposed the match, but Princess Viktoria Luise was her father's favorite and she was ultimately able to obtain his permission. The antagonism between the two families was due to Prussian's annexation of Hanover in 1866.

When Queen Victoria ascended the throne in 1837, the crown of Hanover passed to her uncle Ernest, Duke of Cumberland, as Salic law prevailed in the Hanoverian kingdom. In 1866, however, Ernest's son, the blind King Georg V, was deprived of his throne because he chose the wrong side in the Austro-Prussian war. He retired to his Austrian estates, but continued to lay strenuous claim to the Hanover crown, as well as to the family's private fortune, which had also fallen into Prussia's hands. For the next fifty years, the Hanovers and Hohenzollerns were implacably opposed to one another. Georg's son, Ernst August, married Princess Thyra of Denmark, the younger sister of the Princess of Wales and the Tsarina Marie of Russia. Both Alexandra and Marie were bitter enemies of Prussia, and their hatred was reinforced by their sister marrying into yet another royal house whose fortunes had been blighted by Prussian militarism.

Ernst August's father, who used his British title, Duke of Cumberland, abdicated his rights to the Brunswick duchy, and immediately after their wedding, Ernst August and Viktoria Luise became Duke and Duchess of Brunswick-Lüneburg, where they were sovereigns for a brief five years.

Duchess Viktoria Luise lived until 1980. The present head of the Hanover Royal Family is her eldest son, Prince Ernst August. Educated at Schloss Salem and later at the universities of Oxford, Berlin and Göttingen, he has a degree in law. It may have been this circumstance that gave Prince Ernst August a particular interest in the Act of Settlement passed by the British Parliament in 1701. By persistence, in 1956, he finally managed to establish in the British courts the right of all non-Catholic descendants of the Electress Sophia of Hanover to British citzenship. This proved particularly important in the case of those descendants whose land had been seized in eastern Europe after the war, as they were now able to establish claims for compensation as British subjects.

The Hanover Royal Family has demonstrated a remarkable talent for survival in a hostile world, and their former subjects have retained a strong enthusiasm for the monarchy. On the occasion of Prince Ernst August's wedding in 1951, the celebrations lasted for three days. In 1954, when the Duke died, his funeral procession passed through Hanover with all the honors due to him as though he were still the reigning Duke.

The Duke and Duchess of Brunswick-Lüneburg with their children, 1931. Back: Prince Ernst August; Duke Ernst August; Duchess Viktoria Luise; Prince Georg Wilhelm. Front: Prince Christian; Prince Welf; Princess Friederike.
(HRH Duchess of Brunswick-Lüneburg.)

Viktoria Luise's only daughter, Friederike (Frederika), was married in 1938 to Crown Prince Paul of Greece. Before the wedding, her father, the Duke of Brunswick-Lüneburg, sought permission for her marriage from King George VI, since Frederika was also a Princess of Great Britain and Ireland. The necessary permission was granted at a meeting of the Privy Council in London. At her wedding, Frederika carried a bouquet of orange blossoms sent by her grandfather, Wilhelm II, from Doorn, and myrtle brought from Osborne by Prince Paul's cousin, Princess Marina, the Duchess of Kent.

QUEEN FREDERIKA of the HELLENES
(Private collection)

'I am a barbarian who has come to Greece to be civilized,'
Princess Frederika announced winningly on her arrival in Athens.
For the first twenty years of her life in Greece, her devotion to
charitable and social works won her friends throughout Greece and
the world.   With her youthful good looks, easy public manner and
vivacity, blessed with three charming children, all seemed well with
the Greek monarchy. By the 1960s, however, storm clouds began to
appear.   Frederika, like many royal ladies in the past, acquired a
taste for politics and her hand was evident in many matters.
Seventeen years younger than her husband, King Paul, she always
appeared to be the more dominant of the two, and perhaps unfairly,
she also was the recipient of unwarranted press attention.   King
Paul's early death was a tragedy for Greece and for the monarchy.
Going into exile in 1967, with her son, she eventually moved to
Madras, India, to study philosophy at the university.

The publication of her memoirs in 1971 caused many to reflect that she had perhaps been a much-maligned and misjudged woman. She died of anesthesia poisoning while undergoing eye surgery in 1981 in Madrid. Her funeral took place at Tatoi, the family estate near Athens, were King Paul is buried. While permitting King Constantine to return to Greece for his mother's burial, the government insisted that he leave the same day, fearing demonstrations by the Greek people in his favor.

Viktoria Luise's eldest son, Ernst August, who is the present Duke of Brunswick-Lüneburg, has been married twice. By his first wife, Ortrud, Prince Ernst August has six children. Among them are Marie (a goddaughter of Queen Mary), Ernst August, a film producer who lives in London with his Swiss-born wife, Chantal, and two sons; and a daughter, Alexandra, provides another instance of Victoria's descendants marrying another. In 1981, she married Prince Andreas of Leiningen.

Prince Georg Wilhelm cf Hanover, who is Viktoria Luise's second son, was president of the Internationale Olympische Akademie from 1966 until 1970. A student at Schloss Salem, he became its headmaster in 1948, a position he held until 1959. Continuing family tradition, he too married a descendant of Queen Victoria. In 1946 he wed Princess Sophie of Greece and Denmark, sister of the Duke of Edinburgh, and widow of Prince Christoph of Hesse. (Princess Sophie is one of two descendants of Queen Victoria to have been married to two different descendants.) Their eldest son, Welf, was a classmate of Prince Charles at Gordonstoun. Welf made news when it became known that he and his wife Wibke had become followers of Baghwan Shree Rajneesh, an Indian guru who advocated, among other things, free love. During his 1980 trip to India, Prince Charles visited his cousin in Bombay. Two months later, Prince Welf died of a cerebral hemorrhage after collapsing during karate practice. Princess Welf later followed the Baghwan to the United States; their only daughter Tanya, who is being educated in England, was the subject of a custody battle between her mother and paternal grandparents, Prince and Princess Georg Wilhelm.

Prince and Princess Georg Wilhelm's only daughter, Princess Friederike, was once thought to be a possible bride for Prince Charles. Instead, in 1979, she married a Canadian and now lives in Vancouver with her husband and two children.

Viktoria Luise's youngest son, Prince Christian, broke a long-standing family tradition when in 1963 he married a Belgian commoner. He was forty-four and his bride seventeen. Theirs was the first morganatic marriage in the Hanover family since 1579, when Duke Otto Heinrich of Brunswick-Lüneburg married Marie de Hennin-Lietard.

The wedding of Prince Ernst August of Hanover
and Princess Ortrud of Schleswig-Holstein, 1951
(The Associated Press.)

His elder brother, Ernst August, refused to attend either the civil or the religious ceremonies, but Christian was supported by his mother, Duchess Viktoria Luise, and by his nephew, King Constantine II of the Hellenes. Two daughters were born of the marriage, but Christian and his wife eventually divorced, and just one day before the first anniversary of his mother's death, Prince Christian died of a stroke in a Lausanne hospital.

Prinz Heinrich v. Preussen u. Familie.

Prince Heinrich of Prussia, the second son of Princess Victoria, was the first of Queen Victoria's descendants to marry another descendant. Not unlike his cousin George V in looks and temperament, Prince Heinrich - known in the family as Henry - was in England sailing at Cowes as World War I neared. It was his well-intentioned, but misleading, report to his brother the Kaiser of his conversation with King George V on the morning of July 26, 1914, nine days before hostilities commenced, that helped lull Germany into the belief that Britain would remain neutral.

Heinrich pursued a naval career and lived very much in the shadow of his elder brother, Kaiser Wilhelm II. His marriage to Princess Irene of Hesse and By Rhine was destined to be very happy, but the tragedy of hemophilia hung over two of their three sons. The youngest, Heinrich, died when only four. Their eldest son, Waldemar, also suffered from the disease, but although it severely restricted his life, he married Princess Calixta of Lippe in 1919. During World War II, they lived at Schloss Kamenz in Silesia. Forced to flee ahead of the Soviet advance in 1945, Prince Waldemar became desperately ill and died in a clinic at Tutzing in Bavaria due to the lack of blood transfusion facilities.

The middle son, Prince Sigismund, escaped the fate of his brothers and was able to live a normal, healthy life. In 1922, he moved to Guatemala to start a coffee plantation. Later he moved to Costa Rica where he died in 1979. His daughter, Barbara, is married to Duke Christian Ludwig of Mecklenburg and they live with their two daughters at Hemmelmark, an estate in Holstein which Prince and Princess Henry bought in 1896. Princess Barbara was legally adopted by her paternal grandmother as heir. During the 1960s and 70s, she became the principal opponent of Anna Anderson's attempts to establish her identity as Grand Duchess Anastasia of Russia.

Vicky was mother to four daughters, but her relations with her eldest daughter, Charlotte, were difficult. Charlotte became imbued with the ideas of Bismarck, which set not-at-all well with her mother. In 1891, Empress Friedrich wrote to another daughter, Sophie: 'Charlotte is coming here at Whitsuntide. I do wish I could look forward to her coming with unmixed pleasure but I cannot, considering that she and Bernhard take the *reverse* of what *I* do on almost *every* subject and abuse me right and left behind my back.' Later, in 1893, she wrote: 'It does grieve me to see her so 19th century, thinking so much of her clothes and appearances and smoking so much. She is looking well, but her complexion is so yellow and she smells like a cigar shop, which for ladies is not the thing.'

Charlotte is particularly interesting genealogically. Her marriage in 1878, and the birth of a daughter, Feodora, the following year, made Queen Victoria a great-grandmother at sixty-nine. Queen Victoria lived long enough to see her great-granddaughter marry in 1898, but the marriage was childless and Victoria died before her first great-great-grandchild was born.

Vicky's second daughter, Princess Victoria, had the misfortune to fall in love with Prince Alexander of Battenberg (an older brother of Queen Victoria's son-in-law, Henry), the Prince of Bulgaria. Her engagement became the subject of political controversy involving the British, Prussian and Russian royal families. It caused terrible dissension within the family, and ultimately Victoria was obliged to give up all hope of marrying Alexander. She eventually married Prince Adolf of Schaumburg-Lippe, but the marriage was childless. She became a widow in 1916. Unlike her elder brother, the Kaiser, she was able to live in Germany after the revolution, but it was a bitter, meaningless life until she met a Russian refugee. Alexander Zoubkoff, often described as a penniless waiter, was the son of a university professor of anatomy, but he was twenty-seven and Victoria sixty-two.

The news of her forthcoming marriage shocked her family, and they broke off relations with her. Within two years, her fortune had been dissipated and she began divorce proceedings. Mercifully, Victoria died before the case with all the inevitable publicity came to court. At her funeral the only members of her family present were her sister, Margarete, her sister-in-law, Irene, and her nephew, Prince Adalbert, who placed on her coffin a wreath in the name of the Kaiser.

Vicky's third daughter Sophie married Crown Prince Constantine of Greece in 1889. Sophie, who wore a gown designed by her mother, and Constantine were married in an Orthodox ceremony in Athens on October 27, 1889. The Greek ceremony was followed by a brief Lutheran service, then a family lunch. The wedding festivities, culminated with an opulent dinner.

Sophie's decision two years later to adopt the Greek Orthodox faith caused a public breach between her and her brother the Kaiser, after which he threatened to ban her from Germany for life.

The news of Sophie's conversion came as a shock to Wilhelm's wife, Auguste Victoria, known in the family as 'Dona,' who at the time was pregnant with her sixth son, Joachim. Dona quickly reminded Sophie that Wilhelm, as German Emperor, was head of the Lutheran church and, if she disobeyed him, with her conversion, she would end up in hell.

'Whether I go to hell or not is my own affair,' Sophie retorted in a letter to her mother.

Wilhelm II refused to be moved. 'If my sister enters the Greek Church, than I shall forbid her the country,' he fumed in a letter to Vicky, who along with her mother, Queen Victoria, supported Sophie's decision. Wilhelm also had the temerity to send a telegram to Sophie's father-in-law, King George I, informing the King that he would disown Sophie if she changed her faith.

PRINCESS SOPHIE and CROWN PRINCE CONSTANTINE
(Royal Library of Denmark)

At her mother's insistence, Sophie wrote to Wilhelm to explain her reason for wanting to convert, but the letter fell on deaf ears. Wilhelm remained obdurate. Sophie then sent an open telegram to her mother. 'Received answer, keeps to what he says in Berlin, fixes it to three years. Mad. Never mind. Sophie.'

But the Empress Friedrich did mind. 'You are quite at liberty to do as you like,' she wrote to Sophie. 'You are not his [Wilhelm's] subject, but King George's.'

In June 1891, Sophie traveled to Heidelberg to visit her mother. Her husband, Crown Prince Constantine, had arrived ahead of her to insure that the trip would be safe. Wilhelm made no effort to stop the visit. In fact, he did not say a word about it, at least not in public, as he was about to leave for London for his first state visit there, and he did not want to create a scene by incurring the wrath of his formidable grandmother.

The entire affair is made incomprehensible by the fact that the Greek constitution required the consort to be of the Orthodox faith, which all knew before the marriage.

It is ironic that when Sophie and her husband eventually became sovereigns of Greece, she should have been picked as a scapegoat by supporters of the Entente who spread the rumor that Queen Sophie was in constant contact with her brother in Berlin by means of a radio secreted in the palace. In fact, like all of Vicky's three youngest daughters, Sophie's natural inclinations were more toward England than Prussia, and it was no coincidence that when war broke out her children were on holiday in Eastbourne.

Even today the methods which the Allied Powers used to try and bring Greece into the war on their side leaves one with a feeling of deep injustice. The King and Queen were to bear the main brunt of a campaign of humiliation and vilification which finally led to Constantine leaving Greece in 1917. The Allies insisted that his second son, Prince Alexander, should become king, in the belief that the eldest son, George, had become infected with Prussian militarism during his pre-war training in Potsdam.

Alexander, deprived of all family support, inexperienced and totally untrained for his new position, was a mere puppet of the Greek government, led by Prime Minister Venizelos. It is little wonder that he sought solace in marriage, albeit a morganatic alliance, which he made with Greek-born Aspasia Manos in 1919. Their marriage was brief. The King died in October 1920 from blood poisoning, having been bitten by a monkey. Within weeks, King Constantine returned to Athens as sovereign. He recognized his daughter-in-law as a Princess of Greece, a title that he also accorded to her daughter, Alexandra, born five months after King Alexander's death. In 1944, Alexandra married another descendant of Queen Victoria, the exiled King Peter of Yugoslavia, whose grandmother, Queen Marie of Roumania, was Queen Sophie's first cousin.

Constantine's second reign was of short duration. Military adventures in Turkey ended in disaster, and in 1922, he abdicated, a sad and disillusioned man. His eldest son, King George II, remained in Athens, but he was sovereign in name only. Deposed by the army in 1924, George settled for a time in Roumania where his wife Elisabeth had estates, and where his sister Helen was married to Crown Prince Carol. Unhappily, however, King George II's marriage did not prosper. A cool, classical beauty, Elisabeth's temperament was volatile and vulgar. The pair drifted apart, and George went to live in England where he formed a close relationship with a woman that attracted none of the publicity of that of his cousin Edward VIII. In 1935, Elisabeth obtained a divorce in the Bucharest courts. A few months later a referendum restored George to the Greek throne.

Six years later he was again obliged to leave the country when the Germans invaded Greece. After the war, the monarchy was restored once more in 1946. In April 1947, King George II died of a heart attack, and was succeeded by his youngest brother Paul.

King Paul was in turn succeeded by his only son, King Constantine II. Although King Constantine has been in exile for two decades, the Royal House of Greece has proved amazingly resilient, and it is easy to imagine circumstances in which either Greek politicians or the Greek people, or both, might once again turn to their Royal Family.

King Constantine lives in England with his wife, Danish-born Queen Anne-Marie, and their five children, and is able to maintain a court of some size. Brother of the Queen of Spain and brother-in-law of the Queen of Denmark, he is the least forgotten of exiled monarchs. Queen Elizabeth II, too, seems well disposed toward her fellow monarch and at the christening of his daughter, Theodora, in 1983, she led a gathering of royalties that included Queen Sofia of Spain, Queen Margrethe II of Denmark with Queen Ingrid, King Michael and Queen Anne of Roumania, and Crown Prince Alexander of Yugoslavia, among others. By leading a sober, discreet existence, the exiled monarch ensures that when the time comes, he will be seen to be in every way worthy of the crown he once wore.

His sister Sofia occupies a very special place both in her family and in monarchist circles. If heredity counts for anything, it is not surprising that Queen Sofia is making such a personal success of her position as consort of the Spanish monarch. Beginning with Queen Victoria, she is the latest in a line of Queens on the female side: Vicky, her great-grandmother, Queen of Prussia; Sophie, her grandmother, and then her own mother, Frederika, successively Queens of Greece. Like her brother, she is a favorite of Queen Elizabeth II; the number of her godchildren attests to her popularity in the royal families of Europe, while in Spain itself, it would not be an exaggeration to say that she is probably the most widely-loved Queen Spain has ever known.

The christening of Princess Theodora of Greece and Denmark, 1983. Back row, King Michael of Roumania; Crown Prince Alexander of Yugoslavia; Queen Margrethe II of Denmark; Crown Prince Pavlos; Middle row: Princess Alexia; King Constantine; Queen Sofia of Spain; Prince Nikolaos. Front row: Queen Ingrid of Denmark; Queen Anne Marie with Princess Theodora; Queen Elizabeth II (The Associated Press.)

PRINCESS IRENE OF GREECE
(Private collection)

Queen Sophie's sister, Princess Irene, is unmarried. Talented enough to have been a pupil of the world famous concert pianist, Gina Bachauer, Princess Irene has given a number of public performances. She is now deeply involved with various relief programs to help children.

All of King Constantine I's sons - George, Alexander and Paul- became kings. Of his three daughters, two became queens, while the third renounced her royal title on her marriage. The eldest daughter Helen seems to epitomize in her life the kind of fate which the Greek Royal House has been destined. She was seventeen years old when her grandfather, King George I, was assassinated. Later, she went into exile with her family in 1917, and returned with them to Athens in 1920. Married to Crown Prince Carol of Roumania in 1921, she found herself abandoned four years later when her husband eloped with his mistress, Elena Lupescu, in a blaze of international publicity.

KING MICHAEL and QUEEN ANNE of ROUMANIA
(HM King Michael of Roumania)

In 1927, Princess Helen's only child, Michael, became King of Roumania, only to be set aside three years later when Carol returned to claim the throne. For a time it seemed as though there would be a reconciliation between the couple, but in 1931, Helen was obliged to leave Roumania. She settled with her mother and sister in Italy until 1940 when her son, then aged 19, was again called to the throne. Persuaded by the Fascist dictator Ion Antonescu that her son needed her help, she returned to Roumania and shortly afterward, by a special Act of Parliament, was given the title Queen Mother of Roumania. Since she and Carol had divorced in 1928, she had not become Queen on his accession in 1930.

In December 1947, King Michael was forced by the communists to abdicate and he and his mother left the country. It is not without significance that the communists had to wait three years before they felt confident enough to abolish the monarchy in Roumania. It says much for the influence of Queen Helen, both personally and in respect of her son's upbringing, that together they were able to raise the esteem in which the royal family was held to such levels after King Carol's disastrous ten year reign.

THE DUKE and DUCHESS OF AOSTA - 1987
(HRH The Duke of Aosta.)

Princess Irene, Queen Helen's younger sister, married late in life, in 1939, to Prince Aimone of Savoy, who later became Duke of Aosta. In 1942 her husband was nominated by Mussolini to become King of Croatia, a puppet state set up under Ante Pavelic, a man who organized the assassination of King Alexander of Yugoslavia, to maintain Italian influence in the Balkans. Neither the Duke or his wife were at all enthusiastic about their sudden elevation, and successfully delayed their departure for their new capital until such time as the Italians were no longer able to control Croatia. When the Allies landed in Italy, the Duke was able to escape south, but Irene, then expecting a baby, was trapped behind German lines.

Hitler's fury at the treachery of King Victor Emmanuel III was centered on all the members of the Italian Royal Family he could reach. Princess Irene, with her young son, and her sister-in-law, Anne, Duchess of Aosta, and her two daughters, were interned at a camp at Hirschegg, Austria. They were all freed by French troops in May 1945. Reunited with her husband in Italy, Irene became a widow in 1948 when the Duke died while on a visit to Argentina. Her son, Amadeo, now the 5th Duke of Aosta, lives in Italy with his second wife, Marquesa Silvia Paterno, and his three children from his first marriage to Princess Claude of France, daughter of the Count of Paris, head of the Royal House of France.

Lady Katherine Brandram and Queen Sofia of Spain,
London, 1982 (Paul Brandram.)

The third of the three sisters, Princess Katherine, met her future husband Major Paul Brandram on board the *Ascania* when she was en route to England during World War II. Shortly afterward, they became engaged, but although King George II had given the marriage his blessing, the engagement was kept secret until February 1947. They were married in Athens just two weeks after the King's death in April 1947, and she is now known as Lady Katherine Brandram. Her only son Paul lives in London with his wife and three children, one of whom, Sophie, is a goddaughter of the Queen of Spain.

*Paul and Jennifer Brandram, and daughter, Sophie,
1981 (Paul Brandram.)*

The youngest of Vicky's children was Princess Margarete, known in the family as 'Mossy.' Married to the Landgrave of Hesse, she is the only descendant of Queen Victoria to become the mother of two sets of twins. On the death of her mother, she inherited Schloss Friedrichshof in Kronberg.

Schloss Friedrichshof was to be the setting of a dramatic theft at the end of the second World War. Fearing for the safety of her jewels, the Princess arranged for them to be buried in a sub-cellar of the castle shortly before it was occupied by American troops. The military authorities used the castle as an officers' club, and it was the club's manager, WAC Captain Kathleen Burke Nash, who discovered the jewels, and with the help of Colonel J. W. Durant (whom she later married) and Major D. Watson, managed to smuggle the jewels out of Germany. The princess eventually discovered their loss and reported the theft to the authorities in Frankfurt. Although the three culprits were imprisoned, only one-third of the jewels were ever recovered.

MARGARETE, LANDGRAVINE of HESSE
(HRH Prince Moritz, Landgrave of Hesse.)

Two of Mossy's sons were killed in World War I. Another son lost his life on a bombing raid in World War II, and two of her daughters-in-law also died: Princess Marie-Alexandra in an air raid and Princess Mafalda in Buchenwald concentration camp. Two sons, Philipp and Christoph, embraced Nazism with enthusiasm. The elder, Prince Philipp, married Princess Mafalda, King Victor Emmanuel of Italy's daughter, and was thus ideally placed to play the part of diplomatic messenger between Hitler and Mussolini. Hitler's reaction to the Italian king's capitulation to the Allies in 1943 was strong, and the vengeance he took on Prince Philipp's wife was savage indeed.

Returning to Rome after attending the funeral of her brother-in-law, King Boris III of Bulgaria, who had died mysteriously following a meeting with Hitler at Berchtesgarten, she was taken to Germany on the pretext of joining her husband. Instead, she was thrown into Buchenwald. Eleven months later she was badly burned, and her arm injured, during an Allied air raid. Left unattended for four days, she died of a hemorrhage after her arm was amputated.

Prince Christoph was a major in the Luftwaffe, and is believed to have taken part in some bombing raids on London. At the time of his death, he was on a raid over Italy when his plane crashed. Hitler's attitude toward German royalties had become increasingly hostile and it was suggested that Christoph's death was caused by a bomb placed on his aircraft on the Führer's orders. Nothing, however, has ever been discovered to substantiate such a story. Married to Princess Sophie of Greece and Denmark, Prince Christoph left five children, the last of whom, Princess Clarissa, was born posthumously. Their eldest child, Princess Christina, married Prince Andrej of Yugoslavia (also a descendant of Queen Victoria), and following their divorce, she wed a Dutch painter.

Like her sister-in-law, Princess Irene of Prussia, Margarete lived until the 1950s. Both princesses had been born at the time of the creation of the Second Reich, and they grew to maturity as the Empire reached its glorious, but ephemeral peak. The shock of revolution, the horrors of the Weimar days, and the nightmare of the Third Reich and World War II brought elements of Greek tragedy to their lives - the pathetic death of Prince Waldemar, Princess Mafalda's death in Buchenwald, and the unanswered questions concerning the plane crash that took the life of Prince Christoph. One is tempted to suppose that they may from time to time have looked with nostalgic longing to those halcyon days spent in the company of grandmamma Victoria at Windsor and Balmoral. Perhaps something of her example enabled both Margarete and Irene to survive all the trials they endured with dignity and stoicism.

Princess Mafalda of Hesse with three of her children,
Prince Moritz, Prince Otto and Prince Heinrich (The
Associated Press.)

LANDGRAVE PHILIPP of HESSE,
circ. 1945 (The Associated Press.)

Queen Victoria with four of her great-grandchildren: Left to right: Princess Mary, Prince Edward, Queen Victoria holding Prince Henry; Seated: Prince Albert (George VI) (The Associated Press.)

CHAPTER III

KING EDWARD VII

The British, or Windsor, line, the present Royal Family, descends from Queen Victoria through two second sons and a female (Queen Elizabeth II), breaking the male line of descent to the throne. The eldest son and second child of Victoria and Albert, Albert Edward, was known as 'Bertie'. The relationship between Edward and his parents was long-strained as his puritanical, serious-minded father tried to mould his affable, easy-going, son into his own ideal of a 'modern constitutional monarch'. This fettish of the Prince Consort to 'convert' the more-or-less absolute monarchs of Europe to 'constitutionalism', where they would be little more than figureheads, presents an amusing anomaly, as Queen Victoria was especially energetic in maintaining all of her own power and privilege. The brain-washing efforts of the Prince Consort fell, for the most part, on unheeding ears - as in the case of Bertie, or resulted in disaster - as in the case of Princess Victoria.

When Bertie was twenty, he was shipped off to an army camp at Curragh in northern Ireland, where he promptly had a love affair. His waywardness, gambling and ladies convinced Queen Victoria and Albert that Bertie was unsuited for the Crown, but they didn't quite know what to do about it. Another escapade of Bertie brought Prince Albert to Cambridge to see his son. There he caught a cold which afterwards developed into typhoid, and in 1861 he died at Windsor Castle. Queen Victoria blamed her son, and her dislike for Bertie continued until the end. He once stated, "My mother hated me."

By the time Bertie was thirty, his reputation had become quite tainted. The Queen was continually shocked by stories of his addiction to horse racing, gambling and 'fashionable' society. He was once cited as a correspondent in a well-publicized divorce case.

The Prince of Wales' marriage, arranged by Queen Victoria, in 1863 to Princess Alexandra of Denmark did little to reduce Bertie's love for the fast life, nor his mother's distaste for what she considered a wastral life. At fifty, the Prince of Wales, still going strong, was again cited in a law case, the famous Tranby-Croft trial, where one of his gaming partners was accused of cheating at baccarrat.

49

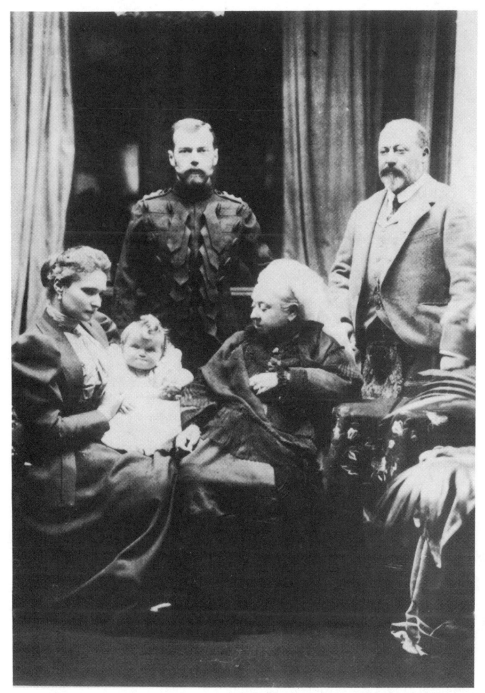

Tsar Nicholas II of Russia, Tsarina Alexandra, holding Grand Duchess Olga of Russia, Queen Victoria and the Prince of Wales (Edward VII) (Author's collection.)

Princess Alexandra was undoubtedly aware of her husband's galaxy of beautiful women and his many love affairs - some brief, and others, like with actress Lily Langtry, of long-duration, but she turned a blind-eye, and devoted her attention to her children and far-flung family.

Perhaps because of her son's reputation, or perhaps because of her own unwillingness to relinquish any of her power, Queen Victoria refused to allow Edward any position of authority or say in affairs of state. He was left to preside over what was called the 'Edwardian years' where he was known as 'Edward the Caresser'!

Even so, the Prince of Wales discharged a full schedule of official functions, including a tour of India in 1875, as a prelude to his mother's proclamation as Empress of India in 1876. He did his share of laying foundation stones, notably the Tower Bridge; helped plan the 1887 and 1897 Jubilee celebrations, and became the first Chancellor of the University of Wales in 1896. Edward's fifty year sojourn as Prince of Wales ended on January 22, 1901, when, on the death of Queen Victoria, he became king as Edward VII.

King Edward and Queen Alexandra had six children: Albert Victor, George (George V), Louise, Victoria, Maud, and John who lived for only a day. The oldest son, Albert Victor, died when he was twenty, and his brother, George, ultimately became king as George V. George V's eldest son, Edward VIII, abdicated and George's second son became king as George VI. The direct male line to the throne ended there, as George VI had only two daughters, the eldest being the present Queen Elizabeth II.

It has already been noted how morganatic marriages affect the lives of continental royalty. In Britain, however, such legal niceties do not exist. Queen Victoria pointed this out when some of her Prussian relatives protested her youngest daughter's marriage to a Battenberg. Writing to her daughter Vicky, whose mother-in-law had been among those to make disparaging comments, Queen Victoria reported that she had written to the Empress Auguste of Germany, saying, 'that morganatic marriages were unknown in England and if a King chose to marry a peasant girl she would be Queen just as much as any princess.' In the same letter, the Queen protests, '. . . that if no fresh blood was infused occasionally the races would degenerate finally - physically and morally - for . . . that almost all the Protestant Royal Families were related to each other and so were the Catholic ones!' In fact, Britain's monarchy has thrived on marrying outside its own caste.

'I also informed the [Privy] Council that May and I had decided some time ago that our children would be allowed tomarryinto British families. It was quite a historical occasion,' King George V wrote in his diary, July 17, 1917, following the meeting where the family's German titles were abandoned and the House of Windsor was born.

Princess Alexandra of Kent and her husband, the Hon. Angus Ogilvy and their children, Marina and James Ogilvy (British Information Services.)

Princess Mary of Teck, who married King George V, had a royal mother (Princess Mary Adelaide of Cambridge), but she would have been totally unacceptable for even the most minor Prussian prince. In more modern times, Lady Elizabeth Bowes-Lyon could not have married into such democratically-inclined families as those of Sweden or Denmark without her husband losing his rights of succession and title. The present Prince of Wales, like his grandfather, King George VI, looked no further than the British aristocracy in choosing a bride, and the practice of contracting marriages with continental royalties seems to have been abandoned. Since the death of King Edward VII in 1910, only two members of foreign royal families have married into the British Royal Family - the late Princess Marina of Greece and her cousin Prince Philip of Greece. The result is that the Royal Family is less royal in terms of lineage than many of its exiled relatives and is likely to become even less so in the future.

For all his keen interest in European politics, King Edward VII was curiously unambitious in the matter of his childrens' marriages. Queen Alexandra's devotion and possessive nature toward her children kept them shy, educationally deprived and shallow.

Society was taken aback, however, when Edward's eldest daughter, Louise (who until the birth of the future Edward VIII was third in the line of succession), became engaged to Lord Fife, who was seventeen years her senior. Although her fiancé had been a Liberal member of Parliament, was rich, a well-known figure on the turf, and a member of the Marlborough House set, he was considered coarse and selfish.

Louise's husband had the distinction of being created the Duke of Fife at the wedding breakfast. In 1905, Louise was created Princess Royal by her father, and the title of Princess (with the rank of Highness) was conferred on her daughters, who had been known until then as Lady Alexandra and Lady Maud Duff. In December 1911, the Duke and Duchess of Fife and their two daughters were on their way to Egypt when their ship, the *Delhi*, was wrecked and their lifeboat went down under them. The Duke caught a chill and a month later died at Aswan.

The Fife dukedom was inherited by his eldest daughter, Alexandra, married Prince Arthur of Connaught, a grandson of Queen Victoria. Widowed in 1938, she was the mother of an only son, Alastair, who in 1942 became the second Duke of Connaught on the death of his grandfather. The title became extinct a year later when the young Duke died while acting as an ADC to the Earl of Athlone in Canada. Two years later, Princess Arthur's sister, Princess Maud (married to the Earl of Southesk), died, and her only son succeeded to the Fife dukedom when his aunt died in 1959. The Duke is also heir to his father's earldom, the Earl of Southesk having recently celebrated his ninety-third birthday.

The Countess of Southesk and her niece, Caroline Bannerman. This was the last photograph taken of Princess Maud (His Grace The Duke of Fife.)

JAMES, 3rd DUKE of FIFE
(His Grace The Duke of Fife.)

King Edward VII's second daughter, Victoria, died unmarried. Once described by a Russian cousin as no more than a 'glorified maid' to her mother, she became increasingly bitter in life, and was a source of much mischief between King George and Queen Mary.

At one point Victoria fancied herself in love with Lord Rosebery, one-time Liberal Prime Minister, but the Princess recalled that 'they wouldn't let me marry him and we could have been so happy.' Throughout his life, King George V telephoned his sister every morning. She died eight weeks before him.

At the time, the marriage of Edward's youngest daughter, Maud, to Prince Carl of Denmark seemed a poor match. The Prince, who was Maud's first cousin, had little in the way of prospects; and for a time it seemed that the marriage would be childless. Maud finally gave birth in 1903 to a son, Alexander. Two years later, Prince Carl was elected King of the newly independent Norway, taking the name Haakon, while his son's name was changed to Olav. Although King Haakon's reign commenced with a brilliant coronation at Trondheim, the King and Queen quickly demonstrated that they were fully in tune with the Norwegians' 'quasi-republican' attitude, and the dynasty has prospered.

When King Olav V ascended the throne in 1957, his wife, the Swedish-born Princess Märtha, was already dead, and although there were for a number of years rumors that he was about to remarry (Princess Marina and Duchess Thyra of Mecklenburg were mentioned), he remains a widower.

After years of opposition, the King's only son, Crown Prince Harald, was permitted to marry Sonja Haraldsen, a draper's daughter.

Theirs had been a bittersweet, ten-year courtship. Although his sisters had married commoners, it was hoped that the heir to the throne would marry a princess; and for some years Harald's name was linked with a succession of suitable princesses. The couple, however, remained faithful to one another.

It has long been speculated that King Olav was the main stumbling block to their marriage. He is said to have feared that marriage to a commoner might become a political matter and damage the throne. Finally, having sounded out members of the Norwegian Parliament and various government officials, the King gave his official consent.

The couple were married at Oslo Cathedral and Sonja became Her Royal Highness Crown Princess Sonja of Norway. The Crown Prince and Princess who live at Skaugum, near Oslo, have two children, Prince Haakon Magnus, who is heir to the throne after his father, and Princess Märtha Louise, who has no rights to the throne, the Salic law still being in force. At her birth, however, there were some suggestions from government officials that the law be repealed. The birth of her younger brother led to the proposal being abandoned for the time being.

PRINCESS VICTORIA
(The Associated Press.)

King Olav V of Norway and his family on the occasion of his Silver Jubilee, 1982. Back: Elisabeth Ferner; Alexander Ferner; Johan Ferner; Princess Ragnhild, Mrs. Lorentzen; Erling Lorentzen. Front: Cathrine Ferner; Carl-Christian Ferner; Princess Astrid, Mrs. Ferner; King Olav V; Princess Märtha Louise, Crown Prince Harald; Hereditary Prince Haakon Magnus; Crown Princess Sonja; Martha Lorentzen; Ingeborg Ribeiro; Haakon Lorentzen; Paulo Ribeiro.

In 1953, Ragnhild married a childhood friend, Erling Lorentzen, the first Norwegian princess to marry in more than six hundred years. The Lorentzens live in Brazil where Erling heads the family's shipping firm. Their children, Haakon and Ingeborg, were born in Norway; the younger daughter, Ragnhild, was born in Brazil.

Haakon Lorentzen received a degree in economics from the Pontifical Catholic University. In 1982, he married Brazilian-born Martha Carvalho de Freitas. The couple, who have one son, Olav, live in Norway where Haakon works as an economist for a bank. He enjoys sailing and surfing and in 1981 was the Brazilian hang-gliding champion. Sport is obviously a much-loved pastime of the Norwegian Royal Family. King Olav V won a gold medal in sailing for his country at the 1928 Olympics, a success repeated in the 1960 games by the then Crown Prince Constantine of the Hellenes.

When King Olav's two daughters, Ragnhild and Astrid, married Norwegian commoners, they were permitted to retain the title of Princess, but lost the style of Royal Highness. Many reference works state they have been accorded the style of Highness, but in fact, they are known quite simply as Princess Ragnhild, Mrs. Lorentzen, and Princess Astrid, Mrs. Ferner.

Ingeborg Lorentzen also married a Brazilian, maritimo lawyer Paulo Ribeiro. Their wedding was attended by several hundred guests, including Crown Princess Sonja and Princess Märtha Louise who was one of the bride's attendants. Ingeborg, who once worked as her father's secretary, and Paulo, now live in Norway.

The death of Crown Princess Märtha in 1954 left her youngest daughter, Astrid, as Norway's first lady, a position she held until her marriage in 1961 to Johan Martin Ferner. The announcement of her engagement caused a stir among Norwegians, and more particularly with the state Lutheran church. Neither the country nor the church objected because Ferner was a commoner, rather because he was divorced. Church officials refused to officiate at the ceremony. As a result, the couple were married at Asker Church just outside Oslo by a retired bishop.

Relations between the British and Norwegian Royal Families continue to be very close. King Olav is a frequent visitor to Britain, coming to London each November for the Remembrance Sunday ceremonies, and one of the first solo visits abroad by the Princess of Wales was to Oslo.

Despite Princess Maud's marriage to Prince Carl, and their elevation to the Norwegian throne, the trend among the British princes and princesses has been not to marry members of foreign royal families. The marriages of the children of King George V continued that trend. All except the late Duke of Kent married British non royal subjects and as a result, his children are, in terms of ancestry, the most purely royal members of the present royal family.

The abandonment of their German titles in 1917, and the change of the family name to Windsor, was an astute political move by King George V to appease popular nationalistic feelings. It wasn't seen in the same light by all. One German nobleman, Count Albrecht von Montgelas, commented, 'The true royal tradition died on that day in 1917 when, for a mere war, King George V changed his name.'

George V's less than enthusiastic effort to rescue his cousin, Tsar Nicholas II and his family, leave one with a feeling of unease. The antithesis of his urbane father, King George V was insular by nature, detested traveling abroad and had little time for his continental relatives, except his Greek and Scandinavian cousins.

On the other hand, though his attitude was of little help to monarchism, it was perfectly in tune with British public opinion, which regarded the European monarchies with whom Britain was at war, as little better than tyrannies. Any suggestion that the King was giving even tacit support to the Kaiser or the Tsar would have dealt a serious blow to the British monarchy. When it came down to a matter of family or the British public, the British won: the Windsor throne was secure, but George's first cousin, Tsar Nicholas, was dead at the hands of Bolshevik executioners.

The Princess Royal with her two sons, George (now the
Earl of Harewood) and the Hon. Gerald Lascelles
(Author's collection.)

The marriage prospects of Princess Mary were the subject of much speculation before the war, but her engagement in 1922 to Viscount Lascelles caused much surprise. Lascelles was ten years older than Mary, and had an austere presence that made him look more like the King's brother than his son-in-law. A few years after her marriage, Princess Mary (who had become the Princess Royal in 1931) seemed to lose her zest for life, and, in the 1930's widespread rumors suggested that she wished to obtain a divorce, but was persuaded not to pursue the matter when her brother abdicated. It perhaps gave more point to Queen Mary's remark at the time, 'Really, this might be Roumania.'

Always particularly fond of her eldest brother, Princess Mary was said to have been unhappy that the Duke of Windsor was not invited to Princess Elizabeth's wedding in 1947. Mary did not attend the marriage, officially being absent due to illness.

THE EARL OF HAREWOOD 1984
(The Record.)

After the deaths of her husband in 1947, and her mother in 1953, the Princess Royal led a semi-retired life. Her death in 1965 was timely. It saved her the anguish of having to watch the publicity about the private lives of her two sons.

'It's very odd about George and music,' the Duke of Windsor once remarked, 'You know his parents were quite normal.' Love of music is indeed a dominating theme in the present Earl of Harewood's life, and it was through music that he met both his wives. Educated at Eton and Cambridge, he was taken prisoner during World War II and imprisoned at Colditz. After the war he served for a time as ADC to the Earl of Athlone, then Governor-General of Canada. After resigning as managing director of the English National Opera in 1985, Lord Harewood took on new duties as President of the National Board of Film Censors. He has also edited the highly successful Kobbe's *Complete Opera Book* published in 1953 and re-issued in 1976. His autobiography, *The Tongs and the Bones*, was published in 1981.

61

Twice appointed as Counsellor of State, Lord Harewood fell out of favor with the Royal Family when it became known that he was the father of a son by the violinist Patricia Tuckwell. Their son, Mark, was born just eight months before the death of the Princess Royal. At the time of Mark's birth, Lord Harewood was still married to pianist Marion Stein (who is now the wife of the former Liberal party leader, Jeremy Thorpe), by whom he had three sons: Viscount Lascelles, a filmmaker, who lives near Bath with his wife and four children; James, an accomplished musician who now resides in New Mexico with his second wife and their children; and Jeremy, an executive with a London record company, who lives in London with his wife and three children. The eventual heir to the Harewood earldom is Lord Lascelles' second son, the Hon. Alexander Lascelles, as his two elder children are prohibited from inheriting because they were born before the marriage. As a result, they also are not listed in the Order of Succession. The same applies to Lord Harewood's youngest son, the Hon. Mark; the Hon. Gerald Lascelles' younger son Martin; and the Hon. James Lascelles' second daughter, Tanit, all of whom were born before their parents were married.

Gerald Lascelles, like his elder brother, has been married twice. After his divorce from his first wife, he married Elizabeth Collingwood in Vienna in 1978. He is an authority on jazz and has a huge collection of records at his Gloucester home. He also enjoys motor racing and is President of the British Racing Drivers Club.

In the last fifty years, divorce has intruded into the British Royal Family in quite a remarkable manner, most spectacularly causing the abdication of Edward VIII. The abdication crisis still fascinates us with its drama, pathos and tragedy. With hindsight, many believe it was both inevitable and fortunate that King Edward gave up the throne. Whoever was responsible for withholding from the Duchess the style of Royal Highness ensured her a unique place in history. No woman before had ever been accorded her husband's title, but been denied his style. When the Duke died, the Royal Family and the Duchess seemed to make peace at last, and shortly thereafter it was announced that on her death, the Duchess would be buried beside her husband. And so the woman the family had shunned when alive is now among them forever.

Princess Margaret's divorce in 1977 was significant in that it finally marked the Royal Family's acknowledgment of a fact of life. The marriage of Prince Michael of Kent, however, reminded everyone of the essentially religious basis of the family's occupation of the throne. The Prince marrying a divorcée could be accepted; that she was a Roman Catholic could not be. Legally required to renounce his rights of succession, Prince Michael, like his cousin Gerald Lascelles, arranged for his marriage to take place abroad.

Had Prince Charles wished to marry a Sikh, Moslem, Hindu or agnostic, he could have done so. If he chose a Roman Catholic, he could no longer remain heir to the throne. Flexible and adaptable in so many other matters, the House of Windsor remains a prisoner of the Act of Settlement. Whatever their personal feelings, neither the Queen nor members of her family can alter this centuries-old antipathy for the Church of Rome.

It is impossible to say if the British Monarchy will survive, and if so, for how long. Queen Victoria, King Edward VII and King George V, were all convinced that they would be the last to reign. Common sense, as republicans never cease reminding us, proclaims the whole concept a sham. But, as Virginia Woolf perceptively remarked, take common sense for a walk through London on the day Princess Marina married, and we realize that monarchy is not purely a matter of reason or logic. It is the response to something more deep-seated in human nature and in man's psyche. That, of course, is another story altogether.

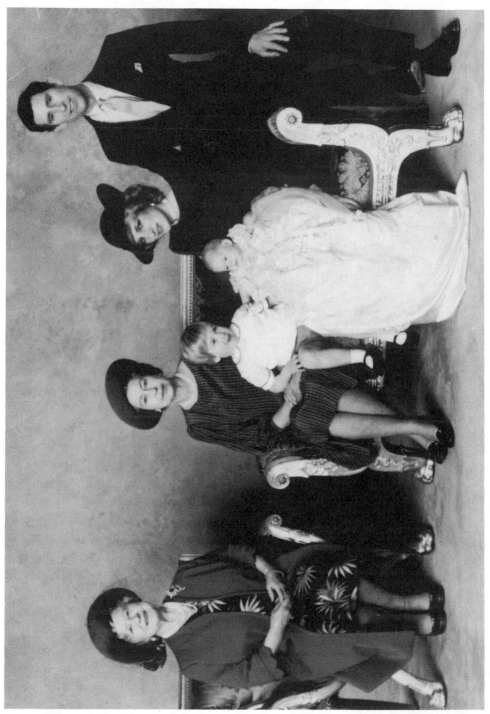

The christening of Prince Henry of Wales, 1984. Left to right: Queen Elizabeth, The Queen Mother; Queen Elizabeth II; Prince William of Wales; The Princess of Wales, holding Prince Henry; and the Prince of Wales (The Associated Press.)

CHAPTER IV

PRINCESS ALICE

The marriage of Princess Alice, the third of the Queen's children, to Prince Ludwig, took place in the drawing room at Osborne House in 1862. It had also been planned by the Prince Consort before his death; fortunately, it turned out to be a love match. At the time of the engagement the Queen wrote to her eldest daughter, Vicky, 'Alice is radiant and only too delighted to be wished joy by everyone. We like darling Louis . . . He is very shy -- and so blushing and bashful when one speaks to him alone about Alice.'

The Prince Consort's death cast a gloom over the wedding. Queen Victoria described it as 'more a funeral than a wedding.' This sad beginning pursued Alice to the grave. She was to enjoy but a brief life, being the first of Victoria's children to die. Two of her children predeceased her, and the fate of her descendants encompassed a series of tragedies of unsurpassed pathos. Intellectually clever, she tended to suffer from comparisons with her elder sister, Vicky. Deeply interested in medical and welfare matters she nursed her children herself, a practice Queen Victoria considered indelicate, and best left to wet nurses.

Her husband, the future Grand Duke Ludwig IV of Hesse and By Rhine, was a straightforward, brave and kindly man, but without the intellectual gifts of his wife. Their sixteen years of marriage were full of domestic bliss, but as each year passed in Darmstadt, increasing difficulties arose. Alice's first three children were all daughters and no doubt there were fears regarding the succession to the Grand Duchy. Lack of money was a constant worry, and in 1866, it seemed that Hesse and By Rhine would be swallowed up by Prussia, having taken the losing side in the Austro-Prussian war. Bismarck appears to have resisted only because of pressure brought by Tsar Alexander II, the brother-in-law of Ludwig's uncle, the reigning Grand Duke.

Four years later while her husband was fighting at Gravelotte in the Franco-Prussian war, Alice was in the forefront organizing hospital facilities, but her effort, coupled with the birth of her children, and the agonizing crisis of religious faith, left her physically and mentally drained. 'I have tried to write as often as I could, but I have only two hours to myself during the whole day. . . . Besides the large Hülfsverein for the "wounded and sick," which is in our palace, I have daily to visit the four hospitals. There is very much to do . . .' Alice wrote to her mother in August 1870.

THE FAMILY OF PRINCESS ALICE
Standing: Prince Ernst Ludwig; Grand Duchess Alice, Grand
Duke Ludwig IV; Princess Elisabeth; Seated: Princess Irene
and Princess Victoria (Broadlands Archives Trust.)

The death of her second son, Friederich ('Frittie') (who suffered from hemophilia), who fell out of a window, was but a prelude of a series of tragedies that marked the family's history over the next seven decades. Princess Alice's death at 35, having nursed her family through diphtheria, mercifully prevented her from witnessing the fate of her children.

After Alice's death, Queen Victoria maintained a close watch on her Hesse grandchildren and their upbringing. As far as she was concerned, there was no question of them being consigned to the care of their other 'very cold, very grand' grandmother, Princess Charles of Hesse and By Rhine.

She also continued to concern herself with her son-in-law who, in his loneliness after Alice's death, found consolation in an affair with the wife of the Russian *charge d'affaires*, Alexandrine de Kolemine. Their timing, however, could not have been more ill-judged. They were eventually married in a secret ceremony on the very evening of the day his eldest daughter, Victoria, married Prince Louis of Battenberg. Darmstadt was full of relatives from his mother-in-law, Queen Victoria, downward. The news burst like a thunderbolt on the assembled family.

'If [your] Papa should feel lonely when you three elder are married -- I should say nothing (though it would pain me) if he chose to make a morganatic marriage with some nice, quiet, sensible and amiable person. . . . But to choose a lady of another religion who has been divorced . . . it would be a *terrible mistake*,' Queen Victoria wrote to her granddaughter, Victoria. To her eldest daughter, the Queen wrote: 'He cannot bear to hear her violently abused to him, for if a man is attracted to a woman and he thinks she is attached to him and has been deceived as to her antecedents he cannot hate her in a day.' Nevertheless, the marriage was impossible. On the instructions of Queen Victoria, the Grand Duke was interviewed by his brother-in-law, the Prince of Wales, and he bowed to family pressure. Madame de Kolemine received 500,000 marks and the marriage was annulled.

The eldest of Alice's children was without a doubt the most remarkable. Born at Windsor Castle in 1863 as Princess Victoria of Hesse and By Rhine, she died at Kensington Palace eighty-seven years later as Dowager Marchioness of Milford Haven. In the intervening period, she was to experience all the tragedies that death saved Princess Alice from witnessing.

Victoria's early life prepared her for what was to come. Assuming responsibility as first lady of the house, she quickly became accustomed in meeting problems and dealing with them without fuss. Practical, without illusions, there was an almost masculine strength about this tobacco-addicted princess (she was still smoking in the year of her death) and it is no surprise that she chose her husband from among the ranks of morganatic princes, nor that he was a naval man, rather than the usual military German princeling.

Princess Victoria's choice of Prince Louis of Battenberg met with the unstinted approval of Queen Victoria, who wrote her eldest daughter, 'Of course people who only care for great matches will not like it. But they do not make for happiness'.

The Battenberg family is a morganatic branch of the Hesse and By Rhine House, having been founded in 1851 when Prince Alexander of Hesse married his sister Marie's lady-in-waiting, Countess Julie von Hauke. Alexander had served in the Russian army, and hoped at one time to marry the Tsar's daughter Olga; having been rebuffed, he was directed toward another Romanov Grand Duchess. Before anything could come of this, however, he met Julie and married her. Outraged, the Tsar banished him from Russia, but when Nicholas died and Alexander's sister and brother-in-law became the new sovereigns of Russia, he was once again welcomed at the court of St. Petersburg. The marriage of his son Louis now brought the Battenberg family into close relationship with the British Royal House, and this was to be reinforced in the following year when his third son, Henry, married the Queen's youngest daughter Beatrice. It was a formidable achievement for a family who were not 'geblüt' and their success carried on into the next generation when the daughters of the house became Queens of Spain and Sweden.

The foundation of this success was due in no small measure to the influence of Countess Julie. Seven years after her marriage, Julie was created Princess of Battenberg; she was a woman of charm, admired by Queen Victoria. Having been a lady-in-waiting at the court of St. Petersburg, she was versed in the vagaries of life among royalty, and realized that the way to success lay not in demanding that which she knew would not be conceded in any case. Unlike the Duke of Teck or other morganatic royals, she never pressed claims to rank or precedence and ultimately had the satisfaction of seeing her children placed alongside the most powerful monarchs in Europe.

Prince Louis of Battenberg entered the Royal Navy in 1868, and steadily made his way up the ladder, but his professionalism and German origin earned him few friends in the service. In 1911, he became Second Sea Lord; the following year he replaced Sir Francis Bridgman as First Sea Lord. Prince Louis was strongly supported by both King George V, and the First Lord of the Admiralty, Winston Churchill. His decision to stop demobilization of Britain's fleet on July 26, 1914 was crucial in ensuring Britain's readiness for war; but when the war came the popular clamor for his removal because of his German connections became too strong to resist, and Prince Louis was forced to resign.

The career of his second son, Earl Mountbatten of Burma, is widely known. His unquenchable ambition and overbearing vanity were less attractive sides of his character, but his achievements in a career that included being Supreme Allied Commander South East Asia, and First Sea Lord like his father were most considerable. It was, however, as last Viceroy of India that he made his most important contribution, bringing to an end the British Raj and ensuring a smooth transfer of power to the subcontinent's new leaders with whom he forged strong links of friendship.

PRINCE and PRINCESS LOUIS OF BATTENBERG

*Princess Louis holding Prince Louis (Earl Mountbatten of Burma);
Princess Alice; Prince George (2nd Marquess of Milford Haven);
Prince Louis; and Princess Louise (Broadlands Archives Trust.)*

The manner of his death was horrible, though his biographer has commented that he would have wished to go out 'with a bang'. It is especially tragic that his grandson, aged fourteen, and two others should have also been killed.

Princess Victoria's marriage to Prince Louis of Battenberg ensured the continuation of the Battenberg family to the present day. In 1947, Princess Victoria's grandson, Prince Philip of Greece, renounced his Greek and Danish titles and took the Battenbergs' anglicized name of Mountbatten prior to his marriage to Princess Elizabeth.

Countess Mountbatten of Burma and Lord Brabourne with their children, 1978. On the stairs: Lord Romsey; Hon. Philip Knatchbull; Lady Amanda Knatchbull; Lady Joanna Knatchbull. In front: Hon. Michael-John Knatchbull; Hon. Timothy Knatchbull and Hon. Nicholas Knatchbull. (Bern Schwartz.)

DAVID, 3rd MARQUESS of MILFORD HAVEN
(The Marchioness of Milford Haven.)

Along with other trials which she faced in her long life, Princess Victoria needed all her strength of character to cope with her two daughters-in-law. The elder, Countess Nada de Torby, was the morganatic daughter of Grand Duke Mikhail Mikhailovitch of Russia, and seemed to have inherited much of his restless spirit; the younger was Edwina Ashley, very much a bright young thing of the 1920s.

Lord Ivar Mountbatten and the 4th Marquess of Milford Haven, 1981 (The Marchioness of Milford Haven.)

Both daughters-in-law figured in contentious trials in the 1930s, and neither emerged from the publicity with untarnished reputations. Nada spent the last twenty years of her life in semi-retirement, having had a son and a daughter; her `grandsons, the present Marquess of Milford Haven and his brother, Lord Ivar Mountbatten, are the sole surviving males of the family.

Edwina's was a personality of strong contrasts. From her grandfather, Sir Ernest Cassel, she inherited great wealth, but like her mother-in-law, she was socialist in her leanings. Before World War II she was a leading socialite; during and after the war she was a tireless worker for the St. John Ambulance Brigade and Save the Children fund, and it was while on tour for them in the Far East that she died in Borneo. Her daughter, Patricia, by special remainder, Countess Mountbatten of Burma, and her husband, Lord Brabourne, were critically injured in the explosion that killed Lord Mountbatten.

Lord Brabourne and his eldest son, Lord Romsey, are active film and television producers; but fittingly, as a goddaughter of Lady Patricia Ramsay (a granddaughter of Queen Victoria), Lady Mountbatten continues to take great interest in the regiment named after her godmother of which she is Colonel-in-Chief - Princess Patricia's Canadian Light Infantry.

Princess Alix and Princess Irene of Hesse and By Rhine,
1887 (David Duff.)

Queen Victoria, Princess Louis of Battenberg, holding her daughter, Princess Alice; Standing behind Princess Louis is Princess Henry of Battenberg (Broadlands Archive Trust.)

Four daughters, Margarita, Theodora, Cecilia and Sophie were born between 1905 and 1914, before Alice gave birth to a son, Philip. Prince Philip was born at the family's Corfu villa, Mon Repos, in June 1921, only a few months before the Greek Royal Family went into exile for the second time. Alice and Andrew eventually separated; he died in Monte Carlo in 1944, and in common with not a few of Queen Victoria's descendants, Alice turned to religion, founding an Order on her return to Greece in 1936. Inheriting the family's tendency to deafness, she had early in life learned to lip read in a number of languages. At the time of the Colonel's *coup d'etat* in Greece in 1967, she was living in a small apartment in Athens. Shortly afterward she returned to England where she lived at Buckingham Palace until her death two years later. Her daughter-in-law, Queen Elizabeth II, is said to have had a special rapport with her.

PRINCE PHILIP and PRINCESS ALEXANDRA OF GREECE
(Ricardo Mateos y Sainz de Medrano.)

Princess Victoria's eldest daughter, Alice, married Prince Andrew of Greece and Denmark in 1903. She was only sixteen when she first met Prince Andrew, and her parents had serious misgivings about the match. Only after Andrew had spent some time at the Battenberg family home, Schloss Heiligenberg, did Louis and Victoria give their permission.

The couple were married in three ceremonies: civil, required by German law, Greek Orthodox, and at the request of the bride's great-uncle, King Edward VII, a Protestant ceremony.

Although she once told a niece that she would never 'marry a king or a widower,' Lady Louise Mountbatten, Victoria's youngest daughter, did both. In 1923, she married the widowed Crown Prince Gustaf Adolf of Sweden. (The Crown Prince's first wife, Princess Margaret of Connaught, had died in 1920.)

The announcement of their engagement provoked a minor controversy because of Louise's title. Although she had become Lady Louise in 1917, she was by birth a Princess of Battenberg. The new title and rank were puzzling to the Swedish government. Swedish princes could only marry royalty; if they married commoners, they forfeited their royal titles and right of succession to the Swedish throne. The Swedish government discreetly inquired about Louise's rank. Prime Minister Stanley Baldwin obliged his counterpart in Stockholm by sending him the official order of precedence at the British court.

Because Sweden was neutral in World War II, Louise was able to act as an intermediary for relatives on both sides of the war. Correspondence would be sent first to her in Stockholm where she would rewrite every letter as if it were coming directly from her, before sending it on to the appropriate cousin.

Princess Alice's second daughter, Elisabeth, was the first of Queen Victoria's granddaughters to change her religion. Although she retained her Lutheran faith when she married Grand Duke Serge of Russia in 1884, Ella, as she was known in the family, ultimately converted to Russian Orthodox in 1891. It was said that she had embraced the Orthodox faith only after she had been persuaded that her failure to convert before her marriage had resulted in her remaining childless. Despite her conversion, she remained childless.

Among the loveliest of Victoria's granddaughters, Ella had an ethereal beauty, charm and sweetness of character that might have done to smooth the abrasive temperament of her cousin Kaiser Wilhelm II, who was one of her most ardent suitors. She chose instead to marry her Russian cousin who she had loved since childhood. The Grand Duke Serge is, even today, a figure of mystery; almost all agree that there was in him a coldness and a streak of cruelty that were noticeably increased by his father's assassination, and made him an even fiercer reactionary. Although he adored his beautiful wife, it was rather in the manner of the love one might lavish on a precious ornament, and he ruled her life with a severity that brooked no contradiction.

Following Serge's assassination in 1905, Ella withdrew from the world, taking the veil and founding an order of nuns. Although she was a well-known figure in Moscow, her charitable work did not save her from the revolution, and like her husband and younger sister, she died a violent death at the hands of the Bolsheviks.

Princess Irene, who was Alice's third child, married her cousin, Prince Heinrich of Prussia. She transmitted hemophilia to two of her three sons.

PRINCESS ELISABETH of HESSE and BY RHINE
and GRAND DUKE SERGE of RUSSIA – 1884
(David Duff.)

Alice's fourth daughter, Alix, (so named because her mother said at the time of her birth 'they pronounce my name dreadfully here') married Tsar Nicholas II. She also transmitted hemophilia to her only son, Tsarevitch Alexis. Alix had undergone much soul-searching about the marriage on account of her religious feelings. Loath to follow her sister, Ella, in abjuring her faith, Alix finally allowed her cousin the Kaiser to win her over to conversion, which is a little surprising considering his violent reaction when his own sister, Sophie, had taken the same course three years before in Greece.

Well-intentioned but weak, immature and politically inexperienced, Nicholas was ill-prepared to reign over turbulent Russia. Alix was even less prepared to be his consort. Shy, reserved, diffident and deeply religious by nature, Alix had little support from her mother-in-law, Empress Marie, whose dominant position at court and in society was reinforced by both law and experience. The fast, gossip-loving, sometimes almost scandalous life in St. Petersburg society had no attraction for her, and both she and her husband preferred a quiet domestic life far from the public eye.

Their joint withdrawal from society robbed Nicholas and Alexandra of much support they might otherwise have enjoyed. The birth of the Tsarevitch in 1904, and the discovery of his illness, threw the Imperial couple back on themselves to an even greater degree. When Tsar Nicholas abdicated in 1917, because of his son's incurable illness, he abdicated not only for himself, but also for Alexis, so that the boy would be allowed to remain with the family. He could not, as Robert Massie wrote in *Nicholas and Alexandra*, 'bring himself to abandon his beloved child to strangers ignorant of all the ramifications of his disease.'

Alexis's illness impelled the Tsarina along a road of religious mysticism and political fanaticism that was in the end to strip the Imperial Family of all its natural resources of support. Accounts of Alix's suffering over her son's illness provokes deep sympathy, but at the same time it is mitigated because of the power held over her by Rasputin. Initially dependent on him because of his supposed healing power, the Tsarina allowed his influence to spread into politics, and her own interference paved the way for destruction of the dynasty.

No one knows exactly what happened at the Ipatiev House in Ekaterinburg on the night of July 16/17, 1918, as the bodies of Nicholas, Alexandra and their children were never recovered. The questions about this event may never be fully resolved unless the Soviet government provides the answers. Since 1918, a number of persons have come forward claiming to be survivors.

The best known of these was Anna Anderson, later Mrs. Manahan, who for many years fought legal battles to establish her identity as the Grand Duchess Anastasia.

E. Uhlenhuth
HOF-PHOTOGRAPH.
COBURG. 1894

PRINCESS ALIX and TSAREVITCH NICHOLAS
(The engagement photograph)
(HRH Princess Margaret of Hesse and By Rhine.)

If the collective fate of these beautiful Hessian princesses, Victoria, Ella, Irene and Alix, seems to have been a story of unending sadness, that of their sole surviving brother was little better. The Grand Duke Ernst Ludwig never recovered from the shock of losing his mother at the age of ten; spoiled and pampered by his parents and sisters, his character had no chance to develop other than in an atmosphere dominated by feminine influence. His accession to the throne when only twenty-three highlights one of the disadvantages of monarchy: succeeding to an inheritance too soon, and therefore being too inexperienced. As a child he had plaintively asked at a time of great anguish why everyone could not join hands and go to heaven. He grew into manhood indecisive, high-spirited, but weak-willed.

Fond of poetry, painting and the gentler pursuits of life, he composed a number of piano pieces and songs, and it was these interest that made many of his family consider that he and his cousin, Victoria Melita of Edinburgh, would make a perfect match. Foremost among the proponents was Queen Victoria herself, but it required all of her persuasive powers to overcome his reluctance to take a wife. 'I have written *twice* to Ernie about the *necessity* of his showing some attention and interest . . . Aunt Marie [Victoria Melita's mother] fears *he* no longer wishes it which I am sure is not the case.'

Victoria Melita appeared ideal. She shared Ernie's love of the arts, but in her case it went far beyond admiration. She was an accomplished practitioner. The fact that Ernie and Victoria Melita shared the same birth date conspired to make the whole idea of marriage perfect.

Their birthday was almost the only thing the couple had in common. An ardent horsewoman, brave and unconventional, Victoria Melita discovered she had married a man whose most remarkable feature was his timidity. For the first few years the disparity between them was drowned in a hectic life of endless parties, journeys, amateur theatricals and socializing. No amount of frenetic activity, however, could disguise the fact that the couple were steadily drifting apart. Their temperaments diametrically opposed, not even the birth of a daughter was able to save the marriage, and the Grand Duchess became determined on divorce. It is said that she laid most of the blame for having married the Grand Duke at the door of her grandmother, Queen Victoria. If so, for once in her life, Victoria Melita showed a measure of mercy that she was rarely to display. To spare the old Queen further anguish in the last year of her life, she waited until Victoria died before proceeding with her divorce.

Prince and Princess Ludwig their niece, Princess Johanna Marina, 1939. (Hessishe Staatarchiv, Darmstadt.)

Whatever his attitude to marriage in general, and women in particular, may have been, the divorce left Ernst Ludwig in a difficult position. All the other male members of the family had made morganatic marriages, and with no heir to succeed him, he was constantly urged to remarry. But with the scandal of his divorce and the underlying reasons for it so well known in Germany, it was no easy task to find a woman of suitable rank to undertake the position. At last, in 1905, he married Princess Eleonore of Solms-Hohensolms-Lich. Then aged thirty-four, Eleonore provided Hesse and By Rhine with a *landesmutter* more in keeping with its past than the extrovert Victoria Melita. More importantly, it was a happy marriage, and she provided the Grand Duke with two sons, Georg, born in 1906, and Ludwig, born two years later.

The family lived a secluded, quiet life until the outbreak of war, when the Grand Duke found himself in a tenuous position. His sister Alix was Tsarina of Russia and his brother-in-law, Prince Louis of Battenberg, was Britain's First Sea Lord. Accusations were made that he sympathized with the enemy. When Hesse declared itself a socialist republic in 1918, Ernst Ludwig, as with all the German monarchs, abdicated, although unlike his first cousin the Kaiser, who was forced into exile, the Grand Duke of Hesse and By Rhine remained at his home, Schloss Wolfsgarten.

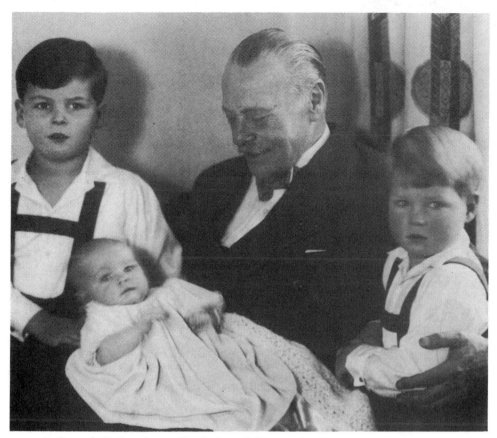

Grand Duke Ernst Ludwig of Hesse and By Rhine with his grandchildren, Prince Ludwig, Prince Alexander and Princess Johanna Marina, 1936 (HRH Princess Margaret of Hesse and By Rhine.)

In 1931, Ernie's son, Georg, married Princess Cecilia of Greece and Denmark (whose mother, Princess Alice of Battenberg, was Ernie's niece), and the birth of three children seemed to ensure the continuation of the Hesse and By Rhine family line. On October 9, 1937, Grand Duke Ernst Ludwig died two weeks before his younger son, Ludwig, had been due to marry the Hon. Margaret Geddes in London. The wedding was postponed until late November, and on November 16, the Grand Duchess Eleonore, with her son, Hereditary Grand Duke Georg and the Hereditary Grand Duchess Cecilia, together with their sons, Alexander and Ludwig, set off by air for London. The plane never reached its destination. Near Ostend in Belgium, fog descended and the plane crashed into a factory chimney. The entire family perished.

As usual, it was the redoubtable Princess Victoria who stepped in at the moment of tragedy and crisis. She persuaded her nephew and his fiancée to go ahead with their wedding, in fact, bringing the date forward to the next day. Though it seemed heartless at the time, afterward everyone agreed that it was the right decision while the family was still in a state of shock and before the full impact of the horror had been able to sink in. The first act of Prince and Princess Ludwig was to visit the scene of the crash and then travel to Darmstadt, where it was announced that they would adopt their orphaned niece, Princess Johanna. Tragically for the couple, Johanna died of meningitis a year later. Prince Ludwig died in 1968, the last of the House of Hesse and By Rhine. He is survived by his widow. Princess Margaret, who continues to live at Schloss Wolfsgarten and who is a special favorite with her British and German relatives.

The Hesse descendant's of Queen Victoria suffered a great variety of tragedies. Two dates stand out remorselessly in the family's story: November 16 and December 14. On November 16, Princess Marie, Alice's youngest daughter died in 1878, at the age of four; it was her mother's kiss during the child's illness that transmitted diphtheria to Princess Alice and led to her own death the next month. November 16 was the date in 1903 when Ernst Ludwig and Victoria Melita's daughter Elisabeth died. It was also the fateful date in 1937 when five members of the family died in the Ostend crash.

December 14, 1878 saw the death of Princess Alice, exactly seventeen years after the death of her father Prince Albert. Little wonder that when the future Queen Mary gave birth to a second son on December 14, 1895, she and her husband should have been apprehensive about Queen Victoria's reaction. Their worries were misplaced; the old Queen preferred to look upon the event as a good augury for the child. Perhaps it was, since the child became King George VI. His daughter, Elizabeth, married Prince Philip, a descendant of Princess Victoria, and through him the Hessian blood still flourishes in the British Royal Family.

PRINCE ALFRED, DUKE OF EDINBURGH
DUKE OF SAXE-COBURG and GOTHA
(Landesbibliotek Coburg)

CHAPTER V

PRINCE ALFRED

The least popular of Victoria's sons, Prince Alfred was nonetheless his father's favorite son. As time passed, however, his mother was to become vividly aware of some of his faults. A Coburger in looks, early in life he formed a passion for the sea and despite being heir to his uncle's landlocked Duchy of Coburg, he was determined to enter the Royal Navy. In reports to his brother, Prince Albert admitted that there was a danger that the navy might create in him a distaste for life at a small German court, but he said, 'we must meet it as we can.'

Queen Victoria went to inordinate lengths to secure the right wife for him. It must, therefore, have been mortifying for her to have to agree that the best, indeed the only suitable princess was a Romanov. The Russians and Prime Minister Gladstone were always the two elements in Queen Victoria's life most likely to arouse her indignation. Even when one of her granddaughters became Tsarina, she was not entirely able to come to terms with Russia.

In every way Marie Alexandrovna's entry into the British royal family was remarkable. The union between the two families was unprecedented: memories of the Crimean war were still vividly alive, as were British apprehensions about Russia's intentions in the Balkans and Asia. The nineteen-year-old Grand Duchess (whose mother was a Hessian princess) brought with her a huge dowry, an immense annual income, magnificent jewels and a Russian priest. Accustomed to being the center of the stage as the Tsar's only daughter, on her marriage to Victoria's second son, Marie found that she was expected to yield precedence not only to the Princess of Wales, but also to the Queen's five daughters. Outraged, the young Duchess of Edinburgh demanded precedence immediately after the Queen herself as the daughter of an Emperor. The Queen indignantly refused, and although following a visit to England by the Tsar, matters were resolved, Marie never really adjusted to life in England. She detested parliamentary government, abhorred the bracing air of Cowes, loathed the London fogs and above all disliked the English language. As a result she made every effort to ensure that her children grew up as Germans. The Princess of Wales was among the many who regretted this. 'It is a pity those children should be brought up as Germans,' she wrote to her son George. 'The last time I saw them they spoke with a very strong accent . . . which I think is a great pity as after all they are English.'

Alfred, Erbprinz von Sachsen Coburg-Goth[a]

In spite of the Duchess, her four daughters never forgot their English origins. Lovers of irony will perhaps see some justice in the fate of the haughty Marie. This proud daughter of a Romanov Tsar, daughter-in-law of a Queen Empress, widow of a German sovereign, died in 1920 in republican Switzerland. Shortly before her death, she received from the socialist German government an envelope containing, of all things, her voting papers. It was addressed to 'Frau Coburg.'

Within a year of their St. Petersburg wedding, the Duke and Duchess of Edinburgh were the proud parents of a son, to be followed over the next ten years by four daughters. Unlike his four sisters, young Alfred's health was not robust, but as the eventual heir to the Duchy of Saxe-Coburg and Gotha, it was decided that he should be brought up in Germany. While the Duke was still pursuing his naval career, his son's upbringing was left largely to his mother, Queen Marie of Roumania has recorded that their father was 'even a little bit of a stranger' to his children.

Young Alfred's brief life lasted only twenty-four years and little has been written about him. Separated from his sisters, he was a lonely young man with a father frequently absent, and a mother who was hard to please and unable to show her feelings. The most significant event in his life was the manner of his death, across which a veil of reticence has been drawn.

In her memoirs his sister Marie simply relates that his health broke down; other writers have attributed it to consumption. *The Times* announced that Prince Alfred's death was due to a tumor, but it seems clear that as *The Complete Peerage* states, he shot himself. Unfortunately, he could not have chosen a more awkward moment for his tragic action, as it occurred in the midst of his parents' silver wedding anniversary celebrations. Though severely wounded, he survived. Angry at so embarrassing an incident occurring when all the family was present, Duchess Marie, against the wishes of the doctors, insisted on having her son moved to Meran, where it was hoped he would recuperate. But the journey proved too much, and young Alfred died alone, except for the presence of a doctor and his manservant.

It is idle to speculate on the reasons for his suicide. A legend has been fostered that he married one Mabel Fitzgerald, but there exists no evidence of this. Whatever the cause, it is an unhappy story. His life is best summed up by his aunt, Empress Friedrich, who wrote to her daughter Sophie, 'I knew how shocked and grieved you would be at the terrible death of your poor cousin. It is indeed terrible. You ask about the cause. It is true that he was giddy and wild, as many young men alas are, and that he contracted an illness of which I know next to nothing, as I have never asked or heard anything about it, one dislikes thinking about it, and still more speaking or writing about it. This was neglected, and the poor boy led a dissipated life besides. Potsdam! -- *there* was not the place for him. He was too inexperienced and heedless and giddy to resist temptations, bad examples, etc. It is not all too miserable! I loved that boy, but there was something irresistibly taking about him. He was one of those who are not fit to take care of themselves, not from evil disposition but from weakness of character.'

The Duke and Duchess of Edinburgh were stunned by their son's death, and Queen Marie of Roumania recorded her astonishment at seeing her mother break down and sink sobbing to her knees as her son's coffin was brought back to Gotha.

When Duke Alfred succeeded his uncle in 1893, his sister Vicky commented, 'Marie will love being Number One,' but as Prince Albert had foreseen, Alfred bitterly missed the Navy and rumors of his wish to abdicate grew. The death of his only son led the Duke to drink more and more heavily and it marked the virtual end of his marriage. He died of the same type of cancer of the throat that caused the death of his brother-in-law, the Emperor Friedrich III.

The daughters of the Duke and Duchess of Edinburgh: Princess Alexandra, Princess Beatrice, Princess Victoria Melita and Princess Marie (HRH Princess Margaret of Hesse and By Rhine)

After Alfred's succession there had been an outcry in Germany that a British Admiral and Prince had become a federal sovereign, a point of view hard to understand when one remembers how many sovereigns and consorts Germany had provided throughout Europe. But Alfred recognized how important it was for his heir to be educated and brought up in Coburg. Following the death of his son, the heir apparent to the Coburg duchy was the Duke of Connaught, but he made it quite clear that he had no intention of giving up his career in the British army. His only son, Arthur, was just as determined to remain in England, and the mantle finally fell upon the fourteen-year-old Duke of Albany, whose father, Leopold, was Queen Victoria's youngest son. Young enough to shed his Englishness and to absorb German ways, the Duke left England, but he and his mother took up residence in Berlin instead of Coburg to avoid Marie's domineering ways.

The marriage between the royal houses of Britain and Russia produced four of the most startling and attractive granddaughters of Queen Victoria. Their beauty, astonishing both in its form and its contrasts, perfectly symbolized the variety of lands in which the princesses were to live. The eldest, Princess Marie, had to adjust to a setting that was totally alien to her. The process took more than twenty years to complete, but in the end she was the one who made the most successful transition. It took Victoria Melita back to the land of her mother's birth, and at one crucial point in her life to the wastes of Finland. As the wife of the Prince of Hohenlohe-Langenburg, Princess Alexandra spent most of her life in the natural heartland of Germany, while the youngest, Princess Beatrice, lived most of her life on the western coast of Spain.

Of the four, the oldest, Marie ('Missy'), was the most radiant. A gifted artist, accomplished writer, fearless horsewoman, she was ardently pursued by her cousin Prince George of Wales and missed becoming Queen of Great Britain only because her mother stepped in to squash the budding romance. Married at seventeen to Crown Prince Ferdinand of Roumania, she spent the first ten years of her married life in a state of semi-isolation, constantly fretting against the restraints imposed by her husband's puritanical uncle, King Carol. Her spirit, however, was never broken, and by 1913, she was the mother of six children, three boys and three girls. More importantly, she had absorbed much of the Latin atmosphere in which she had been living. She gradually came to love deeply the country she adopted through marriage, and when the first Balkan war broke out, Marie was among the first to organize hospital relief and reached the front line with her eldest son and daughter.

The hardships of her early married life proved sterling training for the rigors of what was to come in World War I. Always proud of her British origin, Marie never lost her faith in the ultimate victory of the Entente, and though in public life she always denied that she exerted any influence whatsoever on her rather uninspiring Hohenzollern husband, the world at large knew full well who counted most at the royal palace in Bucharest. Her faith was justified in 1918, when she and her husband returned triumphant to Bucharest, their realm trebled in size and Ferdinand the only Hohenzollern left on a throne.

Unlike her sisters, Victoria Melita and Beatrice, Marie remained stubbornly Protestant to the day of her death. Although she never converted to Orthodoxy (Ferdinand remained a Catholic, but their children were all raised in the Roumanian Orthodox church), no one doubted her patriotism, so staunch had she been in pursuit of Roumania's aims. It must have come as little surprise to Roumanians when they discovered in her will that she had given instructions for her heart to be separated from the rest of her body and buried in a part of Roumania that had been won from Bulgaria in World War I.

CROWN PRINCESS MARIE of ROUMANIA
With her children, Princess Marie and Prince
Nicolas, 1902 (Author's collection.)

Marie sought Roumanian aggrandizement in the Balkans through the marriages of her two eldest children, Carol and Elisabeth, to their cousins, George and Helen of Greece. Neither marriage was a success. Divorce, scandal, rumors and malicious gossip seemed to be the lot of the Roumanian Royal Family, and Queen Marie suffered deeply from the ignominy.

KING CAROL II of ROUMANIA,
Taken shortly before his death
(The Associated Press.)

In due course Carol and Helen were divorced in 1928, but Helen continued to live in Roumania where her only child, Michael, had become king in the previous year under a regency. Elisabeth followed suit in 1935, obtaining her divorce in the Bucharest courts. By then she had begun a liaison with one of her husband's courtiers. She had also gained a reputation for extrovert behavior and language. A self-centered woman, with few friends, her life seemed to be built around frustrations and when she finally left Roumania in 1948, she settled on the Riviera.

Prince Nicolas of Roumania with his first wife, Joana
1932 (The Associated Press.)

QUEEN ELISABETH of the HELLENES
(Claudia Craig.)

Predictably, she met a handsome young Frenchman, Marc Favrat, thirty years her junior, and after passing him off as her chamberlain, she adopted him, trying in vain to persuade the head of the House of Hohenzollern to make him a Prince of Hohenzollern. Not surprisingly, her request was declined, and the former Queen Elisabeth of the Hellenes died in 1956, at the age of sixty two.

In 1918, Carol had an affair with another Roumanian commoner, Zizi Lambrino, the daughter of a Roumanian general. Carol deserted his regiment and fled with Zizi to Odessa (then in German hands) where they were married. Not only had he broken the Roumanian constitution with his marriage, there were also demands for his court martial for desertion. The marriage was annulled, but not before Zizi gave birth to a son, Mircea, named after Carol's youngest brother who had died when only three years old.

Queen Marie's death in 1938 was in many ways fortuitous. Unwaveringly British, she watched with growing anxiety her son King Carol's attempts to withstand increasing Nazi pressure. He was also involved in a public love affair with a Roumanian commoner, the tempestuous Elena Lupescu, much to the displeasure of his family, especially his mother.

In her last years the one consolation granted to Queen Marie centered on her grandson, Michael, the only child of the brief marriage between Carol and Helen of Greece. The exact opposite to herself in temperament, King Michael from his earliest youth had been a reserved character. Keeping his counsel very much to himself, he was able to maintain the dignity of the crown throughout the years of the fascist dictatorship, ably assisted by his mother, Queen Helen. They both had a very English manner, a calm way with dealing with the innumerable difficulties they encountered, and at no time was this better displayed than when the King staged his *coup d'etat* in 1944. The communist government has subsequently tried to play down King Michael's role, but they have never been able to deny his central contribution. Because of the popularity of the King and his mother in Roumania, it took the communists three years before they felt assured enough to force the monarchy's abolition. When they finally acted in December 1947, it was by means of another *coup d'etat* very similar to that which the King himself had staged three years before. It is significant that in Roumania the government did not feel sufficiently certain of the outcome to put the matter to the test of a plebiscite as had been done in neighboring Bulgaria.

Nearly forty years in exile, King Michael has conducted himself with the same discretion and dignity which distinguished him before. He has five daughters, all of whom have been brought up in the Roumanian Orthodox faith.

Unlike other exiled monarchs, King Michael has not taken upon himself the right to name his heir or change the law of succession. Pointing out that such a move required the sanction of the Roumanian parliament, he is content to wait until such matters can be resolved legally. In the meantime, it is clear that his eldest daughter, Princess Margarita, who studied sociology at Edinburgh University, is being prepared to carry on the traditions of the family in the hope that one day they will be recalled to Roumania.

In December 1986, King Michael, accompanied by Queen Anne and Princess Margarita, addressed a meeting of Roumanian exiles in Frankfurt, West Germany. He demanded free self-determination for the Roumanian people. 'The present dictatorial regime . . . could not survive a single day without Moscow's support, the vassal of which it now is, ' he said.

In 1922, Queen Marie of Roumania's second daughter, Marie (Mignon), became the wife of King Alexander I of Yugoslavia. Arranged by Queen Marie, it was a loveless and often stormy marriage, but Mignon produced the longed for heirs. Peter was born in 1923, Tomislav in 1928, and Andrej the following year. Their life together was brought to an abrupt and violent end in 1934, when King Alexander was assassinated in Marseilles. He was enroute to Paris to begin a state visit in the French capital. Marie was spared the event itself; she was traveling to Paris by train, intending to join the king on the outskirts of the city prior to their arrival. From the date of her husband's death, Marie's personality increasingly took on an eccentric air. Morose and careless of her appearance, in 1937 she came to England for an operation and decided to remain for the duration of the war, living with another woman in Bedfordshire. By the time of her death in 1961, she had not been on speaking terms with King Peter for more than eighteen years. The rift between them was the result of Peter's determination to marry his cousin Princess Alexandra of Greece.

The son of a cold and remote father, and a mother indifferent to her children, Peter grew up a lonely young man. He was at an English preparatory school when he succeeded to the throne. He was only eleven, and for the next seven years, Yugoslavia was governed under a regency headed by Peter's cousin, Prince Paul, but despite Paul's pro-British sympathies, Yugoslavia was drawn more and more into the Axis web. In 1941, Yugoslavia was obliged to sign the Tripartite Pact, but the agreement signaled a revolt by the army. The regency was abolished, and at the age of seventeen, Peter assumed full powers as king. Within ten days the German army invaded the country, and twelve days later Yugoslavia was overwhelmed. Peter fled, first to Greece and then to Egypt and finally to England.

Queen Marie of Yugoslavia with her two eldest sons, Peter, age 6 and fifteen-month-old, Tomislav (Author's collection.)

The christening of Crown Prince Alexander of Yugoslavia, 1945: King Peter II, Queen Alexandra, who is holding the Prince. (The Associated Press.)

Throughout the war, King Peter pleaded to be parachuted into Yugoslavia to join the partisans, but the Allies abandoned the monarchist cause and supported the Yugoslav communists who were led by Marshall Tito. In 1945, Yugoslavia became a republic.

In 1944, at the Yugoslav embassy in London, Peter married his cousin Princess Alexandra of Greece. His godfather, King George VI, and Queen Elizabeth were among the witnesses; but without a throne Peter's life became increasingly aimless. A stronger character might have developed in other ways, but the strain of living in exile, the lack of money and the clashes of temperament soon began to take their toll on his marriage. Peter and Alexandra separated, reconciled and separated again. Even more poignant were the circumstances of his death in 1970, at the early age of 47.

The first press announcement stated that King Peter had died in Los Angeles, but in fact, he had died in Colorado General Hospital in Denver. While the original report said he had died of pneumonia, in reality he had died following a liver transplant. It was a friend of King Peter, Eva Marie Lowe, who had released the first inaccurate information, but an astute *Denver Post* reporter unearthed the truth.

The false version of Peter's death had been made up by Mrs. Lowe and Bishop Iriney Kovacevich in an attempt to keep the truth about the liver transplant from the press because they feared that the Yugoslav government would use the death as propaganda. The King's doctors had in fact been waiting for some time for a suitable donor. When a fifteen-year-old California teenager was fatally injured in a motorcycle accident, her body was flown to Denver. There, her parents agreed that her heart, kidneys and liver could be used for transplants. On the same day an unidentified southern California man was flown to Colorado General Hospital.

The transplant was performed the next day; the hospital did acknowledge that the transplant had taken place but refused to identify the patient. On November 4th the hospital announced that the patient died. The following day it was announced that King Peter had died, not in Denver, but in Los Angeles.

When asked by the *Denver Post* about King Peter's death, Mrs. Lowe told the reporter that 'it was impossible' for the King's death certificate to be on file in Denver. She would give no reasons for her statement, but asked that it should not be published. However, his death certificate was found by the Post in Denver, and it appears that the information on it was supplied by Mrs. Lowe. King Peter's name was listed as Peter Petrovich, and according to the certificate, his marital status was given as 'never married.' Further inconsistencies abound. His father's name was given as Alexander Petrovich, his mother's name unknown. Mrs. Lowe later told the press that Queen Alexandra, then living in Italy, although estranged from her husband, had agreed to the operation, and had also wished for the truth to be kept from the press.

Crown Prince Alexander of Yugoslavia with his first wife, Maria da Gloria and their three sons, Peter, Philip and Alexander, 1983 (HRH Crown Prince Alexander of Yugoslavia.)

There was an attempt to have the king's body sent to England for burial rather than entombment in Illinois at a Serb monastery there. An injunction was issued in Los Angeles delaying the burial; in defiance of the court order, plans for the Illinois burial continued. On November 13th, the order was lifted and King Peter was buried at St. Sava Monastery Church in Libertyville, Illinois, the only king to be buried in the United States of America.

There is a sequel to this story. Not long afterward, Mrs. Lowe was divorced from her husband, and in 1974 she married the King's youngest brother, Andrej.

King Peter's only son, Crown Prince Alexander of Yugoslavia, was educated in Switzerland and England. His upbringing was largely supervised by his uncle Prince Tomislav, who until the mid 1980s farmed in Sussex. A godson of Queen Elizabeth II, Alexander served with the 16th/5th The Queen's Royal Lancers, and is now an executive with an international insurance firm. He met his first wife, Princess Maria da Glória of Orléans and Braganca at a party given by her aunt, the Countess of Paris. They have three sons, Prince Peter and twins, Prince Philip and Prince Alexander. After the couple's divorce in 1985, Crown Prince Alexander married Greek-born Katherine Batis.

*Prince Andrej of Yugoslavia with his third
wife, Eva Maria, 1981
(HRH Prince Andrej of Yugoslavia.)*

At the time of his father's death, Alexander declined to be proclaimed King, preferring to await a turn of events in Yugoslavia. 'Both now and in the future, I will be equally ready to accept the free will of the Yugoslav peoples concerning both the destiny of the country and the role of the Karageorgevitch dynasty in it. Even if that decision eventually did not favor a return to constitutional monarchy, I am certain that I and my descendants will continue to play an active role in the political and public life of a country whose history has so reflected the selfless state-building efforts of my family,' the Crown Prince wrote in a May 20, 1980 editorial in *The New York Times*. The editorial was published shortly after the death of President Tito.

Prince Tomislav of Yugoslavia was first married to a niece of Prince Philip, Princess Margarita of Baden, by whom he has two children, Prince Nikolas and Princess Katarina. Katarina, a childhood friend of Prince Andrew, who has worked at several jobs in London, including a five year stint at Harrods where she 'did everything from opening lifts to working as a secretary.' Tomislav's marriage ended in divorce; he is now married to Linda Bonney and they live in Sussex with their two young sons, Prince George and Prince Michael.

Prince Tomislav of Yugoslavia with his second wife, Linda, and his two children, Prince Nikolas and Princess Katarina, 1982 (S. Djukanovic.)

MOTHER ALEXANDRA
(Princess Ileana of Roumania)
(Mother Alexandra)

It was through Queen Marie of Roumania's family that a connection between the House of Habsburg and the descendants of Queen Victoria occurred. Her youngest daughter, Princess Ileana, married Archduke Anton of Austria. Unhappily, the marriage ended in divorce, and the Princess's subsequent marriage to a Roumanian doctor lasted only ten years. Later, the Princess entered a religious order in the United States, and following a period during which she was the Abbess of the monastery, she retired to lead a life of contemplation.

The author of an absorbing book of memoirs, she was also the object of an assassination attempt in the 1960s while she was attending a service at a Roumanian Orthodox church. Her eldest son, Stefan, has become an American citizen and uses the surname Habsburg-Lothringen. He lives in Michigan with his artist wife, Jerrine, where he teaches design and is the director of Education Relations for the General Motors design staff.

Princess Victoria Melita, who was the second daughter of the Duke and Duchess of Edinburgh, was known in the family as 'Ducky.' She was born in Malta, where her father commanded the Mediterranean fleet. Ducky had fearless courage like her sister, Marie, but as Queen Marie herself noted, Ducky could not bring herself to forgive. Her uncompromising nature and inflexibility in the end made her life wretched. Following her divorce from her cousin, Grand Duke Ernst Ludwig of Hesse and By Rhine, she married another first cousin, Grand Duke Kirill of Russia. The news of the marriage did not sit well with Ducky's former sister-in-law, the Tsarina Alexandra. Unable to forgive the scandal that the divorce had brought upon her brother, Alexandra succeeded for a time in having Kirill and Victoria Melita banned from residing in Russia.

After several years the Grand Duke and Grand Duchess were allowed to return, but relations between the two cousins were permanently cold, and it was to be one of the strangest ironies of fate that the murder of so many members of the Imperial Family left Kirill to proclaim himself 'Curator' of the throne.

Their departure from Russia, however, was not the romantic flourish as envisioned by several writers. The couple did not flee, nor did Kirill carry his pregnant wife across the frozen Gulf of Finland to freedom.

'After considerable difficulties I obtained permission from the "Government" to leave for Finland with my family. Our departure was very well and quietly arranged by a commissionaire. In June of the year 1917 I left St. Petersburg by train with my two daughters; Ducky followed me alone,' Kirill wrote in his memoirs, *My Life in Russia's Service,* which was published a year after his death.

In August 1924, Kirill issued a manifesto in which he declared himself 'Curator of the Throne'; in a second manifesto, issued a month later, but never officially proclaimed by the Grand Duke, he pretended to assume the title of Emperor and elevated his two daughters and only son to the rank of Grand Duchesses and Grand Duke with the style of Imperial Highness. According to Romanov House law, however, great-grandchildren of a Tsar were entitled only to the rank of Prince or Princess of Russia with the style of Highness. One of the first mentions of Kirill's second proclamation appeared in *The New York Times* on September 20, 1924. The paper reported a Berlin dispatch to the London *Daily Mail* stating that Kirill had signed a 'proclamation declaring himself "Emperor of All the Russias".' The full text of both manifestos was published in *The New York Times* on December 13, 1924.

'The Russian law of Succession to the Throne,' Kirill stated in the September manifesto, '[does] not permit the Imperial Throne to remain vacant after the death of the previous Emperor and His nearest Heirs has been established. Also, in accordance with our laws the new Emperor becomes such on the strength of the Law of Succession.'

PRINCE AND PRINCESS WLADIMIR OF RUSSIA
(HH Prince Wladimir of Russia.)

But did Grand Duke Kirill have the right to make the declaration? The answer is no.

Romanov House law, which was decreed by Tsar Paul, regarding the succession to the throne is specific, and Kirill was not eligible. Although the Grand Duke was a member of the Imperial Family, he was not entitled to declare himself Emperor or even Curator of the Throne on at least three counts: first, Kirill's wife, Victoria Melita, did not convert to the Orthodox religion until years after their marriage; second, she had been divorced; and, third, Kirill married without the Tsar's permission, which automatically debarred him and his descendants from the succession. As to being 'Curator' of the Throne, at the time he made this declaration, a legitimate heir existed: Grand Duke Dimitri, son of Grand Duke Paul. It is interesting to note that Kirill's heir, Wladimir, has never claimed the title of Emperor, only that of 'Curator' of the Throne.

Grand Duchess Victoria Melita of Hesse and By Rhine, with her daughter, Princess Elisabeth - 1900 (Kunstsammlungen Veste Coburg.)

In the early 1930s, Ducky discovered that her husband had not always been faithful to her, and she never recovered from the shock. It was at this time, too, that misguidedly she gave her support to the Nazi movement in the belief that they offered the best hope for a Romanov restoration.

According to the authors of the book, *Who Financed Hitler,* Victoria Melita contributed 'an enormous sum' of money to German right-wing elements. She also gave 'Hitler some of her jewels'; and in 1924 visited the United States 'to obtain funds for her husband's cause', and although it was never mentioned in the press, for the Nazis as well.

Prince George of Prussia, son of Princess Maria
of Russia and Prince Franz Wilhelm of Prussia
(HH Prince Wladimir of Russia.)

Victoria Melita died in 1936, the first of the four sisters, and was buried at Coburg. Kirill survived her for only two years and was succeeded in his claim by their only son, Wladimir, who was born in 1917 in Finland. Today Prince and Princess Wladimir of Russia divide their time between homes in Spain and France. 'One pretends to nothing. One happens to be born to a certain position,' Wladimir has said concerning his claim as 'Curator of the Throne.' Doubtless this statement, almost autocratical in tone, forms the basis of his belief that he is entitled to alter the law of succession and nominate his only child, Maria, as heiress to the Russian throne. This would be possible under Romanov House Law only if there were no living male heir . . . which there are.

*The wedding of Princess Maria of Russia and The Prince of
Leiningen, 1925. (HSH The Prince of Leiningen.)*

Victoria Melita's two daughters, Maria and Kira, both married into German royal families: Maria to the Prince of Leiningen, and Kira to Prince Louis Ferdinand of Prussia. The present Prince of Leiningen -- Maria's eldest son -- is descended from Queen Victoria as well as from Victoria's half-brother, Carl, 3rd Prince of Leiningen, and her half-sister, Feodora, who married the 5th Prince of Hohenlohe-Langenburg. It was Feodora's granddaughter, Princess Feodora of Hohenlohe-Langenburg, whose marriage in 1894 to Carl's grandson, Emich, reunited the families. Maria's husband, Prince Karl, had the misfortune to fall into Russian hands during World War II, and died a prisoner-of-war in 1946.

The present Prince of Leiningen lives with his wife and children at Schloss Waldleiningen in Amorbach. His elder son, Hereditary Prince Karl-Emich married Princess Margarita of Hohenlohe-Öhringen, while his younger son, Andreas, is married to Princess Alexandra of Hanover. Their marriage in 1981 is the most recent alliance between two descendants of Queen Victoria.

The Prince of Leiningen's younger brother, Prince Karl, emigrated to Canada shortly after his marriage in 1957 to Princess Marie Louise of Bulgaria. Prince Karl's introduction to Canada was made through a Canadian who, during World War II, had been part of the troop in northern Germany that captured the seventeen-year-old Prince. He was then a naval cadet, and spent ten months as a Canadian prisoner-of-war.

Of his move to Canada, the Prince said in a 1983 interview with the *Toronto Star*, 'I have never regretted it for a moment. For the first time we were on our own, free to decide our futures.'

Karl became a stockbroker in the Toronto office of a Wall Street firm, and bought a house in the affluent suburb of Oakville. Two sons, Boris (named for his grandfather, King Boris III of Bulgaria) and Hermann, were born in Canada. Both sons are now married. Prince Boris lives in New Jersey, while Prince Hermann lives in Toronto.

In 1971, Prince Karl settled in Israel. He now lives at Vered Hagalil (Rose of Galilee), a guest ranch near the Golan Heights. Among his duties at the ranch are shopping and chauffeuring. 'The Israelis have been good to me. I'm lucky to have found a place where I got back my piece of mind.'

Karl's family eventually accepted his decision to live in Israel, although at first they thought he was 'crazy,' he said. Every year, however, he still spends time with his family, either with his sister, Margarita, who is married to the Prince of Hohenzollern, or with his elder brother at Schloss Waldleiningen.

THE FAMILY of the PRINCE of LEININGEN
Prince Andreas; The Prince of Leiningen; Hereditary Prince
Kurl-Emich; Princess Stephanie; the Princess of Leiningen
and Princess Melita (HSH The Prince of Leiningen.)

The third of the Duke of Edinburgh's daughters, Alexandra, had perhaps the happiest life of the four sisters. Her beauty was not quite so outstanding as the other three, and her marriage to Prince Ernst of Hohenlohe-Langenburg, ensured that most of her life was conducted far away from the glare of public attention. The present Prince of Hohenlohe-Langenburg, Prince Kraft, is her grandson. He is doubly descended from Queen Victoria, through both his mother, Princess Margarita of Greece, the eldest daughter of Princess Alice of Battenberg, and through his grandmother, Princess Alexandra. The Prince, with his British-born wife, Princess Charlotte of Croÿ, make frequent visits to Britain to see their relatives. The couple live in their medieval castle, Schloss Langenburg, although the Princess spends a good deal of time in Munich where she runs the local office of Christies. They have three children, Princess Cecile, Hereditary Prince Philipp, and Princess Xenia.

Prince Kraft's sister, Princess Beatrix, is private secretary to Princess Margaret of Hesse and By Rhine. His two surviving brothers, Prince Andreas and Prince Albrecht, live respectively in Munich and West Berlin with their wives and children

INFANTA BEATRICE of SPAIN
with her three sons, Alvaro, Alonso and Ataulfo 1913
(HSH The Prince of Hohenlohe-Langenburg.)

The youngest of the four Edinburgh sisters, Princess Beatrice, known in the family as 'Baby Bee,' was described at the time of her marriage as dangerously beautiful. Her marriage in 1909 to Infante Alfonso of the Orléans branch of the Spanish royal family met with strong opposition in Spain. The day following his marriage, Alfonso was deprived of his royal title Infante of Spain, but the dignity was restored to him by Royal Decree, March 12, 1912.

Resistance was principally on religious grounds (unlike her cousin Queen Ena, Beatrice did not become a Catholic until much later); but not a few of the difficulties were due to the ill-feeling in Spain toward her mother-in-law, the Infanta Eulalia, whose fast living and wayward political ideas had made her many enemies. King Alfonso, although privately agreeable to the marriage, did not feel able to give public approval, and as a result, the couple were compelled to live in Coburg and Switzerland for a number of years, during which time Beatrice studied at Lucerne University. Ultimately, they took up residence at the family home in the southwest of the country near Seville, and Alfonso became a general in the Spanish air force. He still enjoyed making solo flights until well into his eighties.

Princess Beatrice appears to have played a less than helpful role in the strained relations between King Alfonso and his wife, and her influence on the King in the 1920s left Queen Ena with the feeling that she had been betrayed by her cousin. The Spanish civil war financially ruined the Infante, and the family moved to England where he worked for the Ford Motor Company. They made their home at Esher and their three sons were educated at Winchester School. During the civil war, their son Alonso was killed by the communists. He was twenty-four. Although Alonso fought on the side of Franco, Beatrice, later in life, was to be unsparing in her scornful comments about General Franco's colorless personality.

Her eldest son, Prince Alvaro, succeeded as the 6th Duke of Galliera on his father's resignation of the title in 1937. He now lives in Monaco with his wife Carla. Their eldest daughter Gerarda's marriage to Harry Freeman Saint in 1963 added another American link to Queen Victoria's descendants. The marriage, which produced two children, ended in divorce, and now Princess Gerarda, who still has business interests in New York City, divides her time between homes in New York and Spain. His second daughter, Beatriz, lives in Switzerland with her Italian husband and two children. Alvaro's elder son was in Spain's diplomatic service, and was Spanish consul in Houston, Texas, when he died in 1975; his younger son, Alvaro-Jaime, is an engineer whose job takes him all around the world. He maintains homes in Monaco and Italy, and is married to Giovanna San Martino de Marchesi di San Germano, whose mother is a sister of Princess Paola of Belgium.

Princess Beatrice died in 1966.

H. R. H. PRINCESS CHRISTIAN
OF SCHLESWIG-HOLSTEIN.

PRINCESS CHRISTIAN OF SCHLESWIG-HOLSTEIN
(Author's collection.)

CHAPTER VI

PRINCESS HELENA

Queen Victoria's fifth child, Princess Helena, presented her with what was probably her most formidable marriage challenge. 'Poor dear Lenchen, though most useful and active and clever and amiable, does not improve with looks and has great difficulties with her figure and want of calm, quite graceful manners.' Ultimately, a suitable partner, from Victoria's point of view, was found in the unprepossessing figure of Prince Christian of Schleswig-Holstein-Sonderburg-Augustenberg. Though prematurely bald and fifteen years older than his bride, Christian had the supreme virtue in Victoria's eyes of being penniless and therefore amenable to her demands.

The principal of these demands was that Christian and his future wife should reside permanently in England 'since useful and active Lenchen' had long ago been marked down to be 'with me for the greater part of the year when she is married and this she knows and wishes.' The couple settled at Cumberland Lodge and speedily set about producing a family. Two boys, Christian Victor, born in 1867, and Albert Victor, in 1869, were followed by two girls, Helena Victoria in 1870, and Marie Louise two years later. Another son, Harold, was born in 1877, but survived for only a day.

Both sons followed military careers. Christian Victor, his mother's 'idol,' served in the Boer War and died unmarried while on active service in South Africa in 1900. Only Princess Marie Louise ever married, but Prince Albert was the father of Princess Helena's only grandchild. It remains unknown if Princess Helena ever knew of Valerie Marie zu Schleswig-Holstein's existence.

Like his cousin, the Duke of Albany, Prince Albert transferred his residence to Germany when it became clear that the marriage of his cousin Duke Ernst Günther of Schleswig-Holstein-Sonderburg-Augustenberg would be childless. He succeed to the Augustenberg estates upon his cousin's death in 1921.

Prince Albert never revealed to anyone, not even his daughter, the name of her mother, although he did tell his two sisters that the woman was of high birth. Born in a part of Hungary now in Czechoslovakia in 1900, Valerie Marie was raised by a Jewish family named Schwalb, whose name she bore until her first marriage to lawyer Johann Wagner. In 1939, she acquired by registration the surname zu Schleswig-Holstein and her birth registration was also changed to include the fact that Prince Albert was her natural father. Valerie Marie knew little of her parentage until she received a letter from Albert in 1931 only a few days before his death.

The change of her name was necessary because Valerie Marie was engaged to marry Duke Engelbert-Charles of Arenberg. As her maiden name was of Jewish origin, Valerie Marie was thought to be Jewish, and under Nazi law, mixed marriages were not permitted. Although her foster parents were Jewish, Valerie Marie was a Roman Catholic.

In July 1938, Valerie Marie's two aunts, Princess Helena Victoria and Princess Marie Louise co-signed a letter acknowledging their niece and attesting to the fact that Valerie Marie was not Jewish.

'We hereby acknowledge and declare that Valerie Wagner is the illegitimate daughter of our brother His Highness Duke Albert of Schleswig-Holstein, who died on the 27th of April 1931. We are entirely ignorant of the names and identity of Valerie Wagner's mother, but we understand that she was a lady of very high rank. Our brother in order to shield this lady's honor never divulged her name to anyone. Valerie Wagner's foster parents, in whose name she was registered, were of Jewish descent, but we desire to emphasize the fact that Valerie Wagner herself is *not* of Jewish birth. Our brother, the Duke of Schleswig-Holstein, in a personal letter to Valerie Wagner, deplored the fact that she had been entrusted to the care of a family of a different race and faith to her own.'

Valerie Marie's first marriage ended in divorce in 1938, and was annulled by the Catholic Church two years later. She married the Duke of Arenberg in a civil ceremony in Berlin in 1939. A Roman Catholic ceremony was performed in October 1940 following the annulment.

In April 1945, the American 9th Army requisitioned the Arenbergs' 300-room castle on the Rhine river. The Duchess was indignant when the officers asked her to give up most of the rooms in the 200-year-old castle. 'I wouldn't put servants in the quarters the Americans asked me to live in. Imagine me getting along in fourteen rooms,' she told an Associated Press reporter.

The Duchess of Arenberg died in 1953. Her aunt, Princess Marie Louise, attended Valerie Marie's funeral at Enghien, Belgium. Born illegitimate, her mother's name unknown, Valerie Marie died a duchess with the style of Serene Highness.

Helena Victoria, known in the family as 'Snipe,' on account of her elongated, doleful features, lived in hope of achieving matrimony one day. She served as her aunt Beatrice's relief companion to Queen Victoria, and then spent the next fifty years in the vigorous pursuit of charitable works. One of the last occasions on which the public saw her was in the film of Queen Elizabeth's wedding in 1947. Seated in a wheelchair, she is seen playfully prodding Prince Richard of Gloucester with her stick. A few months later, Princess Helena died at 77, unmarried.

VALERIE MARIE, DUCHESS of ARENBERG
(Arenberg family archives)

Princess Marie Louise was married in 1891 to Prince Aribert of Anhalt. She returned to England in 1900, having received a message from Queen Victoria while in Canada. Addressed to the Governor-General it simply said 'Tell my granddaughter to come home to me. V.R.'

Back at Cumberland Lodge, she was informed that her marriage had been terminated. She was totally unable to understand why. As she remarked, it was certainly not because of infidelity. For herself, she considered for the rest of her life that her wedding, having been solemnized by the Church of England, was indissoluble and she never regarded herself as being divorced. The *Almanach de Gotha* for 1903 states, however, that the couple were divorced on December 13, 1900. *Whitaker's Peerage*, for the following year, on the other hand, says that 'her marriage was dissolved by joint request on account of a new family law of that ducal house.' The fiction was to be perpetuated ever afterward. The truth, as may be suspected, was embarrassing to all parties concerned. Prince Aribert had been discovered in compromising circumstances with another man, and coming so soon after the Oscar Wilde trials, the British for their part had no wish for the details to become public. Equally, the Germans were anxious to bury the scandal (particularly since Kaiser Wilhelm II had been so instrumental in arranging the marriage) and so the polite fiction was maintained, inevitably giving rise to far more questions than it answered. As usual, King Edward VII summed it all up, succinctly if a shade cruelly. 'Ach, poor Louise,' he remarked, 'she has returned as she went - a virgin.'

In 1956, Princess Marie Louise published her memoirs, *My Memories of Six Reigns*. Delightfully fresh among royal reminiscences, it had the great virtue of being, quite obviously, her own. Time and time again, the princess's own voice comes through, artless, ingenuous, amusing. It was an instant success and was still being reprinted after her death. In her will she left the rights to the book's royalties to the late Prince William of Gloucester.

Though physically very different, both sisters retained a certain unmistakable royal dignity. Perfectly dressed and bejewelled, they acquired a faint air of refined eccentricity, of being slightly removed from everyday reality. Although they had been born Princesses of Schleswig-Holstein-Sonderburg-Augustenberg, their essential Englishness prevailed, so that it was difficult to imagine that they had ever had any connections at all beyond the English Channel.

CHAPTER VII

PRINCESS LOUISE

Born in 1848, the year of revolution, Princess Louise was the prettiest, but least manageable of Queen Victoria's children. She had a determined personality that did not willingly submit to restraint. Named after Prince Albert's mother, she inherited her grandmother's restless spirit. Deeply interested in the arts, Princess Louise was a particularly fine sculptress, who took her work seriously, and as a result was herself taken seriously as an artist. Her best known work is the statue of her mother which stands in Kensington Gardens.

Princess Louise was the object of a number of marriage proposals, among them Prince Albrecht of Prussia, the Crown Prince of Denmark, and the Prince of the Netherlands. None of them appealed to her, and after her sister Helena's wedding it might be thought that she was the ideal person to fill the role of permanent companion to her mother. Instead, Queen Victoria began to groom her youngest daughter for this post, knowing too well that Princess Louise with her independent and difficult moods would be quite unsuitable as a helpmate.

Eventually, it was Louise's artistic talents that led her to meet John, Marquess of Lorne, heir to the Duke of Argyll. Like her, he was a connoisseur of the arts, though in his case literature, and more particularly, poetry, was his great interest. A sensitive, gentle-natured man, three years Louise's senior, he seemed the ideal husband. Initially, Queen Victoria opposed the match, but she was eventually won over when she got to know him more, remarking Louise 'would not marry anyone she did not like.'

Louise's eldest brother, the Prince of Wales, however, proved a stronger opponent of the wedding. Queen Victoria was quick to explain to him her thinking: 'Times have changed; great foreign alliances are looked upon as causes of trouble and anxiety, and are no good . . . . Nothing is more unpopular here or more uncomfortable for *me* and everyone, than the long residence of our married daughters from abroad in my house, with the quantities of foreigners they bring with them, the foreign view they entertain on all subjects; and in beloved Papa's lifetime this was totally different . . . Now that the royal family is so large (you already have five and *what* will these be when your brothers marry?) in these days when you ask Parliament to give money to all the Princesses to be spent *abroad*, when they could perfectly well marry here and the children succeed just as much as if they were children of a Prince or Princess. . . '

PRINCESS LOUISE, DUCHESS of ARGYLL
(Author's collection)

Since it was not in his power to stop the marriage, the Prince of Wales made no further objection, but there is little doubt that his concern was not about his prospective brother-in-law's status, but rather his private life. With his excellent social connections, he no doubt knew more about Lord Lorne than his sister.

The marriage took place in 1871, and was popularly acclaimed, but it was, not surprisingly, childless. An attempt was made at Disraeli's suggestion to give the couple some real purpose in life by appointing Lorne Governor-General of Canada in 1878. When they returned to Britain, Louise spent some time traveling on the Continent and from then on they led separate lives. Her husband died in 1914, but Louise lived for another twenty-five years, taking very little part in public life, although she continued to review the Argyll and Sutherland Highlanders, whose colonel-in-chief she had been named in 1919.

In the aftermath of King George V's illness in 1929, when the Royal Family had been under some strain, Queen Mary wrote to her husband one day, 'To my surprise I hear that dear At. Louise is actually come to court tomorrow, too nice of her and I do feel so touched.'

Princess Louise, Duchess of Argyll, lived until her 91st year, dying in 1939, a year that was to prove even more momentous than the one of her birth.

Admiral Hon. Sir Alexander and Lady Patricia Ramsay on
the their 50th wedding anniversary
(The Countess of Scarbrough/Camera Press.)

CHAPTER VIII

PRINCE ARTHUR

Writing to her eldest daughter, Vicky, in 1858, Queen Victoria mentioned the birth of a third daughter to Prince and Princess Friedrich Karl of Prussia. 'We think perhaps "Mrs. Arthur" may be one of these little girls.' Two years later, Princess Friedrich Karl gave birth to a fourth daughter, Luise Margarete; and in 1879, Princess Luise Margarete became Mrs. Arthur, marrying Prince Arthur, Duke of Connaught, Queen Victoria's third son, and her favorite.

The new Duchess of Connaught settled happily into her new surroundings. She had been glad to leave her Prussian home which had never been congenial. Her father, Prince Friedrich Karl, who was a military martinet with a vicious temper, and her mother lived separate lives that were the talk of Berlin.

Timid, but self-possessed, she was fortunate to have married the most honorable of Victoria's sons. A son, named for his father, and two daughters, Margaret and Patricia, were born of the marriage.

The Duke of Connaught carried out his military duties devotedly, hoping one day to achieve the position of Commander-in-Chief, and though this eluded him, his love of the army never waned throughout his long life. Unlike his elder brothers, he never conducted his extra-marital affairs in public, and though the Duchess of Connaught was no doubt aware of the fact that he had long-standing associations with other women, she was never heard to complain. Chief among these was his attachment to Lady Leslie, which lasted for forty years until his death. Lady Leslie was born Leonie Jerome, sister of the more famous Jennie Jerome who married Lord Randolph Churchill.

Appointed Governor-General of Canada in 1911, the Duke was accompanied to Ottawa by his wife and younger daughter, Princess Patricia. Widely popular on both sides of the Atlantic, Princess Pat, as she was affectionately known, fell in love with one of her father's ADCs, the Hon. Alexander Ramsay, third son of the Earl of Dalhousie. Although the Duchess of Connaught was sympathetic to the romance (knowing all too well the bitterness arranged marriages could produce), the Duke was adamantly opposed to the marriage and withheld his permission.

Princess Pat, however, 'a handsome young woman with a great spirit and a keen sense of humor' as the *New York Times* reported, did not give up hope. In 1916, the Duke's term in Canada was terminated, particularly on account of his wife's failing health, which was little improved by the long, harsh Canadian winters. The Duchess's health continued to decline and she died in 1917, but not before extracting from her husband a promise to allow the marriage to take place once the war ended.

Though this romantic story may not be entirely true, at all events Princess Pat was married in 1919 to Alexander Ramsay. The wedding took place at Westminster Abbey, the first royal marriage to be celebrated there since 1296 when Prince Edmund, son of Henry III, wed Aveline de Forz, and was an extremely popular event. Although she was thirty-two when she married, Princess Pat and her husband lived long enough to celebrate their Golden wedding anniversary. When she married, she chose to relinquish her royal titles, receiving in exchange the title of Lady Patricia Ramsay, with precedence before the Marchionesses of England. Lady Patricia remained an active member in the Royal Family, and was often seen with her husband on state occasions, a tall distinguished, always elegant figure. She enjoyed painting, specializing in watercolors of a sufficiently high standard to merit exhibition. The peaceful, uneventful life she led at her Surrey home was the antithesis of the turbulent existence she would have experienced had she accepted King Alfonso XIII of Spain's proposal of marriage in 1906. Fortunately, for Princess Pat, she had been blessed with good sense rather than a desire for position and wealth.

Her only child, Alexander Ramsay of Mar, who served in World War II and lost a leg in North Africa, lives at Cairnbulg Castle in Aberdeenshire with his wife, Flora, who in her own right is Lady Saltoun. They have three daughters, Katharine, who is heir to her mother's title; Alice, and Elizabeth. Alexander was an ADC to the late Duke of Gloucester, and a page of honor at George VI's coronation. His relations with the Royal Family have always been close, though unobtrusive. He and his wife, Flora Fraser, are guests at major royal occasions, including the wedding of his cousin King Carl XVI Gustaf of Sweden, and more recently at the weddings of the Prince of Wales and the Duke of York. Along with his cousin, the Duke of Fife, Captain Ramsay is a Vice-Patron of the Braemar Royal Highland Society.

The Duke of Connaught's only son, Prince Arthur, had the distinction of serving four sovereigns as ADC; and from 1920 to 1923 he served as Governor-General of South Africa. On his retirement from that post he was succeeded by the Earl of Athlone, brother of Queen Mary, and the husband of his first cousin Princess Alice of Albany. In 1913 he married his first cousin once removed, Princess Alexandra, Duchess of Fife, the elder daughter of Princess Louise.

Prince and Princess Arthur had only one child, a son, Alastair Arthur, born in 1914.

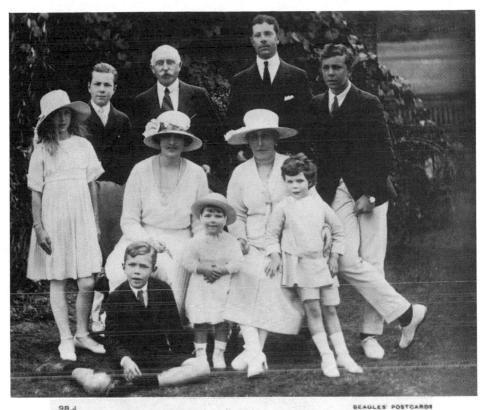

H.R.H. DUKE of CONNAUGHT, H.R.H. Crn. Pce. of SWEDEN and
children, H.R.H. PRINCESS HELENA &
LADY PATRICIA RAMSAY and Son.

With the changes in family name and titles introduced by King George V, the title of Prince and Princess was in future to be restricted to the children and grandchildren of the monarch. Great-grandchildren would bear the surname Windsor with the courtesy title of Lord or Lady before their christian names. So HH Prince Alastair of the United Kingdom of Great Britain and Ireland became Alastair Arthur Windsor, Earl of Macduff, the earldom being the second title of the Fife dukedom.

The death of Prince Arthur of Connaught in 1938 from cancer made Lord Macduff heir to his grandfather, the Duke of Connaught, as well as heir to his mother's dukedom.

Lord Macduff succeeded his grandfather in 1942. The Connaught title became extinct the following year when the second duke died in Canada. The Fife dukedom was inherited by his cousin Lord Carnegie.

The Duke of Connaught's elder daughter, Princess Margaret, also married for love. It was intended that Prince Gustaf Adolf of Sweden would marry Patricia, but when he met Princess Margaret they fell in love and became engaged in Cairo, where the Duke of Connaught was serving as High Commissioner.

THE SWEDISH ROYAL FAMILY - 1917
Front: Prince Sigvard; Prince Bertil; Crown Prince Gustaf Adolf holding Prince Carl Johann, Princess Ingrid. Back: Hereditary Prince Gustaf Adolf and Crown Princess Margaret. (Kungl. Husgeradskammaren.)

Hereditary Prince Gustaf Adolf of Sweden and Hereditary Princess Sibylla with their two eldest daughters, Margaretha and Birgitta (Author's collection.)

Princess Margaret, known as Daisy, initially had to contend with the Swedish court, which for all its French origins, had become thoroughly German in character. The year 1905 was not an easy one for an English Princess to arrive in Sweden as a future Queen. Much to the indignation of her grandfather-in-law, the reigning King Oscar II, his Norwegian subjects had declared their independence. The election to the new throne of the husband of Princess Margaret's cousin Maud can have done little to make things easier for her within the Swedish royal family. Among the Swedes themselves, however, Margaret's natural manners and cheerful disposition made her popular, particularly when contrasted to the haughty attitude adopted by her sister-in-law, the Grand Duchess Marie of Russia, who married Prince Vilhelm in 1908.

When war broke out in 1914, Margaret found herself in a tenuous position. Her mother-in-law, Queen Victoria, was a first cousin of Kaiser Wilhelm II, and she made no secret of her pro-German sympathies. But she and her daughter-in-law (who was also a first cousin of Wilhelm) were able to avoid an open breach.

During the war, Crown Princess Margaret devoted herself to maintaining an open line between the warring factions, not only from her own relatives, but also from prisoners-of-war on both sides. It was a role which her successor, Queen Louise, was to repeat during World War II.

The sudden death of the Crown Princess in 1920, at the early age of thirty-eight, came as a great shock to everyone. She had been expecting her sixth child. Her eldest son, Gustaf Adolf, too, died young, being killed in an air accident in 1947, when only forty-one. Two other sons, Sigvard and Carl Johan married morganatically, and were obliged to renounce their titles and rights of succession. Carl Johan is a businessman. His wife, Kerstin, was a journalist and edited several weekly Swedish magazines, and are among Greta Garbo's few Swedish friends. Sigvard has been married three times; his first wife was a rather tempestuous German, and his second wife, Sonja Robbert, a fashion designer.

Sigvard inherited his mother's artistic talents and is himself a noted industrial designer. His third wife was a well-known stage actress before their marriage. By his second wife he has a son, Michael, who is an architect and lives in Stuttgart, West Germany, with his family. Crown Princess Margaret's other son, Prince Bertil, remained unmarried until 1977.

When King Gustaf VI Adolf, a distinguished archaeologist and authority on Etruscan and Chinese art, died in 1973, he was succeeded by his grandson who took the title Carl XVI Gustaf.

In 1972 Crown Prince Carl Gustaf met a German girl, Silvia Sommerlath, who was working as a translator at the Munich Olympic Games. But, because the Swedish constitution does not permit marriages between a Prince of the Royal House and a commoner, Carl Gustaf and Miss Sommerlath were not married until 1976, three years after he succeeded to the throne. Although Swedish princes lose their right of succession and their titles when they marry commoners, the Swedish monarch can marry whomever he chooses. The following year, Queen Silvia gave birth to a daughter, Princess Victoria. But until the birth of a son, Carl Philip, two years later, the heir to the throne was the King's uncle, Prince Bertil. Even now, should King Carl XVI Gustaf die prematurely, he would be required to act as Regent, or as a close adviser to Queen Silvia if she were designated to that position.

Because of this link to the throne, it was agreed that Prince Bertil, who for many years had been living discreetly with the Welsh-born Lilian Craig, should be allowed to marry without losing either his rank or right of succession. Six months after the King's wedding, Prince Bertil married Mrs. Craig. Not only did Prince Bertil retain his royal rank and place in the succession, his wife became HRH Princess Lilian of Sweden, Duchess of Halland. Their marriage is said to have caused no little resentment among Bertil's brothers and cousins who had had to surrender their rights on marrying commoners. In fact, the special arrangements for Prince Bertil were a recognition of the sacrifice he had made in giving up his marriage plans years before and thereby forfeiting the opportunity of starting a family himself.

King Carl XVI Gustaf and Queen Silvia of Sweden with
their children, Prince Carl Philip, Crown Princess Victoria
and Princess Madeleine, 1986 (Swedish Institute.)

In any case, by the time of Princess Victoria's birth, moves were already being made to amend the Law of Succession. Swedes saw no reason why females should be barred from succeeding to the throne; in 1980 the law was amended so that succession should go to the first-born child regardless of sex. Immediately, Victoria was declared Crown Princess, supplanting her younger brother who had held the position for a few months following his birth. Third in line is their younger sister, Madeleine.

Five years before, another Act of Parliament had stripped the King of almost all his powers, reducing his role to that of a mere representative figure. Nevertheless, he and his Queen remain tireless ambassadors for their country. As Queen Silvia said in an interview with *The New York Times* in 1981, 'We are symbols for the country, a strong means of unifying the people.'

Crown Princess Margaret's only daughter, Princess Ingrid, had experienced a similar development twenty years before. Ingrid, who was born in 1910, married Crown Prince Frederik of Denmark in 1935 (he had first proposed to Princess Olga of Greece and Denmark, but she refused). The couple's first child, Margrethe was born five years later, and was followed by Benedikte in 1944 (for whom Queen Elizabeth of Britain stood as godmother, although Denmark was still under German occupation), and finally Anne-Marie in 1946. By the beginning of the 1950's, it was apparent that there would be no further additions to the family, and proposals were made that the Salic law be abolished, encouraged strongly, it is said, by Queen Ingrid herself. Although objections were made by the then heir, Prince Knud (who was Frederik's younger brother), the Danish parliament in 1953 passed a new Act of Succession, which allowed for female inheritance (and limited the succession to the descendants of Christian X), and Princess Margrethe, then aged thirteen, became Crown Princess.

Queen Margrethe II, who succeeded to the throne in 1972, is known in the family as Daisy. 'It's a family name,' she said in a 1966 interview with *The New York Times*. 'My grandmother - my mother's mother - was called that. Margrethe is a big daisy, I think. Daisy is a small one.'

The Queen speaks fluent Danish, English, French and Swedish and also has a command of German and a little Faroese, enough at least to make a speech in that language. After attending a private school in Copenhagen, Margrethe spent a year as a student at the North Foreland Lodge School for Girls in Kent, England, before going on to Copenhagen and Aarhus Universities, as well as Cambridge and the Sorbonne, and underwent training in the Royal Danish Womens' Air Force. An artist in her own right, the Queen drafted designs for her monogram, and once designed the annual Christmas seals, profits from the sale of which go to charity. She has also illustrated an edition of Tolkien's *Lord of the Rings*.

THE DANISH and GREEK ROYAL FAMILIES, 1980
Back: Prince Henrik of Denmark; Queen Margrethe II; Prince Richard of Sayn-Wittgenstein-Berleburg; King Constantine II; Middle row: Princess Alexia; Queen Ingrid of Denmark; Princess Richard of Sayn-Wittgenstein-Berleburg; Queen Anne Marie; Front row: Prince Joachim; Prince Nikolaos; Crown Prince Frederik of Denmark; Princess Nathalie of Sayn-Wittgenstein-Berleburg; Princess Alexandra of Sayn-Wittgenstein-Berleburg; Crown Prince Pavlos of the Hellenes. (Royal Danish Ministry for Foreign Affairs.)

Married in 1967 to French aristocrat Henri de Laborde de Monpezat (now HRH Prince Henrik), the Queen has two children, Crown Prince Frederik and Prince Joachim. Both attended school in Copenhagen, and while Crown Prince Frederik is in training to assist his mother in her royal duties, Prince Joachim seems destined for a career in agriculture. In 1979, Prince Joachim formally assumed the ownership of Schackenborg, an estate near the German border. The announcement that he was the recipient of a farm caused some controversy in Denmark. The farm had been offered to the Queen by close friends who were childless, but under Danish law estates can only be acquired by those who have agricultural training. Although there was adverse publicity at the time, it was announced shortly afterwards that the Prince intended to study agriculture once his formal education has been completed.

Queen Margrethe and Prince Henrik are determined to keep their sons out of the limelight for as long as possible. She said in one interview 'it is important for children to feel that they have a secure and affectionate home life. That they have - a stable background as I myself have enjoyed.'

Her father, King Frederik IX once said to his wife, 'I have never found a four-leaf clover, but over the years a four-leaf clover has grown up in my family . . . you, my dear, and our three daughters.'

Queen Ingrid's second daughter, Princess Benedikte, is married to Prince Richard of Sayn-Wittgenstein-Berleburg. The Prince, who is a godson of Queen Ingrid, is a forester and manages the family's large estates in West Germany. The Princess, third in line to the Danish throne, followed by her three children, spends about a quarter of the year in Denmark. One of her prime concerns are the problems of the disabled. In 1966, she became Patroness of Project Diadem, a joint program between the U.S.A. and Denmark which enables children from both countries to visit each other. In 1982 she served as patroness of the Fifth Olympic Games for the cerebral-palsied which were held in Denmark.

The youngest of Queen Ingrid's daughters, Princess Anne-Marie, was the first to marry, at 18, in 1964. It was also the first union between the Danish and Greek Royal Families since Prince Wilhelm of Denmark went to Greece in 1863 to become King as George I. A brilliant ceremony in Athens, attended by numerous royalties, a handsome young couple at the start of the new King's reign: everything seemed to presage a renewed life for the Greek Royal Family. Within three years, the family was once again in exile, and Queen Anne Marie joined a long line of Queens without a throne.

The Duke of Connaught was ninety-two when he died in 1942. He had lived longer than any other male member of his family. His had been a life dominated by his strict sense of duty, and a strong sense of family life, which above all had been devoid of excesses and scandal. It is perhaps fitting that his descendants should appear among the most successful and the most enduring of royals today. His great-grandchildren, the King of Sweden and the Queen of Denmark rule over countries where the virtues of restrained politics are the most appreciated and practiced in Europe, and that is something which he would surely have approved.

CHAPTER IX

PRINCE LEOPOLD

Queen Victoria's fourth and youngest son, Prince Leopold, whom she created Duke of Albany in 1881, was the only one of her children to suffer from hemophilia, and it was to circumscribe severely his short life.

The Queen was convinced that he had no prospects of marrying at all, but Leopold, quite naturally, had his own ideas, and to the Queen's great astonishment he set about searching Europe for a suitable partner. Inevitably, he found her at one of the smaller German courts, and it will come as no surprise to learn that his future mother-in-law and wife had come under the scrutiny of his mother many years before.

'Princess Waldeck,' Queen Victoria wrote in 1860, 'is very pleasing and clever and has a very pretty figure. . . but such a plain flat face. She brought her four little girls the day before yesterday . . . enormous, fine children but with cheeks like Eliza Lohlein's[1] children and literally no noses.'

A year after this visit Princess Waldeck gave birth to another daughter, Helen, whom Prince Leopold married in 1882. The new Duchess of Albany's married life was brief. Within two years Leopold had succumbed to his illness, and Helen was a widow with one daughter, Alice. She was also expecting another child who was born a few months later and christened Charles Edward.

Princess Alice lived until 1981, the longest-lived member of the British Royal Family. Married to Prince Alexander of Teck, who was later created Earl of Athlone, she accompanied her husband on his appointments successively as Governor-General of South Africa and of Canada, and she brought to both posts a delightful mixture of modern outlook and manners, skillfully blended with an air of old European royalty that was all the more attractive because it was genuine and natural.

Princess Alice and Lord Athlone had three children: May, who in 1931 married Sir Henry Abel Smith and today lives with her husband near Windsor; Rupert, who took the title of Viscount Trematon following the change of the Royal Family's name in 1917; and Maurice, who lived for only a few months. Both sons inherited hemophilia from their mother. In 1928, Rupert was killed in a car crash in France.

---

[1] Wife of the Prince Consort's valet.

PRINCE LEOPOLD, DUKE OF ALBANY
(Author's Collection.)

THE SAXE-COBURG and GOTHA DUCAL FAMILY, 1930
Princess Sibylla; Prince Johann-Leopold; Duchess Victoria
Adelheid; Prince Friedrich Josias; Princess Caroline
Mathilde; Duke Carl Eduard and Prince Hubertus
(Kuntsammlungen Veste Coburg)

Charles Edward ("Charlie") was brought up quietly in England for the first few years of his life. At age fifteen he was designated heir to his uncle Alfred as the future Duke of Saxe-Coburg and Gotha. It is doubtful if Charles Edward was seriously consulted about this decision, but it was one that was to change the course of his life. 'I have always tried to bring Charlie up as a good Englishman, and now I have to turn him into a good German,' his mother said when she learned that the family would have to move to Germany so that her son could be educated there.

Following the death of his uncle in 1900, Charlie succeeded to the duchy of Saxe-Coburg and Gotha under a regency of Prince Ernst of Hohenlohe-Langenburg, who was married to his cousin, Alexandra, a daughter of the late Duke. To prepare for his future duties, the new Duke, now known to his subjects by the German version of his name, Carl Eduard, studied at Bonn University and at Berlin. In 1905, he married Princess Victoria Adelheid of Schleswig-Holstein-Sonderburg-Glücksburg, a niece of the German Empress Auguste Victoria.

Ernst-Leopold Prinz von Sachsen-Coburg und Gotha and his family: Victoria; Ernst-Josias; Carl-Eduard; Monika; Alice-Sibylla; Ernst-Leopold; and Ferdinand-Christian (Ernst-Leopold Prinz von Sachsen-Coburg and Gotha.)

The outbreak of World War I placed the Duke in an impossible position. Proud of his rank as a Prussian General, he was loath to take up arms against the country of his birth. As his sister, Princess Alice, remarked, he was denounced in Germany for being English, and in England for being German. In November 1918, like all his fellow German sovereigns, he abdicated the ducal throne, although he continued to live in Coburg. A year later, he was stripped of his British titles by an Order in Council, and it seemed that his links with his homeland were broken forever. In the 1930s, as the prospect of another war seemed more certain, there grew on both sides of the channel a movement aimed at burying the enmity between the German and British people. Among those seen to be useful in renewing bonds between the two nations, none was better placed than the Duke of Saxe-Coburg and Gotha. Having joined the Nazi party in 1935, the Duke became president of the Anglo-German fellowship and was a frequent visitor to London, where his talks with influential politicians were of sufficient interest to be brought to the attention of Hitler. But like many of his royal relatives, the Duke was to find that his links with Nazism brought him few advantages (apart from being President of the German Red Cross), but many problems.

Toward the end of World War II, Coburg was taken by the Americans led by General George Patton. Although the general allowed Carl Eduard and his wife to continue living at the family's castle, Veste, the Duke was later interned for a year and a half. After his release in 1946, he was sentenced by a German denazification court and heavily fined. Broken in spirit and racked by arthritis, Carl Eduard lived in seclusion for the rest of his life in Coburg, where he died in 1954.

His eldest son, Johann Leopold, had married morganatically and his second son, Hubertus, died on active service in 1943, so the Coburg duchy was inherited by his youngest son, Prince Friedrich Josias. When the war ended, the Prince, who spent some time as a prisoner-of-war, traveled to Sweden to visit his sister, Sibylla, who had married Prince Gustaf Adolf of Sweden in 1932. There he found employment with the Swedish Johnson line. In 1948 he was sent to San Francisco to work for the American Grace Line, where he was known as 'Mr. Coburg', and after three years was transferred to Brazil. The Prince, who has been married three times, and has four children, now lives on the family estate at Grein, Austria, where he has for some time been working on a biography of his father.

Prince Friedrich Josias' eldest son, Prince Andreas, continues the family tradition by living at Coburg. In 1971, Prince Andreas married Carin Dabelstein; although Carin is a commoner, the marriage is not morganatic, as Prince Friedrich Josias had given his approval. The couple, who live in a private house not far from Schloss Ehrenburg and the Edinburgh Palais (which now houses the Bavarian state archives), have three children.

The Coburgs were once able to boast that the family spanned the entire length and breadth of Europe. Today, they reign in Belgium alone, thus the official visit of Prince Friederich Josias' nephew, King Carl XVI Gustaf, and Queen Silvia of Sweden to Coburg in October 1982 was a happy reminder, both of the family's glorious past, and their continuing influence. It was particularly fitting that the Swedish monarch should tread Coburg soil again, for both his father and mother were descendants of Queen Victoria and Prince Albert of Saxe-Coburg and Gotha. This was the first visit of the king to his mother's home since his childhood, but the King and Queen are frequent visitors to Grein to shoot boar; and Prince Andreas is a godfather of Carl Gustaf's youngest daughter, Madeleine.

PRINCESS BEATRICE
(David Duff)

CHAPTER X

PRINCESS BEATRICE

In the early 1880s a movement was afoot in England to have the law changed to enable women to marry their deceased sisters' husbands. When the Prince of Wales lent his support, it was widely thought that the campaign had been mounted specifically to allow Princess Beatrice, his youngest sister, to marry the Grand Duke Ludwig IV of Hesse and By Rhine. In fact, quite a different fate was in store for her. In 1884, at the wedding of her niece, Princess Victoria of Hesse and By Rhine, to Prince Louis of Battenberg, Beatrice met Louis' younger brother Henry, and instantly fell in love with him.

This was not at all what Queen Victoria had intended for her youngest child, and she was quick to demonstrate her displeasure. For some weeks she refused to even speak to Beatrice, whom she had earmarked to be her permanent companion for the rest of her life. Beatrice was not, however, Victoria's daughter for nothing, and by resolutely declining to abandon the idea of marrying Henry, she won her prince, but not before the Queen had exacted the same kind of undertaking she obtained from Princess Helena's husband, Prince Christian, namely that Henry should live with Beatrice at court.

Prince Henry proved amenable, became a naturalized British subject, received the Garter, was made a Royal Highness, and brought a degree of lightness and gaiety into Queen Victoria's declining years. Inevitably, however, the Battenberg thirst for adventure could not be entirely quenched, and after enduring ten years of court atmosphere Prince Henry begged to be allowed to join the Ashanti campaign. The fever infested African coast broke his health within weeks, and he died aboard ship on his way back to England.

Beatrice was left with four children, three sons, Alexander, Maurice and Leopold, and one daughter, Victoria Eugenie. The two younger sons died unmarried, Maurice of wounds received in action in World War I, while Leopold, who studied at Magdalen College, died after an emergency operation at Kensington Palace in 1922. Both suffered from hemophilia.

In 1917, Alexander relinquished his German titles, and was created Marquess of Carisbrooke. After serving six years in the Royal Navy, Alexander transferred to the Grenadier Guards, with whom he served for the duration of World War I. The first member of the Royal Family to enter the world of commerce, Lord Carisbrooke, although he had no practical experience, was accepted at age

Lady Iris Mountbatten who is holding a photo of her son, Robin Bryan, 1981 (The Associated Press.)

thirty-three into the banking house of Lazards as junior clerk. He later became the director of an Oxford Street store where his duties were described as 'an adviser to buyers of decorative fabrics.' Because there was no special remainder attached to his title, his only child, Lady Iris Mountbatten, was unable to inherit the Marquessate on his death.

At the age of sixteen, Lady Iris was a train bearer at the coronation of King George VI; three years earlier she had been a bridesmaid at the wedding of the Duke of Kent to Princess Marina of Greece.

Lady Iris was married three times. Her first marriage in 1941 to Captain Hamilton O'Malley ended in divorce only five years later. 'If I had divorced him, it would have been okay, but for him to divorce me . . . that was really scandalous,' Lady Iris said in a 1981 interview with *The Toronto Star*.

After the divorce, she went to America in search of work, and had a string of short-lived jobs, including selling brassieres and posing for a bubble-gum advertisement. In 1947, she was arrested for passing a worthless check in a Washington D.C. store. Lady Iris was eventually cleared of the charge, but a check by immigration officials revealed that her visitor's permit had expired and she was working in the United States illegally. After a visit to Canada, she was permitted to return to the U.S. on a permanent visa.

Her second marriage, to American jazz guitarist Michael Neely Bryan, ended after only a few months. Her third marriage, to Canadian William Kemp, took place in Toronto in December 1965. Several weeks later the couple separated, and although they never divorced, Lady Iris continued to live in Toronto until her death.

Her son, Robin Bryan, who was born in the United States, but educated in England, still lives in Canada.

When Lady Iris died in 1982, no member of the Mountbatten family or British Royal Family were present. Her ashes were brought to the Isle of Wight for internment in the Battenberg chapel at Whippingham Church where her grandparents had been married.

The marriage of Princess Beatrice's daughter, Victoria Eugenie, to King Alfonso XIII of Spain was extraordinary in almost every respect. No greater contrast could be imagined than the frail, underdeveloped, black-haired monarch and the magnificently blonde-haired blue-eyed young woman he had chosen as his future Queen. Quite apart from their physical dissimilarities, their backgrounds were totally different. Princess Victoria Eugenie - known in the family as Ena - had grown up at her grandmother's sedate, well-ordered court; Alfonso passed his youth in a country in the last throes of shedding its imperial past. Alfonso counted among his most prized titles that of His Most Catholic Majesty; Ena was a heretic Protestant. Foreign princesses had notoriously failed to become popular Queens of Spain, and it was Ena's fate not to be the exception.

THE ROYAL FAMILY OF SPAIN
Standing, left to right: Infante Jaime (Duke of Segovia); Prince of the Asturias (Count of Covadonga); King Alfonso XIII; Infante Juan (Count of Barcelona.) Seated: Infanta Beatriz (Princess Torlonia); Infanta Isabel Alfonsa (Countess Zamoyska); Queen Maria Cristina (King Alfonso's mother); Infante Gonzalo; Queen Victoria Eugenia; Infanta Maria Cristina (Countess Marone) (The Associated Press, circ. 1928)

There is no doubt that the young couple were deeply in love at the time of their marriage, but it was a love that was completely superficial, as indeed it could scarcely have been otherwise, for they barely knew each other. Their attraction was based purely on external appearance and it was not long before both realized that they had very little in common. The royal pair's dreadful experience of the attempt on their lives while returning from their wedding was considered by many observers to be a fateful augury for the future. Few, however, would have supposed how complete an omen of tragedy that day was to prove.

Shortly after the birth of their first child, Alfonso, Prince of the Asturias, it was discovered that he suffered from hemophilia, following the circumcision that was traditional for Spanish Infantes. Not long afterward, Queen Ena's cousin was to make the same unhappy discovery about her son, Alexis. The reaction of the royal parents says much about their character.

In the case of Nicholas and Alexandra, the crisis served only to bring a loving couple even closer together. But for the Spanish sovereigns, their distress over their son's illness drove them apart: Alfonso turned away from his wife, blaming her for producing a son with such an ailment; Ena was unable to comprehend why fate had dealt her so devastating a blow. Ultimately, the result was the same in both countries. Alexandra developed an almost fierce interest in politics, began to meddle, searched out the faith healer Rasputin, and attempted by every means to protect the absolutist inheritance of her ailing son. Had she been more astute, affairs in Russia might have developed other than they did.

Many critics of Queen Ena subsequently alleged that her mother had kept Alfonso in ignorance of the possibility of hemophilia being passed to any children born of the marriage. There is, however, ample evidence that King Alfonso was well aware of the risk he was taking in marrying Princess Ena.

In Spain, the split between the King and Queen was exploited by aristocrats and politicians for their own purposes, and, at a time when the monarchy should have been showing a united front to the world, it was in fact a battleground of separate factions, each fueled by its own resentments. Alfonso's position might have been different had Ena given birth to a healthy heir. Unhappily, their second son became a deaf mute following an operation. Another son was stillborn in 1910, and the youngest son, Infante Gonzalo, also suffered from hemophilia. Only the middle son, Infante Juan (now the Count of Barcelona) and the two Infantas, Beatriz and Maria Cristina (named for their respective grandmothers) were healthy.

As the monarchy's troubles increased, it became all too apparent that the absence of a healthy heir to succeed the King was a major problem. And yet the royal family continued to maintain the fiction that nothing was amiss. The end, when it came in 1931, was both sudden and surprising. Municipal elections revealed a strong republi-

THE SPANISH ROYAL FAMILY
Standing: Infante Juan Carlos (now King); Infanta Pilar; Prince
Gonzalo. Seated: The Count of Barcelona; Infanta Margarita; Queen
Victoria Eugenia; Infanta Sofía (now Queen) with Infanta Elena on
her lap; the Countess of Barcelona; Prince Alfonso – Switzerland,
1965 (The Associated Press.)

can sentiment in Spain's cities, and overnight the republicans seized their chance. King Alfonso, fearing civil war, went abroad, declaring that he was not abdicating, but merely suspending his royal functions, while the Cortes (Parliament) met to decide the future of the monarchy. It was a fatal mistake.

Once abroad, Alfonso and Ena found little to keep them together and set up separate establishments, parting with some acrimony. Their eldest son, meanwhile, married morganatically, thereby removing himself from the succession. At the same time, the second son, Don Jaime renounced his rights, and the death of Don Gonzalo in a car accident in Austria in 1934, left Don Juan as the heir.

As predicted for so many years, civil war soon broke out in Spain, and though the ultimate victory of General Franco must have given the monarchists some cause to rejoice, they soon discovered that Franco, though royalist in sympathy, like many self-made dictators, had so great an opinion of his own abilities to restore Spain to law and order that he doubted that any other Spaniard could do the job.

It is difficult to disagree. Few would have felt confident in handing power back to King Alfonso, and the complexities of both the political and economic straits in which Spain found itself could certainly not have been solved by the inexperienced and liberal-minded Infante Don Juan.

Juan had married his first cousin in 1935, Princess Maria de las Mercedes of the Two-Sicilies[1]. Shortly before his death in Rome in 1941, King Alfonso formally transferred power to Juan, no doubt in an attempt to emphasize the legitimacy of his son's succession, and though Don Juan pressed Franco to step down and proclaim restoration of the monarchy, Franco continued to rule Spain. The downfall of the other European dictators in 1945 appeared to weaken Franco's position. Don Juan was so convinced that his time had come that he had postage stamps printed showing his portrait with the words Juan III. Franco, however, was too astute a politician to be so easily disposed of. In 1947 a Law of Succession was promulgated restoring the monarchy. However, the General was left by the terms of the act to designate both his successor and the time of return. The only stipulation being that the new king should be of 'royal lineage.'

Finally, at a meeting in 1948 between Franco and the Count of Barcelona, it was agreed that Juan's elder son, Juan Carlos, should be brought to Spain to be educated at a preparatory school in Madrid. He would later attend the military, naval and air academies as well as Madrid's university. Juan Carlos' position was further strengthened

---

[1] Maria de las Mercedes' mother, Infanta Maria de las Mercedes (1880-1904) was King Alfonso XIII's eldest sister.

in 1962 when he married Princess Sophie of Greece and Denmark. The couple were given the Zarzuela Palace outside Madrid as their official residence. Three children, the Infantas Elena and Cristina, and a son, Infante Felipe, were born, thus assuring the succession.

Despite the obvious grooming he was undergoing, Juan Carlos was still not certain that he would be named as the future monarch. At any time, for any reason, General Franco could change his mind. The Carlist specter loomed up once again when the Carlist pretender, Carlos-Hugo of Bourbon-Parma, married Princess Irene of the Netherlands. A few years later, Franco's own granddaughter, Carmen, married Prince Alfonso, the eldest son of Don Jaime, and though the latter had renounced his rights, there was a basis for arguing that he could not renounce rights for descendants who were unborn at the time. Alternative successors were therefore available.

The birth of the Infante Felipe in 1968, however, seems to have decided Franco. Perhaps he had been waiting merely to ensure that a male heir was forthcoming. On the occasion of Felipe's birth, his great-grandmother, Queen Ena, still in exile in Switzerland, announced her intention of attending his christening. Assured of a warm welcome, she landed at Madrid's airport and had a tremendous reception as she drove into the capital. It is given to few Queens driven into exile to return as she did, and perhaps this happy event in the evening of her life gave her some measure of joy to compensate for the life of tragedy that had pursued her from the day she arrived in Spain. Of more significance to the Queen was her private meeting with Franco. Though the two had never had any particular sympathy for one another, they both understood the position of the other. Queen Ena was adept enough not to raise the question of her grandson's succession, but she is said to have returned to Switzerland confident that Juan Carlos would be the first monarch of the restored dynasty. On July 22, 1969, a few months after her death, Franco finally designated Juan Carlos as Spain's future king. On November 22, 1975, two days after Franco's death, Juan Carlos was proclaimed King Juan Carlos I of Spain.

(Although the King's father, the Count of Barcelona, permitted his son to be groomed as the future monarch, he did not renounce his own claim to the throne until May 14, 1977. He said that the Spanish monarchy was once again 'installed and consolidated.')

Long before Juan Carlos's accession, politicians of both the right and the left (as well as many of the center) had predicted that he would be known to history as 'Juan the Brief.' Considered by most to be a mere pawn of Franco, possessing none of Franco's astuteness, Juan Carlos had in fact spent many years in a position which called for tact and diplomacy. Treading carefully between the differing factions that made up Franco's Spain, he managed to survive without offending any, and without becoming the client of any. Today, King Juan Carlos has more power than any other European

KING JUAN CARLOS and QUEEN SOFIA of SPAIN
(The Associated Press)

monarch (the Prince of Liechtenstein and the Grand Duke of Luxembourg excepted) and he has managed to consolidate that power, but in such a way as to be demonstrably doing so in the interests of all Spaniards. In his first speech as King, Juan Carlos expressed 'respect and gratitude to Franco,' but he also expressed his hope to promote a 'free and modern society.'

Democracy, so often fought over in Spain, so rarely enjoyed, has begun to take root under the restored monarchy. With growing confidence, Juan Carlos has presided over the introduction of a new constitution, free elections, the installation of a Socialist government - all steps along the road toward democracy, tentative but real. The attempt in 1981 by right-wing military leaders to seize power was thwarted by the King's call to the rest of the army to crush the revolt. His success is ample proof of the widespread support he enjoys in Spain. Not only support, but genuine popularity, exceeded perhaps only by that which is shown for the Queen.

It is particularly felicitous to end this story on such a note. Nowhere in recent years has monarchy demonstrated not only its ability to adapt to modern times but to provide the lead. That it should be in the persons of two of Queen Victoria's descendants, Their Most Catholic Majesties King Juan Carlos and Queen Sofia of Spain would surely have pleased Queen Victoria immensely, but would also have gratified her beloved Albert to see his ideal of Constitutional Monarchy being realized in Spain today.

THE CHILDREN OF QUEEN VICTORIA

HM Alexandrina VICTORIA, QUEEN OF GREAT BRITAIN AND IRELAND, EMPRESS OF INDIA, succeeded her uncle, HM King William IV, June 20, 1837: Born May 24, 1819 at Kensington Palace, London; Died January 22, 1901 at Osborne House, Isle of Wight; Only daughter of HRH Prince Edward of Great Britain and Ireland, Duke of Kent and Strathearn, Earl of Dublin, Duke of Brunswick and Lüneburg[1] and HSH Princesss Marie Luise <u>Victoire</u> of Saxe-Coburg-Saafeld.[2] Married February 10, 1840 at the Chapel Royal, St. James's Palace, her first cousin HSH Prince Franz August Karl <u>Albert</u> Emanuel of Saxe-Coburg and Gotha. Created HRH Prince Albert, February 6, 1840 and Prince Consort, June 26, 1857. Born August 26, 1819 at Schloss Rosenau, near Coburg; Died December 14, 1861 at Windsor Castle, younger son of HSH Ernst I (Anton Karl Ludwig), Duke of Saxe-Coburg and Gotha[3] and HSH Princess Dorothea <u>Luise</u> Pauline Charlotte Friederike Auguste of Saxe-Gotha-Altenburg.[4]

ISSUE: Victoria (Chapter XII)
      Edward VII (Chapter XIII)
      Alice (Chapter XIV)
      Alfred (Chapter XV)
      Helena (Chapter XVI)
      Louise (Chapter XVII)
      Arthur (Chapter VIII)
      Leopold (Chapter XIX)
      Beatrice (Chapter XX)

1. Born November 2, 1767 at Buckingham Palace; died January 23, 1820 at Sidmouth, Devon. Married May 29, 1818 at Coburg and July 11, 1918 at Kew Palace. Fourth son of King George III (William Frederick) of Great Britain and Ireland and Duchess Sophie Charlotte of Mecklenburg-Strelitz.

2. Born August 17, 1786 at Coburg; died March 16, 1861 at Frogmore House, Windsor. Married (1) December 21, 1803 at Coburg, as his second wife, Emich Carl, 2nd Prince of Leiningen, born December 27, 1763 at Dürckheim; died July 4, 1814 at Amorbach, son of Carl Friedrich Wilhelm, 1st Prince of Leiningen and Countess Christiane Wilhelmine of Solms-Rödelheim and Assenheim, by whom she had a son and daughter (who were half brother and half sister to Queen Victoria.)

   1. Carl Friedrich Wilhelm Emich, 3rd Prince of Leiningen, born September 12, 1804 at Amorbach; died November 13, 1856 at Amorbach. Married February 13, 1829 at Amorbach (div. 1848), Countess Marie von Klebelsberg, born March 27, 1806 at Dirna, Bohemia; died October 28, 1880 at Bonn, daughter of Count Maximilian von Klebelsberg and Maria Anna von Turba, leaving issue two sons.

   2. Princess Anna Feodorovna (Feodora) Auguste Charlotte Wilhelmine of Leiningen, born December 7, 1807 at Amorbach; died September 23, 1872 at Baden-Baden. Married February 18, 1828 at Kensington Palace, HSH Ernst Christian Carl, 4th Prince of Hohenlohe-Langenburg, born May 7, 1794 at Langenburg; died April 12, 1860 at Baden-Baden, son of HSH Carl Ludwig, 3rd Prince of Hohenlohe-Langenburg and Countess Amalie Henriette Charlotte of Solms-Baruth, leaving issue three sons and three daughters.

3. Born January 2, 1784; died January 29, 1844 at Gotha. Married (1) July 31, 1817 at Gotha (div. 1826). Married (2) December 23, 1832 at Coburg, his niece, Duchess Antoinette Friederike Auguste Marie Anna of Württemberg, born September 17, 1799 at Coburg; died September 24, 1860 at Gotha, daughter of Duke Alexander Friedrich Carl of Württemberg and Princess Antoinette Ernestine Amalie of Saxe-Coburg-Saafeld.

4. Born December 21, 1800 at Gotha; died August 30, 1831 at Paris. Following her divorce, Princess Luise married (2) October 18, 1826, Baron Maximilian Elisaus Alexander von Hanstein. Created Count von Polzig, July 19, 1826 by the Duke of Saxe-Hildburghausen. Born June 9, 1804 at Bayreuth; died April 18, 1884 at Schmöllin.

CHAPTER XII

THE DESCENDANTS OF PRINCESS VICTORIA OF GREAT BRITAIN
AND IRELAND, EMPRESS OF GERMANY AND QUEEN OF PRUSSIA

HRH Princess <u>Victoria</u> Adeldaide Mary Louisa of Great Britain and Ireland. Created Princess Royal, January 19, 1841. Born November 21, 1840 at Buckingham Palace; died August 5, 1901 at Friedrichshof. Married January 25, 1858 at the Chapel Royal, St. James's Palace, HIM FRIEDRICH III (Wilhelm Nikolaus Karl), GERMAN EMPEROR AND KING OF PRUSSIA. Succeeded his father, March 9, 1888. Born October 15, 1831 at Neues Palais, Potsdam; died June 15, 1888 at Neues Palais, Potsdam, only son of HIM WILHELM I (Ludwig), GERMAN EMPEROR AND KING OF PRUSSIA and HH Princess Marie Luise <u>Auguste</u> Catharine of Saxe-Weimar-Eisenach. Issue:

    A. Wilhelm
    B. Charlotte
    C. Heinrich
    D. Sigismund
    E. Victoria
    F. Waldemar
    G. Sophie
    H. Margarete

A

HIM (Friedrich) <u>WILHELM II</u> (Viktor Albert), GERMAN EMPEROR AND KING OF PRUSSIA. Succeeded his father June 15, 1888. Abdicated November 28, 1918. Born January 27, 1859 at Berlin; died June 4, 1941 at Haus Doorn, The Netherlands. Married (1) February 27, 1881 at Berlin, HH Princess <u>Auguste Viktoria</u> Friederike Luise Feodora Jenny of Schleswig-Holstein-Sonderburg-Augustenburg, born October 22, 1858 at Dolzig; died April 11, 1921 at Haus Doorn, The Netherlands, eldest daughter of HH <u>Friedrich</u> Christian August, Duke of Schleswig-Holstein-Sonderburg-Augustenburg[1] and HSH Princess <u>Adelheid</u> Viktoria Amalie Luise Marie Konstanze of Hohenlohe-Langenburg.[2]

A1 HI & RH Friedrich <u>Wilhelm</u> Viktor August Ernst, Crown Prince of the German Empire and of Prussia. Renounced his rights to the throne December 1, 1918. Born May 6, 1882 at Marmorpalais, Potsdam; died July 20, 1951 at Hechingen. Married June 6, 1905 at Berlin, HH Duchess <u>Cecilie</u> Auguste Marie of Mecklenburg-Schwerin, born September 20, 1886 at Schwerin; died May 6, 1954 at Bad Kissingen, younger daughter of HRH <u>Friedrich Franz III</u> (Paul Nikolaus Ernst Heinrich, Grand Duke of Mecklenburg-Schwerin and HIH Grand Duchess Anastasia Mikhailovna of Russia.

1. HRH Prince <u>Wilhelm</u> Friedrich Franz Joseph Christian Olaf of Prussia, born July 4, 1906 at Marmorpalais, Potsdam; died May 26, 1940 at Nivelles, France, of wounds received in action. Married June 3, 1933 at Bonn, Dorothea von Salviati, born September 10, 1907 at Bonn; died May 7, 1972 at Bonn-Bad Godesberg, only daughter of <u>Alexander</u> Hermann Heinrich August von Salviati and Helene Crasemann.

    1) HRH Princess <u>Felicitas</u> Cecilie Alexandrine Helene Dorothea of Prussia, born June 7, 1934 at Bonn. Married (1) September 12, 1958 at Bonn (div. 1972), <u>Dinnies</u> Karl Friedrich von der Osten, born May 21, 1929 at Köslin, second son of Karl August von der Osten and <u>Wilhelmine</u> Gottliebe Jenny von Boddion.

        (1) <u>Friederike</u> Thyra Marion Wilhelmine Dorothea von der Osten, born July 14, 1959 at Bad Godesburg. Married August 17 (civil) at Ismaning, near Munich and September 1, 1984 (religious) at Aümuhle, <u>Bernhard</u> Ernst Dieter von Reiche, born April 26, 1956 at Celle, son of Otto Paul Hermann <u>Hans</u> von Reiche and Astrid-Eleonore Gartner.
            a. <u>Felicitas</u> Catharini Malina Johanna von Reiche, born October 28, 1986 at Munich.
        (2) <u>Dinnies</u> Wilhelm Karl Alexander von der Osten, born February 15, 1962 at Bad Godesburg
        (3) <u>Hubertus</u> Christoph Joachim Friedrich von der Osten, born May 5, 1964 at Reinbek
        (4) <u>Cecilie</u> Felicitas Katherina Sophie von der Osten, born March 12, 1967 at Hamburg

        Princess Felicitas married (2) October 27, 1972 at Aümuhle, <u>Jörg</u> Hartwig von Nostitz-Wallwitz, born September 26, 1937 at Verden/Aller, second son of General Gustav Adolf von Nostitz-Wallwitz and Renata Rachals.
        (5) <u>Diana</u> Renata Friederike von Nostitz-Wallwitz, born October 7, 1974 at Hamburg
    2) HRH Princess <u>Christa</u> Friederike Alexandrine Viktoria of Prussia, born October 31, 1936 at Schloss Klein-Obisch, Silesia. Married March 24, 1960 at Wahlschied, Siegkries, <u>Peter</u> Paul Eduard Maria Clemens Maximilian Franz von Assis Liebes, born January 18, 1926 at Munich; died May 5, 1967 at Bonn, son of Martin Liebes and Countess <u>Clementine</u> Pauline Nadine Maria Josepha Eduardina Magdalena Elisabeth Antonia Eulalia Ottilie von Montegelas.

2. HI & RH Prince <u>Louis Ferdinand</u> Viktor Eduard Albert Michael Hubertus of Prussia, born November 9, 1907 at Marmorpalais, Potsdam. Married May 2 (civil and Orthodox) at Potsdam and May 4, 1938 (Lutheran) at Doorn, HH Princess Kira Kirillovna of Russia,* born May 9, 1909 at Paris; died September 8, 1967 at St, Briac-sur-mer, France, younger daughter of HIH Grand Duke Kirill Vladimirovitch of Russia and HRH Princess Victoria Melita of Great Britain and Ireland, Princess of Saxe-Coburg and Gotha, Duchess of Saxony.

    1) HRH Prince Louis Ferdinand <u>Friedrich Wilhelm</u> Hubertus Michael Kirill of Prussia, born February 9, 1939 at Berlin-Grünewald. Married (1) August 22, 1967 at Plön, Holstein (div. 1975), Waltraud Freydag, born April 14,

1940 at Kiel, daughter of Dr. Alois Freydag and Annemarie Rolfs.

(1) <u>Philip</u> Kirill Friedrich Wilhelm Moritz Boris Tanko Prinz von Preussen,[3] born April 23, 1968 at Eutin, Holstein

Prince Friedrich Wilhelm married (2) April 23 (civil) at Hechingen and April 24, 1976 (religious) at Burg Hohenzollern, <u>Ehrengard</u> Insea Elisabeth von Reden, born June 7, 1943 at Berlin, elder daughter of Lt. Colonel <u>Günther</u> Ludwig Jobst Johann von Reden and <u>Ehrengard</u> Johanna von Hülsen.

(2) <u>Friedrich Wilhelm</u> Louis Ferdinand Kirill Prinz von Preussen, born August 16, 1979 at Berlin

(3) <u>Viktoria-Luise</u> Kira Ehrengard Prinzessin von Preussen, born May 2, 1982 at Berlin

(4) <u>Joachim Albrecht</u> Bernhard Christian Ernst Prinz von Preussen, born June 26, 1984 at Berlin

2) HRH Prince Wilhelm Heinrich <u>Michael</u> Louis Ferdinand Friedrich Franz Wladimir of Prussia, born March 22, 1940 at Berlin. Married (1) September 23 (civil) at Düsseldorf-Kaiserwerth and September 25, 1966 (religious) at Bremen-Borgfeld (div. 1982), Jutta Jörn, born January 27, 1943 at Giessen, daughter of Otto Jörn and Ernestine Prübenau.

(1) <u>Micaela</u> Maria Prinzessin von Preussen, born March 5, 1967 at Berlin

(2) <u>Nataly</u> Alexandra Caroline Prinzessin von Preussen, born January 13, 1970 at Frankfurt-am-Main

Prince Michael married (2) June 23, 1982 at Bad Soden am Mittwoch, Birgitte (<u>Gitta</u>) Dallwitz-Wegner, born September 17, 1939 at Kitzbühel, Tyrol, daughter of Hans Viktor Dallwitz-Wegner and Elisabeth Heimann.

3) HRH Princess <u>Marie-Cecilé</u> Kira Viktoria Luise of Prussia, born May 28, 1942 at Cadinen. Married December 3 (civil) and December 4, 1965 (religious) at Berlin, HH Duke <u>Friedrich August</u> Wilhelm Christian Ernst of Oldenburg, born January 11, 1936 at Rastede, fourth son of HH Duke <u>Nikolaus</u> Friedrich Wilhelm of Oldenburg[4] and HSH Princess <u>Helene</u> Bathildis Charlotte Marie Friederike of Waldeck and Pyrmont.

(1) HH Duke <u>Paul-Wladimir</u> Nikolaus Louis Ferdinand Peter Max Karl-Emich of Oldenburg, born August 16, 1969 at Lübeck

(2) HH Duchess <u>Rixa</u> Marie-Alix Kira Altburg of Oldenburg, born September 17, 1970 at Lübeck

(3) HH Duchess <u>Bibiane</u> Maria Alexandra Gertrud of Oldenburg born June 24, 1974 at Oldenburg

4) HRH Princess <u>Kira</u> Auguste Viktoria Friederike of Prussia, born June 27, 1943 at Cadinen. Married September 10 (civil) at Munich and September 11, 1973 (religious) at Felizenweil (div. 1984), <u>Thomas</u> Frank Liepsner, born January 20, 1945 at St. Louis, Missouri, son of <u>Robert</u> Frank Liepsner and Lorene Wonsetler.

(1) <u>Kira-Marina</u> Liepsner, born January 22, 1977 at Munich

(1) Kira-Marina Liepsner, born January 22, 1977 at Munich

5) HRH Prince Louis Ferdinand Oskar Christian of Prussia, born August 25,
    1944 at Golzow, Neumark; died July 11, 1977 at Bremen. Married May 23
    (civil) and May 24, 1975 (religious) at Rüdenhausen, H Ill H Countess
    Donata Emma of Castell-Rüdenhausen, born June 21, 1950 at Rüdenhausen,
    only daughter of H Ill H Siegfried Casimir Friedrich, 4th Prince of
    Castell-Rüdenhausen and H Ill H Countess Irene of Solms-Laubach.
    (1) HRH Prince Georg Friedrich Ferdinand of Prussia, born June 10,
         1976 at Bremen
    (2) HRH Princess Cornelie-Cecilé Viktoria Luise of Prussia, born January
         30, 1978 at Bremen (posthumously)

6) HRH Prince Christian-Sigismund Louis Ferdinand Kilian of Prussia, born
    March 14, 1946 at Bad Kissingen. Married September 27 (civil) and
    September 29, 1984 (religious) at Gut Damp an der Ostsee, Countess Nina
    Helene Lydia Alexandra von Reventlow, born March 13, 1954 at Kiel, only
    daughter of Count Carl Ludwig Erich Ernst Victor Christian Detlev
    Alexander von Reventlov and Nina Pryadkin.
    (2) HRH Prince Christian Ludwig Michael Friedrich Ferdinand of Prussia,
         born May 16,1986 at Bremen

    Prince Christian-Sigismund also has a natural daughter by Christiane
    Grandmontagne, daughter of Daniel Grandmontagne
    (1) Isabelle-Alexandra von Preussen, born September 18, 1969 at
         Sarreguemines, Moselle, France

7) HRH Princess Xenia Sophie Charlotte Cecilie of Prussia, born December 9,
    1949 at Bremen-Oberneuland. Married January 27, 1973 at Bremen (div.
    1978), Per-Edvard Lithander, born September 10, 1945 at Wasa/Götesburg,
    Sweden, son of Patrik Edvard Lithander and Kerstin Ingrid Britta Beck
    Aurell.
    (1) Patrick Edvard Christian Lithander, born June 25, 1973 at Bremen
    (2) Wilhelm Sebastian Lithander, born November 21, 1974 at Bremen

3. HRH Hubertus Karl Wilhelm of Prussia, born September 30, 1909 at Marmor-
    palais, Potsdam; died April 8, 1950 at Windhoek, South-West Africa; Married (1)
    December 29, 1941 at Oels, Silesia (div. 1943), Baroness Maria Anna Sybilla
    Margaretha von Humboldt-Dachroeden, born July 9, 1916 at Bromberg, only
    daughter of Baron Alexander Wilhelm Ernst Bernhard von Humboldt-Dachroeden
    and Katharina Daum. (No Issue).

    Married (2) June 5, 1943 at Schloss Prillwitz, Mecklenburg, HSH Princess
    Magdalene Pauline Reuss, born August 20, 1920 at Leipzig, elder daughter of
    HSH Prince Heinrich XXXVI Reuss and HSH Princess Hermine of Schönburg-
    Waldenburg.

1) HSH Princess Anastasia Viktoria Cecilie Hermine of Prussia, born February 14, 1944 at Brieg. Married October 8 (civil) at Bronnbach an der Tauber and November 8, 1965 (religious) at Erbach, Rheingau HSH Hereditary Prince Aloys-Konstantin Karl Eduard Joseph Johann Konrad Antonius Gerhard Georg Benediktus Pius Eusebius Maria of Löwenstein-Wertheim-Rosenberg, born December 16, 1941 at Würzburg, only son of HSH Karl Friedrich Franz Xaver Joseph Aloysius Antonius Ignatius Expeditus Maria Scholastica, 8th Prince of Löwenstein-Wertheim-Rosenberg and Carolina dei Conti Rignon.

   (1) HSH Prince Carl-Friedrich Georg Eduardo Paolo Nickolos Franz Alois Ignatius Hieronymous Maria of Löwenstein-Wertheim-Rosenberg, born September 30, 1966 at Frankfurt-am-Main

   (2) HSH Prince Hubertus Maximilian Gabriel Franz Louis Konstantin Dominik Wunibald Maria of Löwenstein-Wertheim-Rosenberg, born December 18, 1968 at Frankfurt-am-Main

   (3) HSH Princess Christina Maria Johanna Caroline Magdalene Osy Cecilie Hermine Isidora Anastasia of Löwenstein-Wertheim-Rosenberg, born April 4, 1974 at Frankfurt-am-Main

   (4) HSH Prince Dominik-Wilhelm Nikolaus Sturmius Antonius Charles Benedikt Felix Maria of Löwenstein-Werthheim-Rosenberg, born March 7, 1983 at Frankfurt-am-Main

2) HSH Princess Marie-Christine of Prussia, born July 18, 1947 at Gelnhausen; died May 29, 1966 in an auto accident at Giessen.

4. HRH Prince Friedrich Georg Wilhelm Christoph of Prussia,[5] born December 19, 1911 at Berlin; died April 20, 1966 at Reinhartshausen. Married July 30, 1945 at Little Hadham, Hertfordshire, Lady Brigid Katharine Rachel Guinness,[6] born July 30, 1920 at London, youngest daughter of Rupert Edward Cecil Lee Guinness, 2nd Earl of Iveagh and Lady Gwendolen Florence Mary Onslow.

   1) HRH Prince Frederick Nicholas of Prussia, born May 3, 1946 at London. Married February 27, 1980 at London, Honourable Victoria Lucinda Mancroft, born March 7, 1952 at London, elder daughter of Stormont Mancroft Samuel Mancroft, 2nd Baron Mancroft and Diana Elizabeth Lloyd.

      (1) Beatrice Victoria von Preussen, born February 10, 1981 at London

      (2) Florence Jessica von Preussen, born July 28, 1983 at London

      (3) Augusta Lily von Preussen, born December 15, 1986 at London

   2) HRH Prince William Andrew of Prussia, born November 14, 1947 at London. Married January 2, 1979 at London, Alexandra Blahova,[7] born December 28, 1947 at Brno, Czechoslovakia, daughter of Frantisek Blaha and Vlasta Dokoupilova.

      (1) Tatiana Brigid Honor von Preussen, born October 16, 1980 at London

      (2) Frederick Alexander von Preussen, born November 15, 1984 at London

   3) HRH Princess Victoria Marina Cecilie of Prussia, born February 22, 1952 at London. Married May 3, 1976 at Albury, Hertfordshire, Philippe Alphonse Achache, born March 25, 1945 at Toulouse, France, son of Jean Robert Achache and Jacqueline Henriette Andrieu.

        (1)   <u>George</u> Jean Achache, born June 8, 1980 at London

        (2)   <u>Francis</u> Maximilian Frederick Achache, born April 30, 1982 at London

  4)   HRH Princess <u>Antonia</u> Elizabeth Brigid Louise of Prussia, born April 28, 1955 at London. Married February 3, 1977 at London, Arthur <u>Charles</u> Valerian Wellesley, Marquess of Douro, born August 19, 1945 at London, eldest son of Brigadier <u>Arthur</u> Valeria Wellesley, 8th Duke of Wellington and <u>Diana</u> Ruth McConnel.

        (1)   <u>Arthur</u> Gerald Wellesley, Earl of Mornington, born January 31, 1978 at London

        (2)   Lady <u>Honor</u> Victoria Wellesley, born October 25, 1979 at London

        (3)   Lady <u>Mary</u> Luise Wellesley, born December 16, 1986 at London

  5)   HRH Prince <u>Rupert</u> Alexander Frederick of Prussia, born April 28, 1955 at London (twin of Princess Antonia). Married January 5, 1982 at London, Ziba Rastegar-Javaheri, born December 12, 1954 at Teheran, Iran, daughter of Mortéza Rastegar-Javaheri and Rabeéh Baghaii-Kermani.

        (1)   <u>Brigid</u> Elizabeth Soraya von Preussen, born December 24, 1983 at London

        (2)   <u>Astrid</u> Katherine Rabeéh von Preussen, born April 16, 1985 at London

5.   HRH Princess <u>Alexandrine</u> Irene of Prussia, born April 7, 1915 at Berlin; died October 2, 1980 at Starnberg, West Germany.

6.   HRH Princess <u>Cecilie</u> Viktoria Anastasia Zita Thyra Adelheid of Prussia, born September 5, 1917 at Schloss Cecilienhof, Potsdam; died April 21, 1975 at Schloss Königstein, Taunus. Married June 21, 1949 at Burg Hohenzollern <u>Clyde</u> Kenneth Harris, born April 18, 1918 at Maud, Oklahoma; died March 2, 1958 at Amarillo, Texas, son of Bert Harris and Aurora Vandevere.

  1)   <u>Kira</u> Alexandrine Brigid Cecilie Ingrid Harris, born October 20, 1954 at Amarillo, Texas. Married May 22, 1982 at Las Acequias Farms, Santa Fe, New Mexico, John <u>Mitchell</u> Johnson, born May 12, 1951 at Dallas, Texas, son of Joseph <u>Edward</u> Johnson and Blanche Dabney.

        (1)   <u>Philip</u> Louis Johnson, born October 18, 1985 at Fort Worth, Texas

A2   HRH Prince Wilhelm <u>Eitel-Friedrich</u> Christian Karl of Prussia, born July 7, 1883 at Marmorpalais, Potsdam; died December 8, 1942 at Potsdam. Married February 27, 1906 at Berlin (div. 1926), HH Duchess Sophie Charlotte of Oldenburg,[8] born February 2, 1879 at Oldenburg; died March 29, 1964 at Westerstede, Oldenburg, eldest daughter of HRH Friedrich August, Grand Duke of Oldenburg and HRH Princess <u>Elisabeth</u> Anna of Prussia. (No Issue.)

A3   HRH Prince <u>Adalbert</u> Ferdinand Berengar Viktor of Prussia, born July 14, 1884 at Marmorpalais, Potsdam; died September 22, 1948 at La Tour de Peilz, Switzerland. Married August 3, 1914 at Wilhelmshaven, HH Princess <u>Adelheid</u> Erna Karoline Marie Elisabeth of Saxe-Meiningen, Duchess of Saxony, born August 16, 1891 at Cassel; died April 25, 1971 at La Tour de Peilz, Switzerland, second daughter of HH Prince <u>Friedrich</u> Johann Bernhard Hermann Heinrich Moritz of Saxe-Meiningen, Duke of

Saxony[9] and HSH Princess Adelheid Karoline Mathilde Emilie Agnes Ida Sophie of Lippe.

1. HRH Princess Victoria Marina of Prussia, born September 4, 1915 at Berlin; died September 4, 1915 at Berlin

2. HRH Princess Victoria Marina of Prussia, born September 11, 1917 at Kiel; died January 21, 1981 at Taos, New Mexico. Married September 26, 1947 at Springfield, Missouri, Kirby William Patterson, born July 24, 1907 at Springfield, Missouri; died June 4, 1984 at Springfield, Missouri, son of Orin Patterson and Emily Robards.
   1) Berengar Orin Bernhard Kirby Patterson, born August 21, 1948 at Springfield, Missouri
   2) Marina Adelaide Emily Patterson, born August 21, 1948 at Springfield, Missouri (twin of Berengar). Married September 24, 1982 at Las Vegas, Nevada, John William Engel, born September 22, 1946 at Norwalk, California, son of Clarence Engel and Madea Pearl Moore.
      (1) William John Engel, born February 17, 1983 at Downey, California

   3) Dohna Maria Patterson, born August 7, 1954 at Springfield, Missouri. Married July 28, 1974 at Scottsdale, Arizona, Stephen Leroy Pearl, born August 15, 1951 at Camden, New Jersey, son of Leroy Pearl and Abigail Corson

3. HRH Prince Wilhelm-Victor Ernst Freund Friedrich Georg Adalbert of Prussia, born February 15, 1919 at Kiel. Married July 20, 1944 at Donaueschingen, Countess Marie-Antoinette Franziska Ladislaja Josepha Paula Bernhardine Agnes Hoyos, Baroness zu Stichsenstein, born June 27, 1920 at Hohenthurm, eldest daughter of Count Friedrich Heinrich Joseph Maria Gregor Kolumbus Hoyos, Baron zu Stichsenstein and Wilhelmine Pauline Sidonie Marie Julitta von Wuthenau.
   1) HRH Princess Marie Louise Marina Franziska of Prussia, born September 18, 1945 at Konstanz. Married May 19 (civil) at Hechingen and May 22, 1971 (religious) at Donaueschingen, H Ill H Count Rudolf Maria Emil Franz Friedrich Carl Antonius Christopherus Hubertus Wenzel Michael von Schönburg-Glauchau, born September 25, 1932 at Wechelsberg, second son of H Ill H Count Friedrich Carl Heinrich Ludwig Bohuslaw Anton Jakob Joseph Joachim Maria von Schönburg-Glauchau and Countess Maria Anna von Barorów-Baworowska.
      (1) H Ill H Countess Sophie Anastasia Wilhelmine Marie Antoinette von Schönburg-Glauchau, born May 17, 1979 at Malaga, Spain
      (2) H Ill H Count Friedrich Wilhelm Simeon Dionysius Joachim Rudolf Maria Adalbert von Schönburg-Glauchau, born April 27, 1985 at Malaga, Spain
   2) HRH Prince Adalbert-Adelhart Alexander Friedrich Joachim Christian of Prussia, born March 4, 1948 at Konstantz. Married June 14, 1981 at Glentorf, near Brunswick, Eva Maria Kudicke, born June 30, 1951 at Teheran, Iran, daughter of Günther Kudicke and Barbara Ziegler.

(1) <u>Alexander</u> Markus Wilhelm-Victor Prinz von Preussen, born October 3, 1984 at Munich

(2) <u>Christian</u> Friedrich Wilhelm Johannes Prinz von Preussen, born July 3, 1986 at Munich

(3) <u>Philipp</u> Heinrich Adalbert Günther Prinz von Preussen, born July 3, 1986 at Munich (twin of Prince Christian)

A4 HRH Prince <u>August Wilhelm</u> Heinrich Günther Viktor of Prussia, born January 29, 1887 at Stadtschloss, Potsdam; died March 25, 1949 at Stuttgart. Married October 22, 1908 at Berlin (div. 1920), HH Princess <u>Alexandra Viktoria</u> Auguste Leopoldine Charlotte Amalie Wilhelmine of Schleswig-Holstein-Sonderburg-Glücksburg,[10] born April 21, 1887 at Grünholz; died April 15, 1957 at Lyon, second daughter of HH <u>Friedrich Ferdinand</u> Georg Christian Karl Wilhelm, Duke of Schleswig-Holstein-Sonderburg-Glücksburg and HH Princess Viktoria Friederike Auguste Marie <u>Caroline Mathilde</u> of Schleswig-Holstein-Sonderburg-Augustenburg.[11]

1. HRH Prince <u>Alexander Ferdinand</u> Albrecht Achilles Wilhelm Joseph Viktor Karl Feodor of Prussia, born December 26, 1912 at Berlin; died June 12, 1985 at Wiesbaden. Married December 19, 1938 at Dresden, Irmgard Weygand,[12] born August 22, 1912 at Mainz, daughter of Friedrich Weygand and <u>Karla</u> Franziska Oheim.

1) <u>Stephan</u> Alexander Dieter Friedrich Prinz von Preussen, born September 30, 1939 at Dresden. Married (1) February 28, 1964 at Wiesbaden (div. 1976), Heide Schmidt, born February 6, 1939 at Frankfurt-am-Main, daughter of Dr. <u>Ernst</u> Arthur Julius Schmidt and <u>Gertrud</u> Elisabeth Auguste Gundlach.

(1) <u>Stephanie</u> Viktoria Luise Irmgard Gertrud Prinzessin von Preussen, born September 21, 1966 at Mannheim-Neckarau.

Stephan married (2) June 19, 1981 at Kochel-am-See, Bavaria, Hannelore-Maria Kerscher, born October 26, 1952 at Passau, daughter of Leo Kerscher and Martha Sufcak.

A5 HRH Prince <u>Oskar</u> Karl Gustav Adolf of Prussia, born July 27, 1888 at Marmorpalais, Potsdam; died January 27, 1958 at Munich. Married July 31, 1914 at Berlin, Countess <u>Ina-Marie</u> Helene Adele Elise von Bassewitz. Created Countess von Ruppin, 1914 and Princess of Prussia with the qualification of Royal Highness, 1920. Born January 27, 1888 at Bristow; died September 17, 1973 at Munich, younger daughter of Count <u>Karl</u> Heinrich Ludwig von Bassewitz-Levetzow and Countess <u>Margarete</u> Cäcilie Luise Alexandrine Friederike Susette von der Schulenburg.

1. HRH Prince <u>Oskar</u> Wilhelm Karl Hans Kuno of Prussia, born July 12, 1915 at Potsdam; died September 5, 1939 in action in Poland.

2. HRH Prince <u>Burchard</u> Friedrich Max Werner Georg of Prussia, born January 8, 1917 at Potsdam. Married January 30 (civil) and January 31, 1961 (religious) at Munich, H Ill H Countess <u>Eleonore</u> Vera Alexia Anna Maria Fugger von Babenhausen,[13] born January 31, 1925 at Babenhausen, eldest daughter of Major General Count <u>Leopold</u> Heinrich Carl Friedrich Maria Fugger von

Babenhausen and Countess <u>Vera</u> Aloysia Emma Theresia Maria Josefine Czernin von und zu Chudenitz.

3. HRH Princess <u>Herzeleide-Ina-Marie</u> Sophie Charlotte Else of Prussia, born December 25, 1918 at Bristow, Mecklenburg. Married August 15 (civil) and August 16, 1938 (religious) at Potsdam, HSH <u>Karl</u> Peter Franz Andreas Alexander, Prince Biron von Curland, born June 15, 1907 at Schloss Wartenberg, Gross Wartenberg, Silesia; died February 28, 1982 at Munich, eldest son of HSH <u>Gustav</u> Peter Johan, Prince Biron von Curland and Francoise Lévisse de Montigny de Jaucourt.

    1) HSH Princess Viktoria-<u>Benigna</u> Ina-Maria Cecilie Friederike-Luise Helene Biron von Curland, born July 2, 1939 at Schloss Wartenberg, Silesia. Married May 3 (civil) and May 6, 1968 (religious) at Munich, Baron <u>Johann</u> Christoph Robert von Twickel, born July 25, 1940 at Berlin, elder son of Baron <u>Ludwig</u> Joseph Maria Ferdinand Hubertus Georg Ignatius Antonius Thomas Eustachius von Twickel and <u>Ann</u> Barbara Throckmorton.

        (1) Baron <u>Nikolaus</u> Maximilian Ludwig Karl Ernst-Johann Maria von Twickel, born April 1, 1969 at Munich

        (2) Baron <u>Tassilo</u> Heinrich Alexander von Twickel, born December 8, 1976 at Munich

    2) HSH <u>Ernst-Johann</u> Karl Oskar Franz Eitel-Friedrich Peter Burchard, Prince Biron von Curland,[14] born August 6, 1940 at Berlin. Married August 14 (civil) and August 15, 1967 (religious) at Munich, Countess <u>Elisabeth</u> Victoria Raimonda of Ysenburg-Philippseich, born December 9, 1941 at Rome, younger daughter of Count <u>Ludwig</u> Joseph Albert Franz Heinrich Dieter of Ysenburg-Philippseich and Nobile Mariangela Aloisi.

    3) HSH Prince <u>Michael</u> Karl August Wilhelm Biron von Curland, born January 20, 1944 at Gross Wartenberg, Silesia. Married July 1 (civil) and July 2, 1969 (religious) at Munich, Kristin von Oertzen, born November 6, 1944 at Liessow, near Schwerin, second daughter of Joachim von Oertzen and Gerda von Siemens.

        (1) HSH Princess Veronika Biron von Curland, born January 23, 1970 at Munich

        (2) HSH Prince Alexander Biron von Curland, born September 18, 1972 at Munich

        (3) HSH Princess Stephanie Biron von Curland, born September 24, 1975 at Munich

4. HRH Prince <u>Wilhelm-Karl</u> Adalbert Erich Detloff of Prussia, born January 30, 1922 at Potsdam. Married March 1, 1952 at Destedt, near Brunswick, <u>Armgard</u> Else Helene von Veltheim, born February 17, 1926 at Destedt, only daughter of <u>Friedrich</u> Bertram Hans von Veltheim and <u>Ottonie</u> Luise Sophie von Alvensleben.

    1) HRH Princess <u>Donata</u>-Viktoria Ina-Marie Ottonie of Prussia, born December 24, 1952 at Bonn

    2) HRH Prince <u>Wilhelm-Karl</u> Oskar Friedrich of Prussia, born August 26, 1955 at Bonn

3) HRH Prince <u>Oskar</u> Hans Karl Michael of Prussia, born May 6, 1959 at Bonn

A6 HRH Prince <u>Joachim</u> Franz Humbert of Prussia, born December 17, 1890 at Berlin; died July 18, 1920 at Potsdam. Married March 11, 1916 at Schloss Bellevue, near Berlin, HH Princess <u>Marie Auguste</u> Antoinette Friederike Alexandra Hilda Luise of Anhalt,[15] born June 10, 1898 at Schloss Ballenstedt; died May 22, 1983 at Essen, younger daughter of HH <u>Eduard</u> Georg Wilhelm Maximilian, Duke of Anhalt[16] and HH Princess Marie Agnes <u>Luise</u> Charlotte of Saxe-Altenburg, Duchess of Saxony.

1. HRH Prince <u>Karl Franz Joseph</u> Wilhelm Friedrich Eduard Paul of Prussia, born December 15, 1916 at Potsdam; died January 22, 1975 at Arica, Chile. Married (1) October 1 (civil) at Doorn, The Netherlands and October 5, 1940 (religious) at Berlin, (div. 1946) HSH Princess <u>Henriette</u> Hermine Wanda Ida Luise of Schönaich-Carolath, born November 25, 1918 at Berlin; died March 16, 1972 at Neuendettelsau, younger daughter of HSH Prince <u>Johann Georg</u> Ludwig Ferdinand August of Schönaich-Carolath and HSH Princess Hermine Reuss (Elder Line.)[17]

   1) HRH Prince <u>Franz Wilhelm</u> Viktor Christoph Stephan of Prussia, born September 3, 1943 at Grünberg, Silesia. Married September 4 (civil) at Dinard, France and September 22, 1976 (religious) at Madrid (div. 198?),[18] HSH Princess Maria Wladimirovna of Russia,* born December 23, 1953 at Madrid, only daughter of HH Prince Wladimir Kirillovitch of Russia and Princess Leonida Georgievna Bagration-Mukhransky.

      (1) HRH Prince Georg of Prussia, born March 13, 1981 at Madrid

   2) HRH Prince Franz Joseph <u>Friedrich Christian</u> Carl Erdmann Louis Ferdinand Oskar of Prussia, born September 3, 1943 at Grünberg, Silesia; died September 26, 1943 at Schloss Saabor.

   3) HRH Prince <u>Franz Friedrich</u> Christian of Prussia, born October 17, 1944 at Grünberg, Silesia. Married October 23, 1970 at Neuwied, Gudrun Winkler, born January 29, 1949 at Ischenrode, daughter of Horst Winkler and Edith Salz.

      (1) Christine Prinzessin von Preussen, born February 22, 1968 at Koblenz

Prince Karl Franz Joseph married (2) November 9, 1946 at Hamburg (div. 1959), <u>Luise</u> Dora Hartmann,[19] born September 5, 1909 at Hamburg; died April 23, 1961 at Hamburg, daughter of <u>Max</u> Emil Theodor Hartmann and Dora Wandel. (No Issue.) Prince Karl Franz Joseph married (3) July 20, 1959 at Lima, Peru, Eva Maria Herrera y Valdeavellano, born June 10, 1922 at Lima; died March 6, 1987 at Lima, daughter of Norberto Herrera y Carraczco and Juana Valdeavellano y Otero.

   4) <u>Alexandra</u> Maria Augusta Juana Consuelo Prinzessin von Preussen, born April 29, 1960 at Lima

   5) <u>Désirée</u> Anastasia Maria Benedicta Prinzessin von Preussen, born July 13, 1961 at Lima, married May 25, 1983 at Lima, Juan Carlos Gamarra y Skeels, born November 15, 1954 at Lima, son of Carlos Gamarra y Vargas and Edwina Skeels.

(1) Juan Francisco Gamarra y von Preussen, born March 1, 1987 at Montevideo, Uruguay

A7   HRH Princess <u>Viktoria-Luise</u> Adelheid Mathilde Charlotte of Prussia, born September 13, 1892 at Marmorpalais, Potsdam; died December 11, 1980 at Hanover. Married May 24, 1913 at Berlin, HRH Prince <u>Ernst August</u> Christian Georg of Hanover, Prince of Great Britain and Ireland, Duke of Brunswick and Lüneburg,[20] born November 17, 1887 at Penzing, Austria; died January 30, 1953 at Schloss Marienburg, Nordstemmen, third son of HRH Prince <u>Ernst August</u> Wilhelm Adolf Georg Friedrich of Hanover, Prince of Great Britain and Ireland, Duke of Brunswick and Lüneburg, 3rd Duke of Cumberland and Teviotdale, Earl of Armagh[21] and HRH Princess <u>Thyra</u> Amelia Caroline Charlotte Anne of Denmark.[22]

1.   HRH Prince <u>Ernst August</u> Georg Wilhelm Christian Ludwig Franz Joseph Nikolaus of Hanover, Prince of Great Britain and Ireland, Duke of Brunswick and Lüneburg, born March 18, 1914 at Brunswick. Married (1) August 31 (civil) at Schloss Marienburg and September 4, 1951 (religious) at Hanover, HH Princess <u>Ortrud</u> Bertha Adelheid Hedwig of Schleswig-Holstein-Sonderburg-Glücksburg, born December 19, 1925 at Flensburg; died February 6, 1980 at Schulenburg-an-der-Leine, second daughter of HH Prince <u>Albert</u> Christian Adolf Karl Eugen of Schleswig-Holstein-Sonderburg-Glücksburg and HSH Princess Hertha of Ysenburg and Büdingen.

1)   HRH Princess <u>Marie</u> Viktoria Luise Hertha Friederike of Hanover, born November 26, 1952 at Hanover. Married June 4 (civil) at Pattenson and June 5, 1982 (religious) at Schloss Marienburg, Count <u>Michael</u> Georg Botho von Hochberg,[23] born December 5, 1943 at Züllichau, only son of Count <u>Konrad</u> Eberhard Georg Richard von Hochberg and <u>Eleonore</u> Kunigunde Charlotte von Czettritz und Neuhaus.

(1) Count <u>Conrad</u> Hans-Heinrich Ernst-August von Hochberg, born June 17, 1985 at Hamburg

2)   HRH Prince <u>Ernst August</u> Albert Paul Otto Rupprecht Oskar Berthold Friedrich-Ferdinand Christian Ludwig of Hanover, born February 26, 1954 at Hanover. Married August 28, (civil) at Pattenson and August 30, 1981 (religious) at Schloss Marienburg, Chantal Hochuli, born June 2, 1955 at Zurich, daughter of <u>Johann</u> Gustav Hochuli and Rosmarie Lembeck.

(1) HRH Prince <u>Ernst August</u> Andreas Philipp Konstantin Maximilian Rolf Stephan Ludwig-Rudolph of Hanover, born July 19, 1983 at Hildesheim, near Hanover

(2) HRH Prince <u>Christian</u> Heinrich Clemens Paul Frank Peter Welf Wilhelm-Ernst Friedrich Franz of Hanover, born June 1, 1985 at Hildesheim

3)   HRH Prince <u>Ludwig</u> Rudolph Georg Wilhelm Philipp Friedrich Wolrad Maximilian of Hanover, born November 21, 1955 at Hanover

4)   HRH Princess <u>Olga</u> Sophie Charlotte Anna of Hanover born February 17, 1958 at Hanover

5)   HRH Princess <u>Alexandra</u> Irene Margaretha Elisabeth Bathildis of Hanover, born February 18, 1959 at Hanover. Married October 5 (civil) at Amorbach and October 11, 1981 (religious) at Gmunden-am-Traunsee, Austria, HSH Prince Andreas of Leiningen,* born November 27, 1955 at Frankfurt-am-

Main, second son of HSH Emich Cyril Ferdinand Hermann, 7th Prince of
Leiningen and HH Duchess Eilika Stephanie Elisabeth Thekla Juliana of
Oldenburg. (For Issue, see Chapter XV)

6) HRH Prince Heinrich Julius Christian Otto Friedrich Franz Anton Günther
of Hanover, born April 29, 1961 at Hanover

Prince Ernst August, Duke of Brunswick and Lüneburg married (2) July 16
(civil) and July 17, 1981 (religious) at Laubach, H Ill H Countess Monika of
Solms-Laubach, born August 8, 1924 at Laubach, daughter of H Ill H Count
Georg Friedrich of Solms-Laubach and H Ill H Countess Johanna Marie of
Solms-Hohensolms-Lich.

2. HRH Prince Georg Wilhelm Ernst August Friedrich Axel of Hanover, Prince of
Great Britain and Ireland, born March 25, 1915 at Brunswick. Married April 23
(civil) and April 24, 1946 (religious) at Salem, Baden, HRH Princess Sophie of
Greece and Demnark,* born June 26, 1914 at Corfu, Greece, youngest daughter
of HRH Prince Andrew of Greece and Demark and HSH Princess Victoria Alice
Elisabeth Julia Marie of Battenberg; and widow of HH Prince Christoph of
Hesse.

1) HRH Prince Welf Ernst August Andreas Philipp Georg Wilhelm Ludwig
Berthold of Hanover, born January 25, 1947 at Schloss Marienburg; died
January 10, 1981 at Poona, India. Married May 23 (civil) at Munich and
May 25, 1969 (religious), at Essen-Bredeney Wibke van Gunsteren, born
November 26, 1948 at Lübeck, daughter of Harry van Gunsteren and
Ursula Schmidt-Prange.

(1) Tania Saskia Viktoria-Luise Prinzessin von Hannover, born July 24,
1970 at Duisburg

2) HRH Prince Georg Paul Christian of Hanover, born December 9, 1949 at
Salem, Baden. Married September 15, 1973 at Rottach-am-Tegernsee,
Victoria Anne Bee,[24] born March 6, 1951 at New York City, younger
daughter of Robert Bee and H Ill H Countess Eleonore Vera Alexia Anna
Maria Fugger von Babenhausen.

(1) Vera Alice Prinzessin von Hannover, born November 5, 1976 at
Munich

(2) Nora Sophie Prinzessin von Hannover, born January 15, 1979 at
Munich

3) HRH Princess Friederike (Frederica) Elisabeth Viktoria-Luise Alice Olga
Theodora Helena of Hanover, born October 15, 1954 at Salem, Baden.
Married August 17, 1979 at Vancouver, British Columbia, Jerry William
Cyr, born January 16, 1951 at Port Alberni, British Columbia, son of
Gordon Paul Cyr and Emma Grandbois.

(1) Julia Emma Cyr, born September 17, 1982 at Vancouver, British
Columbia

(2) Jean-Paul Welf Cyr, born March 6, 1985 at Vancouver, British
Columbia

3. HRH Princess Friederike Luise Thyra Margarete Sophie Olga Cecile Isabelle Christa of Hanover, Princess of Great Britain and Ireland, born April 18, 1917 at Blankenburg, Harz; died February 6, 1981 at Madrid. Married January 9, 1938 at Athens, HM PAUL I, KING OF THE HELLENES,* born December 14, 1901 at Athens, third son of HM Constantine I,King of the Hellenes and HRH Princess Sophie Dorothea Ulricke Alice of Prussia; died March 6, 1964 at Tatoi, near Athens. (For issue see Chapter XII).

4. Prince Christian Oskar Ernst August Wilhelm Viktor Georg Heinrich of Hanover, born September 1, 1919 at Gmünden; died December 10, 1981 at Lausanne, Switzerland. Married November 23 (civil) at Salzburg, Austria and November 25, 1963 (religious) at Brussels, (div. 1976) Mireille Dutry, born January 10, 1946 at London, daughter of Armand Dutry and Tinou Soinne.
    1) Caroline-Luise Mireille Irene Sophie Prinzessin von Hannover, born May 3, 1965 at Wels, Austria
    2) Mireille Viktoria Luise Prinzessin von Hannover, born June 3, 1971 at Brussels

5. HRH Prince Welf-Heinrich Ernst August Georg Christian Berthold Friedrich Wilhelm Louis Ferdinand of Hanover, born March 11, 1923 at Gmünden. Married September 20 (civil) and September 21, 1960 (religious) at Büdingen, HSH Princess Alexandra Sophie Cecilie Anna Maria Friederike Benigna Dorothea of Ysenburg and Büdingen, born October 23, 1937 at Frankfurt-am-Main, only daughter of HSH Otto Friedrich Viktor Ferdinand Maximilian Gustav Richard Bogislav, 3rd Prince of Ysenburg and Büdingen and Princess Felicitas Anna Eleonore Cecilie Reuss.

Kaiser Wilhelm II married (2) November 5, 1922 at Haus Doorn, The Netherlands, HSH Princess Hermine Reuss (Elder Line),[25] born December 17, 1887 at Greiz; died August 7, 1947 at Frankfurt-am-Oder, 4th daughter of HSH Prince Heinrich XXII Reuss (Elder Line) and HSH Princess Ida Mathilde Adelheid of Schaumburg-Lippe. (No Issue.)

B
HRH Princess Viktoria Elisabeth Auguste Charlotte of Prussia, born July 24, 1860 at Neues Palais, Potsdam; died October 1, 1919 at Baden-Baden. Married February 18, 1878 at Berlin, HH Bernhard III (Friedrich Wilhelm Albert Georg, Duke of Saxe-Meiningen. Succeeded his father June 25, 1914 as Duke of Saxe-Meiningen. Abdicated November 10, 1918. Born April 1, 1851 at Meiningen; died January 16, 1928 at Meiningen, eldest son of HH Georg II, Duke of Saxe-Meiningen and HRH Princess Friederike Luise Wilhelmine Marianne Charlotte of Prussia.

B1 HH Princess Feodora Viktoria Augusta Marianne Marie of Saxe-Meiningen, Duchess of Saxony, born May 12, 1879 at Potsdam; died August 26, 1945 at Schloss Neuhoff. Married September 24, 1898 at Breslau HSH Prince Heinrich XXX Reuss (Younger Line), born November 25, 1864 at Schloss Neuhoff; died March 23, 1939 at Schloss Neuhoff, fifth son of HSH Prince Heinrich IX Reuss (Younger Line) and Baroness Anna Marie Wilhelmine Helene von Zedlitz und Leipe auf Zülzendorf. (No Issue.)

C

HRH Prince Albert Wilhelm Heinrich of Prussia, born August 14, 1862 at Neues Palais, Potsdam; died April 20, 1929 at Hemmelmark, near Eckernförde. Married May 24, 1888 at Charlottenburg, HGDH Princess Irene Luise Maria Anna of Hesse and By Rhine,* born July 11, 1866 at Darmstadt; died November 11, 1953 at Hemmelmark, near Eckernförde, third daughter of HRH (Friedrich Wilhelm) Ludwig IV (Karl), Grand Duke of Hesse and By Rhine and HRH Princess Alice Maud Mary of Great Britain and Ireland.

C1   HRH Prince Waldemar Wilhelm Ludwig Friedrich Viktor Heinrich of Prussia, born March 20, 1889 at Kiel; died May 2, 1945 at Tutzing, Bavaria. Married August 14, 1919 at Hemmelmark, near Eckernförde, HSH Princess Calixta Agnes Adelheid Irmgard Helene Karole Elise Emma of Lippe, born October 14, 1895 at Potsdam; died December 15, 1982 at Schloss Reinhartshausen, Erbach, Rheingau, elder daughter of HSH Prince Friedrich Wilhelm Franz Julius Ludwig Kalixt of Lippe and H Ill H Countess Gisela Berta Adelheid Klothilde Emma Klementine of Ysenburg and Büdingen in Meerholtz. (No Issue.)

C2   HRH Prince Wilhelm Viktor Karl August Heinrich Sigismund of Prussia, born November 27, 1886 at Kiel; died November 14, 1978 at Puntarenas, Costa Rica. Married July 11, 1919 at Hemmelmark, near Eckernförde, HH Princess Charlotte Agnes Ernestine August Bathildis Marie Therese Adolfine of Saxe-Altenburg, Duchess of Saxony, born March 4, 1899 at Potsdam, elder daughter of HH Ernst II (Bernhard Georg Johann Karl Friedrich Peter Albert, Duke of Saxe-Altenburg and HSH Princess Friederike Adelheid Marie Luise Hilda Eugenie of Schaumburg-Lippe.

1.   HRH Princess Barbara Irene Adelheid Viktoria Elisabeth Bathildis of Prussia,[26] born August 2, 1920 at Hemmelmark, near Eckernförde. Married July 5 (civil) and July 11, 1954 (religious) at Glücksburg, HRH Duke Christian Ludwig Ernst August Maximilian Johann Albrecht Adolf Friedrich of Mecklenburg, born September 29, 1912 at Ludwigslust, second son of HRH Friedrich Franz IV (Michael) of Mecklenburg-Schwerin[27] and HRH Princess Alexandra Luise Marie Olga Elisabeth Therese Vera of Hanover, Princess of Great Britain and Ireland.[28]
1)   HH Duchess Donata of Mecklenburg, born March 11, 1956 at Kiel
2)   HH Duchess Edwina of Mecklenburg, born September 25, 1960 at Kiel

2.   HRH Prince Alfred Friedrich Ernst Heinrich Conrad of Prussia, born August 17, 1924 at Finca Santa Sofia, Guatemala. Married December 15, 1984 at Southampton, New York, Maritza Farkas,[29] born August 6, 1929 at Gombaszog, Czechoslovakia, daughter of Julius Farkas and Ilona von Literaty.

C3   HRH Prince Heinrich Viktor Ludwig Friedrich of Prussia, born January 9, 1900 at Kiel; died February 26, 1904 at Kiel.

D

HRH Prince Franz Friedrich Sigismund of Prussia, born September 15, 1864 at Potsdam; died June 18, 1866 at Potsdam.

E

HRH Princess Friederike Amalia Wilhelmine <u>Victoria</u> of Prussia, born April 12, 1866 at Neues Palais, Potsdam; died November 13, 1929 at Bonn. Married (1) November 19, 1890 at Berlin, HSH Prince <u>Adolf</u> Wilhelm Karl of Schaumburg-Lippe, born July 20, 1850 at Bückeburg; died July 9, 1916 at Bonn, fourth son of HSH <u>Adolf I</u> Georg, Prince of Schaumburg-Lippe and HSH Princess Hermine of Waldeck and Pyrmont. (No Issue). Princess Victoria married (2) November 19 (civil) at Bonn and November 21, 1927 (religious) at Berlin, Alexander Anatolievitch Zoubkoff, born September 25, 1901 at Ivanovo-Woznessensk, Russia; died January 28, 1936 at Luxembourg, son of Anatol Zoubkoff and Mary Kornelia Frykberg. (No Issue.)

F

HRH Prince Joachim Friedrich Ernst <u>Waldemar</u> of Prussia, born February 10, 1868 at Berlin; died March 27, 1879 at Potsdam.

G

HRH Princess <u>Sophie</u> Dorothea Ulrike Alice of Prussia, born June 14, 1870 at Neues Palais, Potsdam; died January 13, 1932 at Frankfurt-am-Main. Married October 27, 1889 at Athens, HM CONSTANTINE I, KING OF THE HELLENES,[30] born August 2, 1868 at Athens; died January 11, 1923 at Palermo, Sicily, eldest son of HM GEORGE I, KING OF THE HELLENES[31] and HIH Grand Duchess Olga Constantinova of Russia.

G1   HM GEORGE II, KING OF THE HELLENES. Succeeded to the Greek throne upon his father's abdication, September 27, 1922, but left Greece March 24, 1924. Restored to the throne, November 3, 1935, but again left Greece following the German invasion, April 23, 1941. Recalled to the throne September 28, 1946. Born July 19, 1890 at Tatoi, near Athens, died April 1, 1947 at Athens. Married February 27, 1921 at Bucharest (div. 1935), HRH Princess <u>Elisabeth</u> Charlotte Josephine Alexandra Victoria of Roumania,* born October 12, 1894 at Castle Pelesch, Sinaia; died November 15, 1956 at Cannes, eldest daughter of HM FERDINAND I, KING OF ROUMANIA and HRH Princess <u>Marie</u> Alexandra Victoria of Great Britain and Ireland, Princess of Saxe-Coburg and Gotha, Duchess of Saxony. (No Issue.)

G2   HM ALEXANDER I, KING OF THE HELLENES. Succeeded to the throne following his father's departure from Greece, June 11, 1917. Born August 1, 1893 at Tatoi, near Athens; died October 25, 1920 at Athens. Married November 4, 1919, at Athens, Aspasia Manos,[32] born September 4, 1896 at Athens; died August 7, 1972 at Venice, daughter of Colonel Petros Manos and Maria Argyropoulos.

    1.   HRH Princess Alexandra of Greece, born March 25, 1921 (posthumously) at Athens. Married March 20, 1944 at the Yugoslav Embassy, London, HM PETER II, KING OF YUGOSLAVIA,* born September 6, 1923 at Belgrade; died November 3, 1970 at Denver, Colorado, eldest son of HM ALEXANDER I, KING OF YUGOSLAVIA and HRH Princess Marie of Roumania. (For issue see Chapter XV.)

G3   HRH Princess Helen of Greece and Denmark, born May 3, 1896 at Athens; died
     November 28, 1982 at Lausanne, Switzerland. Married March 10, 1921 at Athens (div.
     1928), HM CAROL II, KING OF ROUMANIA,* born October 15, 1893 at Castle
     Pelesch, Sinaia; died April 4, 1953 at Estoril, Portugal, eldest son of HM FER-
     DINAND I, KING OF ROUMANIA and HRH Princess Marie Alexandra Victoria of
     Great Britain and Ireland, Princess of Saxe-Coburg and Gotha, Duchess of Saxony.
     (For issue, see Chapter XV.)

G4   HM PAUL I, KING OF THE HELLENES. Succeeded to the throne following the death
     of his eldest brother, King George II, April 1, 1947. Born December 14, 1901 at
     Tatoi, near Athens; died March 6, 1964 at Athens. Married January 9, 1938 at
     Athens, HRH Princess Friederike Luise Thyra Viktoria Margarete Sophie Olga Cecilie
     Isabelle Christa of Hanover, Princess of Great Britain and Ireland,* born August 18,
     1917 at Blankenburg, Harz; died February 6, 1981 at Madrid, only daughter of HRH
     Prince Ernst August Christian Georg of Hanover, Duke of Brunswick and Lüneburg
     and HRH Princess Viktoria Luise Adelheid Mathilde Charlotte of Prussia
     1.   HRH Princess Sophie of Greece and Denmark, born November 2, 1938 at
          Psychiko. Married May 14, 1962 at Athens, HM JUAN CARLOS I (Alfonso
          Victor Maria), KING OF SPAIN,* born January 5, 1938 at Rome, eldest son of
          HRH Infante Don Juan Carlos Teresa Silvestre Alfonso of Spain, Count of
          Barcelona and HRH Priness Maria de las Mercedes Cristina Januaria Isabel
          Luisa Carolina Victoria of the Two-Sicilies, Infante of Spain. (For issue, see
          Chapter XIX.)

     2.   HM CONSTANTINE II, KING OF THE HELLENES. Succeeded to the throne on
          the death of his father. Left Greece December 13, 1967.[33] Born June 2, 1940
          at Psychiko. Married September 18, 1964 at Athens, HRH Princess Anne Marie
          Dagmar Ingrid of Denmark,* born August 30, 1946 at Amalienborg Palace,
          Copenhagen, youngest daughter of HM (Christian) FREDERIK IX (Franz Michael
          Carl Valdemar Georg), KING OF DENMARK and HRH Princess Ingrid Victoria
          Sofia Louise Margareta of Sweden.
          1)   HRH Princess Alexia of Greece and Denmark,[34] born July 10, 1965 at Mon
               Repos, Corfu
          2)   HRH Pavlos, Crown Prince of Greece, Prince of Denmark, born May 20,
               1967 at Tatoi, near Athens
          3)   HRH Prince Nikolaos of Greece and Denmark, born October 1, 1969 at
               Rome
          4)   HRH Princess Theodora of Greece and Denmark, born June 9, 1983 at
               London
          5)   HRH Prince Philippos of Greece and Denmark, born April 24, 1986 at
               London

     3.   HRH Princess Irene of Greece and Denmark,[35] born May 11, 1942 at Cape
          Town, South Africa

G5   HRH Princess Irene of Greece and Denmark, born February 13, 1904 at Athens; died
      April 15, 1974 at Florence, Italy. Married July 1, 1939, at Florence HRH Prince
      Aimone Roberto Margherita Giuseppe Torino of Savoy, Duke of Spoleto, 4th Duke of
      Aosta,[36] born March 9, 1900 at Turin; died January 29, 1948 at Buenos Aires,
      Argentina, second son of HRH Prince Emanuele Filiberto Vittorio Eugenio Genova
      Giuseppe Maria of Savoy, 2nd Duke of Aosta and HRH Princess Hélène Louise
      Henriette of Orléans.

1.   HRH Prince Amadeo Umberto Constantino Giorgio Paolo Maria Fiorenzo of
      Savoy, 5th Duke of Aosta, born September 27, 1943 at Florence. Married (1)
      July 22, 1964 at Sintra, Portugal (div. 1982; annulled 1987), HRH Princess
      Claude Marie Agnes Catherine of Orléans,[37] born December 11, 1943 at
      Larache, Morocco, fifth daughter of HRH Prince Henri Robert Ferdinand Marie
      Louis Philippe of Orléans, Count of Paris and HRH Princess Isabelle Marie
      Amélie Louise Victoire Thérèse Jeanne of Orléans and Braganca.[38]

      1)   HRH Princess Bianca Irene Elena Isabella Fiorenza Maria of Savoy, born
           April 2, 1966 at Florence
      2)   HRH Prince Aimone Umberto Emanuele Filiberto Luigi Amadeo Gustavo
           Elena Maria Fiorenzo of Savoy, Duke of Apulia, born October 13, 1967 at
           Florence
      3)   HRH Princess Mafalda Giovanna Shams Maria Fiorenza Isabella of Savoy,
           born September 20, 1969 at Florence

      The Duke of Aosta married (2) March 30, 1987 at Bagheria, near Palermo,
      Sicily, Marquesa Donna Silvia Ottavia Costanza Maria Paterno di Spedalotto,
      born December 31, 1953 at Palmero, younger daughter of Don Vincenzo dei
      Marchesi Regiovanni, Conti di Prades, Baroni de Spedalotto and Rosanna
      Bellardo.

G6   HRH Princess Katherine of Greece and Denmark,[39] born May 4, 1913 at Athens.
      Married April 21, 1947 at Athens, Richard Campbell Andrew Brandram, born August
      5, 1911 at Bexhill-on-Sea, Sussex, only son of Richard Andrew Brandram and Maud
      Campbell.

1.   Richard Paul George Andrew Brandram, born April 1, 1948 at London. Married
      February 12, 1975 at London, Jennifer Diane Steele, born August 23, 1951 at
      London, daughter of Lieutenant-Colonel Robert Steele and Gyllian Diane
      Greville-Williams.

      1)   Sophie Eila Brandram, born January 23, 1981 at Wimbledon, London
      2)   Nicholas George Brandram, born April 23, 1982 at Wimbledon, London
      3)   Alexia Katherine Brandram, born December 6, 1985 at Wimbledon, London

H
HRH Princess Margarete Beatrice Feodora of Prussia, born April 22, 1872 at Potsdam;
died January 22, 1954 at Schönberg, near Kronberg. Married January 25, 1893, HRH Prince
Friedrich Karl Ludwig Konstantin of Hesse, Landgrave of Hesse,[40] born May 1, 1868 at
Panker, Holstein; died May 28, 1940 at Cassel, third son of HRH Prince Friedrich Karl
Georg Adolf of Hesse, Landgrave of Hesse and HRH Princess Maria Anna Friederike of
Prussia.

H1 HH Prince <u>Friedrich Wilhelm</u> Sigismund Viktor of Hesse, born November 23, 1893 at Frankfurt-am-Main; killed in action September 12/13, 1916 at Kara Orman, Roumania.

H2 HH Prince <u>Maximilian</u> Friedrich Wilhelm Georg Eduard of Hesse, born October 20, 1894 at Rumpenheim, near Offenbach; killed in action October 13, 1914 at St. Jean-Chappel, near Bailleul, France.

H3 HRH Prince Philipp of Hesse, Landgrave of Hesse, born November 6, 1896 at Rumpenheim, near Offenbach; died October 25, 1980 at Rome. Married September 23, 1925 at Racconigi, Italy, HRH Princess <u>Mafalda</u> Maria Elisabetta Anna Romana of Savoy, born November 19, 1902 at Rome; died August 28, 1944 at Buchenwald, near Weimar, second daughter of HM VITTORIO EMANUELE III, KING OF ITALY and HRH Princess Elena of Montenegro.

1. HRH Prince <u>Moritz</u> Friedrich Karl Emanuel Humbert of Hesse, Landgrave of Hesse,[41] born August 6, 1926 at Racconigi, Italy. Married June 1 (civil) and June 3, 1964 (religious) at Kronberg, Taunus (div. 1974), HSH Princess <u>Tatiana</u> Louise Ursula Therese Elsa of Sayn-Wittgenstein-Berleburg,[42] born July 31, 1940 at Giessen, second daughter of HSH <u>Gustav Albrecht</u> Alfred Franz Friedrich Otto Emil Ernst, 5th Prince of Sayn-Wittgenstein-Berleburg and Margareta Fouché d'Otrante.

   1) HH Princess <u>Mafalda</u> Margarethe of Hesse, born July 6, 1965 at Kiel
   2) HH Prince <u>Heinrich</u> Donatus Philipp Umberto of Hesse, born October 17, 1966 at Kiel
   3) HH Princess <u>Elena</u> Elisabeth Madeleine of Hesse, born November 8, 1967 at Kiel
   4) HH Prince <u>Philipp</u> Robin of Hesse, born September 10, 1970 at Kiel

2. HRH Prince <u>Heinrich</u> Wilhelm Konstantin Viktor Franz of Hesse,[43] born October 30, 1927 at Rome.

3. HRH Prince <u>Otto</u> Adolf of Hesse, born June 3, 1937 at Rome. Married April 5 (civil) at Munich and April 6, 1965 (religious) at Trotsberg, Upper Bavaria (div. 1969), <u>Angela</u> Mathilde Agathe von Doering,[44] born August 12, 1940 at Goslar, daughter of Major General Bernd von Doering and Eleonore Wrede. (No Issue.)

4. HH Princess <u>Elisabeth</u> Margarethe Elena Johanna Maria Jolanda Polyxene of Hesse, born October 8, 1940 at Rome. Married February 26 (civil) and February 28, 1962 (religious) at Frankfurt-am-Main, Count <u>Friedrich Carl</u> Eduard Wilhelm Franz Eusebius Michael Hubert von Oppersdorff, born January 30, 1925 at Oberlogau, Upper Silesia; died January 11, 1985 at Gravenbruch-Neu Isenburg, youngest son of Count <u>Wilhelm Hans</u> Georg Mathias Eduard Anton von Oppersdorff and HSH Princess <u>Marie Louise</u> Antoinette Elisabeth Eulalie Josepha Wilhelmine of Isenburg.

   1) Count <u>Friedrich</u> Karl Philipp Wilhelm Hans Moritz Maria von Oppersdorff, born December 1, 1962 at Frankfurt-am-Main
   2) Count <u>Alexander</u> Wolfgang Johannes Georg Viktor Emanuel Maria von Oppersdorff, born August 3, 1965 at Frankfurt-am-Main

H4   IIII Prince <u>Wolfgang</u> Moritz of Hesse,[45] born November 6, 1896 at Rumpenheim, near Offenbach (twin of Prince Philipp). Married (1) September 17, 1924 at Salem, Baden, HGDH Princess <u>Marie Alexandra</u> Thyra Viktoria Luise Carola Hilda of Baden,[46] born August 1, 1902 at Salem, Baden; died January 29, 1944 in an air raid on Frankfurt-am-Main, only daughter of HRH Maximilian (<u>Max</u>) Alexander Friedrich Wilhelm, Margrave of Baden [47] and HRH Princess <u>Marie Louise</u> Victoria Caroline Amalie Alexandra Augusta Friederike of Hanover, Princess of Great Britain and Ireland.[48] (No Issue.) Prince Wolfgang married (2) September 7, 1948 at Frankfurt-am-Main, Ottilie Moeller, born June 24, 1903 at Frankfurt-am-Main, daughter of Ludwig Moeller and Eleanore Steinmann.

H5   HH Prince <u>Richard</u> Wilhelm Leopold of Hesse,[49] born May 14, 1901 at Frankfurt-am-Main; died February 11, 1969 at Frankfurt-am-Main.

H6   HH Prince <u>Christoph</u> Ernst August of Hesse, born May 14, 1901 at Frankfurt-am-Main; killed October 7, 1943 in an air crash in the Appenines while on active service (twin of Prince Richard). Married December 15, 1930 at Kronberg, HRH Princess Sophie of Greece and Denmark,* born June 26, 1914 at Corfu, youngest daughter of HRH Prince Andrew of Greece and Denmark and HSH Princess Victoria <u>Alice</u> Elisabeth Julia Marie of Battenberg. Princess Sophie married (2) Prince Georg Wilhelm of Hanover.)

1.   HH Princess <u>Christina</u> Margarethe of Hesse, born January 10, 1933 at Kronberg. Married (1) August 1 (civil) and August 2, 1956 (religious) at Kronberg (div. 1962), HRH Prince Andrej of Yugoslavia,* born June 28, 1929 at Bled (For issue, see Chapter XV.) Princess Christina married (2) December 3, 1962 at London (div. 1986) <u>Robert</u> Floris van Eyck, born May 3, 1916 at The Hague, The Netherlands, son of <u>Pieter</u> Nicolaus van Eyck and <u>Nelly</u> Estelle Benjamins.
   1)   <u>Helene</u> Sophia van Eyck, born October 25, 1963 at London. Married January 24, 1986 at Hastings, East Sussex, <u>Roderick</u> Alan Harman,[50] born July 18, 1942 at Chang-chou, China, son of <u>Douglas</u> John Harman and <u>Gladys</u> Mary Gunstone.
      (1)   <u>Sascha</u> Alexandra Sophia Harman, born July 26, 1986 at St. Leonards-on-Sea, East Sussex
   2)   <u>Mark</u> Nicholas van Eyck, born February 16, 1966 at Oxford

2.   HH Princess <u>Dorothea</u> Charlotte Karin of Hesse, born July 24, 1934 at Panker. Married March 31 (civil) at Schliersee, Upper Bavaria and April 1, 1959 (religious), at Munich HSH Prince <u>Friedrich</u> Karl Hugo Maximilian Maria Cyrillus Felix Hubertus of Windisch-Graetz, born July 7, 1917 at Heilgenberg, Baden, youngest son of HSH <u>Hugo</u> Vincenz Alexander Maria, Prince of Windisch-Graetz and HSH Princess <u>Leontine</u> Irma Maximiliane Egona Elisabeth Aktinea Wenzeslavia Huberta of Fürstenberg.
   1)   HSH Princess <u>Marina</u> Margherita Sophia Leontina Christiana of Windisch-Graetz, born December 3, 1960 at Milan, Italy
   2)   HSH Princess <u>Clarissa</u> Elisabetta Fiore of Windisch-Graetz, born August 5, 1966 at Erba, Prov. Como, Italy. Married November 16, 1985 at Alserio, near Como, <u>Eric</u> Michel Jacques de Waele, born January 6, 1962 at Etterbeek, Belgium, son of <u>Jean</u> August de Waele and Annemarie Ponsar.

(1) Michel Jean Henri de Waele, born May 18, 1986 at New York City

3. HH Prince Karl Adolf Andreas of Hesse, born March 26, 1937 at Berlin. Married March 26 (civil) and April 18, 1966 (religious) at The Hague, The Netherlands, Countess Yvonne Margit Valerie Szapáry von Muraszombath, Széchysziget and Szapár, born April 4, 1944 at Budapest, Hungary, only daughter of Count Béla György Janos Amand Maria Szapáry von Muraszombath, Széchysziget and Szapár and Baroness Wally Olga Vera Elisabeth Ursula (Ulla) von Richtofen.
    1) Christoph Prinz von Hessen, born June 18, 1969 at Munich
    2) Irina Verena Prinzessin von Hessen, born April 1, 1971 at Munich

4. HH Prince Rainer Christoph Friedrich of Hesse, born November 18, 1939 at Kronberg

5. HH Princess Clarissa Alice of Hesse, born February 6, 1944 at Kronberg (posthumously). Married July 20, 1971 at Paris (div. 1976), Claude-Jean Derrien,[51] born March 12, 1948 at Boulogne-sur-Seine, France, son of Jean Guillaume Derrien and Jacqueline Marie Therese Adele Laine. No issue, but Princess Clarissa has a natural daughter
    1) Johanna von Hessen, born August 25, 1980 at Munich

ENDNOTES

1. Elder brother of Prince Christian of Schleswig-Holstein-Sonderburg-Augustenberg, husband of Queen Victoria's third daughter, Princess Helena.
2. Daughter of Queen Victoria's elder half sister, Princess Feodora of Leiningen and her husband, Carl Ludwig, 3rd Prince of Hohenlohe-Langenburg.
3. The descendants of Kaiser Wilhelm II who are surnamed Prinz or Prinzessin von Preussen rather than HRH Prince or Princess of Prussia are children of morganatic marriages. Under present German law (since 1919), titles are a part of one's surname. But to distinguish between the royal and non-royal, I have used the traditional titles (HRH Prince or Princess of Prussia) for the royal descendants and the legal surname (Prinz or Prinzessin von Preussen) for those who are the issue of unequal marriages. This also apply to other German royal and princely families including Hanover, Hesse, and Saxe-Coburg and Gotha.
4. Half-brother of Duchess Sophie Charlotte of Oldenburg, who married Kaiser Wilhelm II's son Prince Eitel-Friedrich.
5. Prince Friedrich of Prussia became a British citizen and his descendants use the surname von Preussen
6. Married (2) June 3, 1967 at Old Windsor, Berkshire, Major Anthony Patrick Ness, born June 15, 1914 at Boscombe, Bournemouth.
7. Married (1) November 17, 1972 at Kensington, London (div.) Tom Aisbett, born March 7, 1949 at Warworth, Northumberland.
8. Married (2) November 24, 1927 at Rastede, Harald von Hedemann, born September 22, 1887 at Cologne; died June 12, 1951 at Hankhausen-Rastede.
9. Younger brother of Duke Bernhard II of Saxe-Meiningen, who married Kaiser Wilhelm's sister Charlotte.
10. Married (2) January 7, 1922 at Grünholz (div. 1933) Arnold Rümann, born December 1, 1884 at Hannover; died December 6, 1951 at Rheme. Princess Alexandra Viktoria was not the only child of Duke Friedrich Ferdinand to marry a descendant of Queen Victoria. Her elder sister, Victoria Adelheid married Victoria's grandson, Charles Edward, Duke of Albany, Duke of Saxe-Coburg and Gotha, and her brother, Duke Friedrich, married a great-granddaughter, Princess Marie Melita of Hohenlohe-Langenburg.

11. Younger sister of Princess Auguste Viktoria, who was Kaiser Wilhelm II's first wife.
12. Married (1) Werner Rosendorff (div. 1933.)
13. Married (1) February 14, 1946 at Mittleberg (div. 1959), Robert Bee, born September 2, 1918 at New York City. Their younger daughter Victoria Anne Bee is also married to a descendant of Queen Victoria, HRH Prince Georg of Hanover.
14. Prince and Princess Ernst-Johann Biron von Curland have two adopted daughters:
    1. Anja Prinzessin Biron von Curland, born January 25, 1975 at Munich.
    2. Christiana Prinzessin Biron von Curland, born May 23, 1977 at Munich.
15. Married (2) September 27, 1926 at Berlin-Schöneburg (div. 1935) Baron Johann Michael von Loën, born September 6, 1902 at Dessau.
16. Elder brother of Prince Aribert of Anhalt, who married Princess Marie Louise of Schleswig-Holstein-Sonderburg-Augustenberg.
17. Princess Hermine was the second wife of Kaiser Wilhelm II, who was Prince Karl Franz Joseph's grandfather. Hermine was Karl Franz Joseph's mother-in-law, as well as stepgrandmother.
18. According to several sources, including Ivan Bilibin, who is the head of Prince Wladimir's Chancellery, Franz Wilhelm and Maria are divorced, but the exact year has not been determined.
19. Married (1) Fritz Simon (div. 1940.)
20. Succeeded to the duchy of Brunswick following his father's renunication (October 24, 1913) and annullment (October 27) of the impeachment of his House by the Federal Diet, November 1, 1913. Abdicated November 8, 1918. Deprived of his British titles by Order in Council, March 28, 1919.
21. Only son of King Georg V of Hanover, who was the only son of King Ernst August of Hanover and 1st Duke of Cumberland (fifth son of King George III of Great Britain), whose descendants in the male line until 1919 enjoyed the style and title of HRH Prince or Princess of Great Britain and Ireland.
22. Youngest sister of Queen Alexandra, consort of Edward VII, King George I of the Hellenes and Tsarina Marie Feodorovna of Russia.
23. Married (1) October 15, 1971 at Lütjenburg (div. 1972), Rixa Lage, born November 9, 1944 at Neu-Brandenburg, Mecklenburg.
24. See note 13.
25. Married (1) January 7, 1907 at Greiz, Prince Johann Georg of Schönaich-Carolath, born September 11, 1873 at Saabor; died April 7, 1920 at Wöfelsgrund.
26. Princess Barbara was legally adopted by her grandmother, Princess Heinrich of Prussia by deed dated September 17, 1952. The adoption was legally recognized January 23, 1953.
27. Elder brother of Duchess Cecilie of Mecklenburg-Schwerin who married Crown Prince Wilhelm of Germany, Kaiser Wilhelm II's eldest son.
28. Princess Alexandra was the elder sister of Ernst August, Duke of Brunswick and Lüneburg, who was married to Princess Viktoria Luise of Prussia.
29. Married (1) Dirk van Wilpe (div. 1963).
30. Succeeded to the throne of Greece on March 18, 1913 following his father's assassination. He left the country on June 11, 1917 while his second son Alexander was named acting king in his father's absence. Returned to the throne, December 19, 1920 after a plebiscite following Alexander's death. Constantine abdicated September 22, 1922 in favor of his eldest son George.
31. Second son of King Christian IX of Denmark and brother of Queen Alexandra, wife of King Edward VII.

32. Recognized as HRH Princess Alexander of Greece by Royal Decree, September 10, 1922.
33. King Constantine II was deposed June 1, 1973. The monarchy was abolished by plebiscite, December 8, 1974.
34. Crown Princess of Greece from July 10, 1965 until May 20, 1967.
35. Princess Irene was Crown Princess of Greece from March 6, 1964 until July 10, 1965.
36. Created Duke of Spoleto, September 22, 1904. Succeeded his brother Amadeo as 4th Duke of Aosta, March 3, 1942. Proclaimed as Tomislav II, King of Croatia, May 11, 1941, but abandoned all claims in 1943.
37. Married (2) April 27, 1982 at Port-au-Prince, Haiti, Arnaldo de la Cagnina, born June 26, 1929 at Rome.
38. Sister of Prince Pedro of Orléans and Braganza, whose daughter, Maria da Gloria, married Crown Prince Alexander of Yugoslavia.
39. Granted the rank of a duke's daughter in Great Britain, September 9, 1947 by King George VI and is known as Lady Katherine Brandram.
40. Adopted by Prince Ludwig of Hesse and By Rhine, December 24, 1960, and upon his death, Prince Moritz became Head of all the House of Hesse. The adoption was ratified at Langen, Hesse, December 4, 1961.
41. Princess Tatiana's elder brother Richard is married to a descendant of Queen Victoria as well, Princess Benedikte of Denmark.
42. Better known as Enrico d'Assia, the international opera and theatre set designer.
43. Married (1) July 31, 1959 at Munich (div. 1965), Hans Peter Schmiedler, born March 14, 1914; married (3) June 20, 1969 at Bennigsen, Wilbrand von Reden, born October 21, 1937 at Hannover.
44. Adopted his nephew, Prince Karl of Hesse, July 7, 1952.
45. Elder sister of Berthold, Margrave of Baden, who married Princess Theodora of Greece and Denmark.
46. Last Chancellor of the German Empire, October 3-November 10, 1918.
47. Elder sister of Ernst August, Duke of Brunswick and Lüneburg, who married Princess Viktoria Luise of Prussia
48. Following Finland's independence from Russia after the Russian revolution, Friedrich Karl was elected King of Finland on October 9, 1918 by the Finnish Parliament. Because of the iminent German collapse at the end of World War I, the new king informed the Finnish people on November 4th, that he wished to wait the outcome of the peace negotiations before accepting the throne. As a result of Allied pressure and so as not to embarrass the peace talks he withdrew his candidature on December 20, 1918 at Finland became a republic.
49. Adopted his nephew, Prince Rainer of Hesse, July 7, 1952.
50. Married (1) July 2, 1965 Mary Clarke (div. 1980)
51. Married (2) December 1, 1980 at Paris, Hendrika Christina Koffeman, born February 17, 1947.

CHAPTER XIII

THE DESCENDANTS OF EDWARD VII
KING OF GREAT BRITAIN AND IRELAND, EMPEROR OF INDIA

HM (Albert) EDWARD VII, KING OF GREAT BRITAIN AND IRELAND, EMPEROR OF INDIA. (Duke of Cornwall and Duke of Rothesay, etc., November 9, 1841. Created Prince of Wales and Earl of Chester, December 8, 1841. Created Earl of Dublin, January 17, 1850. Born November 9, 1841 at Buckingham Palace; died May 6, 1910 at Buckingham Palace. Married March 19, 1863 at St. George's Chapel, Windsor Castle, HRH Princess <u>Alexandra</u> Caroline Marie Charlotte Louise Julia of Denmark, born December 1, 1844 at the Yellow Palace, Copenhagen; died November 20, 1925 at Sandringham, daughter of HM Christian IX, King of Denmark and HH Princess <u>Louise</u> Wilhelmine Friederike Caroline Augusta Julia of Hesse-Cassel.

A

HRH Prince <u>Albert Victor</u> Christian Edward of Great Britain and Ireland.[1] Created Duke of Clarence and Avondale and Earl of Athlone, May 24, 1890. Born January 8, 1864 at Frogmore House, Windsor; died January 14, 1892 at Sandringham House.

B

HM GEORGE V (Frederick Ernest Albert), KING OF GREAT BRITAIN AND IRELAND, EMPEROR OF INDIA. Created Duke of York, Earl of Inverness and Baron Killarney, May 24, 1892. Upon his father's accession to the throne, May 6, 1910 succeeded as Duke of Cornwall and Duke of Rothesay, Earl of Carrick, Baron of Renfrew, Lord of the Isles and Great Steward of Scotland. Created Prince of Wales and Earl of Chester, November 9, 1901. Born June 3, 1865 at Marlborough House, London; died January 20, 1936 at Sandringham House. Married July 6, 1893 the Chapel Royal, St. James's Palace, HSH Princess Victoria <u>Mary</u> Augusta Louisa Olga Pauline Claudine Agnes of Teck, born May 26, 1867 at Kensington Palace; died March 24, 1953 at Marlborough House, only daughter of HSH Franz (<u>Francis</u>) Paul Karl Ludwig Alexander, 1st Prince and Duke of Teck[2] and HRH Princess <u>Mary Adelaide</u> Wilhelmine Elizabeth of Cambridge.[3]

B1 HM EDWARD VIII (Albert Christian George Andrew Patrick <u>David</u>), KING OF GREAT BRITAIN AND IRELAND, EMPEROR OF INDIA.[4] Succeeded on his father's accession as Duke of Cornwall and Duke of Rothesay, etc. Created Prince of Wales and Earl of Chester, June 2, 1910. Succeeded to the throne on the death of his father, January 20, 1936. Abdicated December 10, 1936. Created HRH Duke of Windsor, March 8, 1937. Born June 23, 1894 at White Lodge, Richmond Park; died May 28, 1972 at Paris. Married June 3, 1937 at Chateau de Candé, Monts, France, Bessie <u>Wallis</u> Warfield,[5] born June 19, 1896 at Blue Ridge Summit, Pennsylvania, only daughter of Teackle Wallis Warfield and Alice Montague. (No Issue.)

171

B2 HM (Albert Frederick Arthur) GEORGE VI, KING OF GREAT BRITAIN AND IRELAND, EMPEROR OF INDIA (until 1947). Created Duke of York, Earl of Inverness and Baron Killarney, June 3, 1920. Succeeded to the throne on his elder brother's abdication, December 10, 1936. Born December 14, 1895 at York Cottage, Sandringham House; died February 6, 1952 at Sandringham House. Married April 26, 1923 at Westminster Abbey, Lady <u>Elizabeth</u> Angela Marguerite Bowes-Lyon,[6] born August 4, 1900 at London, youngest daughter of <u>Claude</u> George Bowes-Lyon, 14th Earl of Strathmore and Kinghorne and <u>Nina</u> Cecilie Cavendish-Bentinck.

1. HM ELIZABETH II (Alexandra Mary) (1952-), QUEEN OF GREAT BRITAIN AND NORTHERN IRELAND. Succeeded to the throne on her father's death, February 6, 1952. Born April 21, 1926 at London. Married November 20, 1947 at Westminster Abbey, HRH Prince Philip of Greece and Denmark.* Relinquished his titles of Prince of Greece and Prince of Denmark and assumed the surname Mountbatten, February 28, 1947; granted the qualification of Royal Highness, November 19, 1947. Created Duke of Edinburgh, Earl of Merioneth and Baron Greenwich, November 20, 1947. Granted the style and dignity of a Prince of the United Kingdom of Great Britain and Northern Ireland, February 22, 1957. Born June 10, 1921 at Mon Repos, Corfu, only son of HRH Prince Andrew of Greece and Denmark and HSH Princess Victoria <u>Alice</u> Elisabeth Julie Marie of Battenberg.

   1) HRH The Prince <u>Charles</u> Philip Arthur George of Great Britain and Northern Ireland. Succeeded on his mother's accession to the throne as Duke of Cornwall and Duke of Rothesay, etc. Created Prince of Wales and Earl of Chester, July 26, 1958. Born November 14, 1948 at Buckingham Palace. Married July 29, 1981 at St. Paul's Cathedral, London, Lady <u>Diana</u> Frances Spencer, born July 1, 1961 at Park House, Sandringham, youngest daughter of Edward <u>John</u> Spencer, 8th Earl Spencer and Hon. <u>Frances</u> Ruth Burke Roche.

      (1) HRH Prince <u>William</u> Arthur Philip Louis of Wales, born June 21, 1982 at St. Mary's Hospital, Paddington, London

      (2) HRH Prince Henry <u>(Harry)</u> Charles Albert David of Wales, born September 15, 1984 at St, Mary's Hospital, Paddington, London

   2) HRH The Princess <u>Anne</u> Elizabeth Alice Louise of Great Britain and Ireland. Created Princess Royal, June 13, 1987. Born August 15, 1950 at Clarence House, London. Married November 14, 1973 at Westminster Abbey, <u>Mark</u> Anthony Peter Phillips, born September 22, 1948 at Tetbury, Gloucestershire, only son of Major <u>Peter</u> William Garside Phillips and <u>Anne</u> Patricia Tiarks.

      (1) <u>Peter</u> Mark Andrew Phillips, born November 15, 1977 at St. Mary's Hospital, Paddington, London

      (2) <u>Zara</u> Anne Elizabeth Phillips, born May 15, 1981 at St. Mary's Hospital, Paddington, London

   3) HRH The Prince <u>Andrew</u> Albert Christian Edward of Great Britain and Northern Ireland. Created Duke of York, Earl of Inverness and Baron Killyleagh, July 23, 1986. Born February 19, 1960 at Buckingham Palace. Married July 23, 1986 at Westminster Abbey, <u>Sarah</u> Margaret Ferguson, born October 15, 1959 at Welbeck Street Nursing Home, London, younger daughter of <u>Ronald</u> Ivor Ferguson and <u>Susan</u> Mary Wright.

4) HRH The Prince Edward Antony Richard Louis of Great Britain and Northern
Ireland; born March 10, 1964 at Buckingham Palace.

2. HRH The Princess Margaret Rose of Great Britain and Northern Ireland. Born
August 21, 1930 at Glamis Castle, Forfarshire. Married May 6, 1960 at Westminster Abbey (div. 1978), Antony Charles Robert Armstrong-Jones.[7] Created
Earl of Snowdon and Viscount Linley, October 6, 1961; born March 7, 1930 at
London, only son of Ronald Owen Lloyd Armstrong-Jones and Anne Messel.
   1) David Albert Charles Armstrong-Jones, Viscount Linley, born November 3,
   1961 at Clarence House
   2) Lady Sarah Frances Elizabeth Armstrong-Jones, born May 1, 1964 at
   Clarence House

B3 The HRH Princess Victoria Alexandra Alice Mary of Great Britain and Ireland.
Created Princess Royal, January 1, 1932. Born April 25, 1897 at York Cottage,
Sandringham; died March 28 1965 at Harewood House, Leeds. Married February 28,
1922 at Westminster Abbey, Henry George Charles Lascelles, 6th Earl of Harewood,
Viscount Lascelles and Baron Harewood,[8] born September 9, 1882 at London; died May
23, 1947 at Harewood House, Leeds, elder son of Henry Ulick Lascelles, 5th Earl of
Harewood and Lady Florence Katharine Bridgeman.
1. George Henry Hubert Lascelles, 7th Earl of Harewood, born February 7, 1923 at
   Chesterfield House, London. Married (1) September 29, 1949 at St. Mark's,
   North Audley Street, London, Maria Donata (Marion) Nanetta Paulina Gustava
   Erwina Wilhelmina Stein,[9] born October 18, 1926 at Vienna, only daughter of
   Erwin Stein and Sofie Bachmann.
   1) David Henry George Lascelles, Viscount Lascelles, born October 21, 1950
   at London. Married February 12, 1979 at Paddington, London, Margaret
   Rosalind Messenger, born April 15, 1948 at Cheltenham, Gloucestershire,
   daughter of Edgar Frank Messenger and Margaret Alice Black.
      (1) Honourable Emily Tscring Lascelles, born November 23, 1975 at Bath,
      Somerset
      (2) Honourable Benjamin George Lascelles, born September 19, 1978 at
      Bath
      (3) Honourable Alexander Edgar Lascelles,[10] born May 13, 1980 at Bath
      (4) Honourable Edward David Lascelles, born November 19, 1982 at Bath
   2) Honourable James Edward Lascelles, born October 4, 1953 at London.
   Married (1) April 4, 1973 at Wortham, Norfolk (div. 1985), Fredericka
   Ann Duhrsson, born June 12, 1954 at Newport, Maine, daughter of Alfred
   Duhrsson and Elizabeth Buntt.
      (1) Sophie Amber Lascelles, born October 1, 1973 at Thorpness, Suffolk
      (2) Rowan Nash Lascelles, born November 6, 1977 at Church Farm,
      Sotherton, Suffolk
   James Lascelles married (2) May 4, 1985 at Albuquerque, New Mexico, Lori
   (Shadow) Susan Lee,[11] born August 29, 1954 at Albuquerque, New Mexico,
   only child of John Robert Lee and Marianne Lee Bennett.
      (3) Tanit Lascelles, born July 1, 1981 at Santa Eulalia, Ibiza, Spain
      (4) Tewa Ziyane Robert George Lascelles, born June 8, 1985 at Edgewood,
      New Mexico

3) Honourable Robert <u>Jeremy</u> Hugh Lascelles, born February 14, 1955 at London. Married July 4, 1981, at London Julie Baylis, born July 19, 1957 at Droitwich, Worcestershire, daughter of Robert Baylis and Valerie Smart.
   (1) <u>Thomas</u> Robert Lascelles, born September 7, 1982 at London
   (2) <u>Ellen</u> Mary Lascelles, born December 17, 1984 at London
   (3) <u>Amy</u> Rose Lascelles, born June 26, 1986 at London
The Earl of Harewood married (2) July 31, 1967 at New Canaan, Connecticut, <u>Patricia</u> Elizabeth Tuckwell,[12] born November 24, 1926 at Melbourne, Australia, daughter of Charles Tuckwell and <u>Elizabeth</u> Jane Norton.
4) Honourable <u>Mark</u> Hubert Lascelles, born July 5, 1964 at London

2. Honourable <u>Gerald</u> David Lascelles, born August 21, 1924 at Goldsborough Hall, Knaresborough, Yorkshire. Married (1) July 15, 1952 at St. Margaret's, Westminster (div. 1978), Angela Dowding, born April 20, 1919 at Hanwell, daughter of <u>Charles</u> Stanley Dowding and Lilian Lawlor.
   1) <u>Henry</u> Ulick Lascelles, born May 19, 1953 at London. Married August 25, 1979 at Chapel Royal, Windsor Great Park, Windsor, <u>Alexandra</u> Clare Ruth Morton, born April 15, 1953 at London, daughter of <u>Charles</u> Peter Morton and <u>Pauline</u> Dorothy Edwards.
Gerald Lascelles married (2) November 17, 1978 at Vienna, <u>Elizabeth</u> Evelyn Collingwood, born April 23, 1924 at Wimbledon, London, daughter of Brigadier Sydney Collingwood and <u>Charlotte</u> Annie Oughterson.
   2) <u>Martin</u> David Lascelles, born February 9, 1962 at London

B4 The HRH Prince <u>Henry</u> William Frederick Albert of Great Britain and Ireland. Created Duke of Gloucester, Earl of Ulster and Baron Culloden, March 31, 1928. Born March 31, 1900 at York Cottage, Sandringham. Died June 10, 1974 at Barnwell Manor, Northamptonshire. Married November 6, 1935 at Buckingham Palace, Lady <u>Alice</u> Christabel Montagu-Douglas-Scott,[13] born December 25, 1901 at Montagu House, London, third daughter of <u>John</u> Charles Montagu-Douglas-Scott, 7th Duke of Buccleuch and 9th Duke of Queensbury, Earl of Dalkeith and Lady <u>Margaret</u> Alice Bridgeman.
1. HRH Prince <u>William</u> Henry Andrew Frederick of Gloucester, born December 18, 1941 at Barnet, Hertfordshire; died August 28, 1972 in a flying accident at Halfpenny Green, near Wolverhampton.
2. HRH Prince <u>Richard</u> Alexander Walter George of Gloucester. Succeeded his father as 2nd Duke of Gloucester, Earl of Ulster and Baron Culloden. Born August 26, 1944 at Northampton. Married July 8, 1972 at Barnwell Parish Church, Northamptonshire, <u>Birgitte</u> Eva van Deurs,[14] born June 20, 1946 at Odensee, Isle of Funen, Denmark, younger daughter of <u>Asger</u> Preben Wissing Henriksen and Vivian van Deurs.
   1) <u>Alexander</u> Patrick Gregers Richard Windsor, Earl of Ulster, born October 24, 1974 at St. Mary's Hospital, Paddington, London
   2) Lady <u>Davina</u> Elizabeth Alice Benedikte Windsor, born November 19, 1977 at St. Mary's Hospital, Paddington
   3) Lady <u>Rose</u> Victoria Birgitte Louise Windsor, born March 1, 1980 at St. Mary's Hospital, Paddington

B5 The HRH Prince George Edward Alexander Edmund of Great Britain and Ireland. Created Duke of Kent, Earl of St. Andrews and Baron Downpatrick, October 12, 1934. Born December 20, 1902 at Sandringham House; died August 25, 1942 in an air crash at Morven, Scotland while on active service. Married November 29, 1934 at Westminster Abbey, HRH Princess Marina of Greece and Denmark,[15] born December 13, 1906 at Athens; died August 27, 1968 at Kensington Palace, third daughter of HRH Prince Nicholas of Greece and Denmark and HIH Grand Duchess Helen Vladimirovna of Russia.

1. HRH Prince Edward George Nicholas Paul Patrick of Kent. Succeeded his father as 2nd Duke of Kent, Earl of St. Andrews and Baron Downpatrick. Born October 9, 1935 at London. Married June 8, 1961 at York Minster, York, Katharine Lucy Mary Worsley, born February 22, 1933 at Hovingham Hall, York, only daughter of Colonel Sir William Arthington Worsley, 4th Baronet and Joyce Morgan Brunner.

    1) George Philip Nicholas Windsor, Earl of St. Andrews,[16] born June 26, 1962 at Coppins, Iver, Buckinghamshire

    2) Lady Helen Marina Lucy Windsor, born April 28, 1964 at Coppins

    3) Lord Nicholas Charles Edward Jonathan Windsor, born July 25, 1970 at London

2. HRH Princess Alexandra Helen Elizabeth Olga Christabel of Kent, born December 25, 1936 at London. Married April 24, 1963 at Westminster Abbey, Honourable Angus James Robert Bruce Ogilvy, born September 28, 1928 at London, second son of David Lyulph Gore Wolseley Ogilvy, 12th Earl of Airlie and Lady Alexandra Marie Bridget Coke.

    1) James Robert Bruce Ogilvy, born February 29, 1964 at Thatched House Lodge, Richmond Park

    2) Marina Victoria Alexandra Ogilvy, born July 31, 1966 at Thatched House Lodge, Richmond Park

3. HRH Prince Michael George Charles Franklin of Kent,[17] born July 4, 1942 at Coppins, Iver, Buckinghamshire. Married June 30, 1978 (civil) at Vienna and July 29, 1983 (religious) at Archbishop House, London, Baroness Marie Christine Agnes Hedwig Ida von Reibnitz,[18] born January 15, 1945 at Karlsbad (now Karlovy Vary, Czechoslovakia), only daughter of Baron Günther Hubertus von Reibnitz and Countess Maria Anna Carolina Franziska Walpurga Bernadette Szapáry von Muraszombath, Széchysziget und Szapár.

    1) Lord Frederick Michael George David Louis Windsor, born April 6, 1979 at St. Mary's Hospital, Paddington, London

    2) Lady Gabriella (Ella) Marina Alexandra Ophelia Windsor, born April 23, 1981 at St. Mary's Hospital, Paddington, London

B6 The HRH Prince John Charles Francis of Great Britain and Ireland, born July 12, 1905 at York Cottage, Sandringham; died January 18, 1919 at Wood Farm, Wolferton, Norfolk.

C

HRH Princess Louise Victoria Alexandra Dagmar of Great Britain and Ireland. Created Princess Royal, November 9, 1905. Born February 20, 1867 at Marlborough House; died January 4, 1931 at London. Married July 27, 1889 at Buckingham Palace, Alexander William George Duff, 6th Earl and 1st Duke of Fife,[19] born November 10, 1849 at Edinburgh; died January 29, 1912 at Aswan, Egypt, only son of James Duff, 5th Earl of Fife and Lady Agnes Georgiana Elizabeth Hay.[20]

C1 A son, stillborn, June 16, 1890 at East Sheen Lodge, Richmond.

C2 Lady Alexandra Victoria Alberta Edwina Louise Duff.[21] Created HH Princess Alexandra of Fife, November 9, 1905 by her grandfather, HM King Edward VII. Succeeded her father as 2nd Duchess of Fife and Countess of Macduff, January 29, 1912. Born May 17, 1891 at East Sheen Lodge, Richmond; died February 26, 1959 at London. Married October 15, 1913 at the Chapel Royal, St. James's Palace, HRH Prince Arthur Frederick Patrick Albert of Connaught,* born January 13, 1883 at Windsor Castle; died September 12, 1938 at London, only son of HRH Prince Arthur William Patrick Albert of Great Britain and Ireland, Duke of Connaught and Strathearn and HRH Princess Luise Margarete Alexandra of Prussia. (For issue, see Chapter XVII.)

C3 Lady Maud Alexandra Victoria Georgina Bertha Duff. Created HH Princess Maud of Fife, November 9, 1905 by her grandfather, HM King Edward VII. Born April 3, 1893 at East Sheen Lodge, Richmond; died December 14, 1945 at London. Married November 12, 1923 at London, Charles Alexander Carnegie, 11th Earl of Southesk, Lord Carnegie of Kinnaird and Leuchards, and Baron Balinhard of Farnell;[22] born September 23, 1893 at Edinburgh, son of Charles Noel Carnegie, 10th Earl of Southesk and Ethel Mary Elizabeth Bannerman.
1. James George Alexander Bannerman Carnegie, Lord Carnegie. Succeeded his maternal aunt as 3rd Duke of Fife and Earl of Macduff, February 26, 1959. Born September 23, 1929 at London. Married September 11, 1956 at Perth (div. 1966), Hon. Caroline Cecily Dewar,[23] born February 12, 1934 at Bardowie Castle, Milngavie, elder daughter of Alexander Dewar, 3rd Baron Forteviot and Cynthia Monica Starkie.
    1) A son, stillborn, April 4, 1958.
    2) Lady Alexandra Clare Carnegie, born June 20, 1959 at London
    3) David Charles Carnegie, Earl of Macduff, born March 3, 1961 at London. Married July 16, 1987 at Guards Chapel, Wellington Barracks, London Caroline Anne Bunting, born November 13, 1961 at Windsor, daughter of Martin Brian Bunting and Veronica Mary Cope.

D

HRH Princess Victoria Alexandra Olga Mary of Great Britain and Ireland, born July 6, 1868 at Marlborough House; died December 3, 1935 at Coppins, Iver, Buckinghamshire.

E

HRH Princess Maud Charlotte Mary Victoria of Great Britain and Ireland, born November 26, 1869 at Marlborough House; died November 20, 1938 at London. Married July 22, 1896 at Buckingham Palace, HRH Prince Christian Frederik Carl Georg Valdemar Axel of

Denmark.[24] Elected King of Norway, November 18, 1905 and ascended the throne as HM HAAKON VII, KING OF NORWAY. Born August 3, 1872 at Charlottenlund, Denmark; died September 21, 1957 at Oslo, second son of HM (Christian) FREDERIK VIII (Vilhelm Carl), KING OF DENMARK and HRH Princess Louise Josephine Eugènie of Sweden.

E1 HRH Prince Alexander Edward Christian Frederik of Denmark. Following the succession of his father as King of Norway, Prince Alexander became HRH Prince Olav of Norway, November 18, 1905. Succeeded to the throne on the death of his father as HM OLAV V, KING OF NORWAY, September 21, 1957. Born July 2, 1903 at Appleton House, Sandringham. Married March 21, 1929 at Oslo, HRH Princess Märtha Sofie Lovisa Dagmar Thyra of Sweden,[25] born March 28, 1901 at Stockholm; died April 5, 1954 at Oslo, second daughter of HRH Prince Oskar Carl Vilhelm of Sweden, Duke of Västergötland and HRH Princess Ingeborg Charlotte Caroline Frederikke of Denmark.

1. HRH Princess Ragnhild Alexandra of Norway,[26] born June 9, 1930 at Oslo. Married May 15, 1953 at Asker, near Oslo, Erling Sven Lorentzen, born January 28, 1923 at Oslo, son of Øivind Lorentzen and Ragna Nilsen.
   1) Haakon Lorentzen, born August 23, 1954 at Oslo. Married April 14, 1982 at Rio de Janeiro, Brazil, Martha Carvalho de Freitas, born April 5, 1958 at Rio de Janeiro, daughter of José Maria Gomes de Freitas and Maria Bernadete Aragao Carvalho.
      (1) Olav Alexander Lorentzen, born July 11, 1985 at Rio de Janeiro
   2) Ingeborg Lorentzen, born February 27, 1957 at Oslo. Married June 4, 1982 at Rio de Janeiro, Paulo César Ribeiro Filho, born November 29, 1956 at Rio de Janeiro, son of Paulo César Ribeiro and Ercilia Cabral Pereira.
   3) Ragnhild Alexandra Lorentzen, born May 8, 1868 at Rio de Janeiro

2. HRH Princess Astrid Maud Ingeborg of Norway,[27] born February 12, 1932 at Oslo. Married January 12, 1961 at Asker, near Oslo, Johan Martin Ferner,[28] born July 22, 1927 at Oslo, son of Ferner Jacobsen and Ragnhild Olsen.
   1) Cathrine Ferner, born July 22, 1962 at Oslo
   2) Benedikte Ferner, born September 27, 1963 at Oslo
   3) Alexander Ferner, born March 15, 1965 at Oslo
   4) Elisabeth Ferner, born March 30, 1969 at Oslo
   5) Carl Christian Ferner, born October 22, 1972 at Oslo

3. HRH Crown Prince Harald of Norway, born February 21, 1937 at Skaugum. Married August 29, 1968 at Oslo, Sonja Haraldsen, born July 4, 1937, daughter of Carl August Haraldsen and Dagny Ulrichsen.
   1) HRH Princess Märtha Louise of Norway, born September 22, 1971 at Oslo
   2) Hereditary Prince Haakon Magnus of Norway, born July 20, 1973 at Oslo

F

HRH Prince Alexander John Charles Robert Albert of Great Britain and Ireland,[29] born April 6, 1871 at Sandringham House; died April 7, 1871 at Sandringham House.

1. He became engaged to Princess Victoria Mary of Teck, December 3, 1891, who following his death married his younger brother, the future George V.

2. Son of Duke Alexander of Württember and his morganatic wife Countess Claudine Rhédey von Kis-Rhéde, created Countess von Hohenstein, May 2, 1835 by Emperor Ferdinand I of Austria. Franz was created Prince of Teck with the qualification of Serene Highness by King Wilhelm I of Württemberg. Created Duke of Teck by King Carl I of Württemberg, December 16, 1871. Granted the qualification of Highness by Queen Victoria, July 11, 1887.

3. First cousin of Queen Victoria. Daughter of HRH Prince Adolphus, Duke of Cambridge, seventh son of King George III.

4. Created Duke of Windsor, March 8, 1937, but the Letters Patent dated May 27, 1937 which reconferred on him the 'title, style or attribute of Royal Highness' specifically stated that 'that his wife and descendants, if any, shall not hold said title or attribute.'

5. Married (1) January 8, 1916 at Baltimore, Maryland (div. 1927), Earl Winfield Spencer, born September 20, 1888 at Kinsley, Kansas; died May 29, 1950 at Coronado, California. Married (2) July 21, 1928 at Chelsea, London (div. 1937), Ernest Aldrich Simpson, born May 6, 1897 at New York City; died November 30, 1958 at London.

6. Formerly believed to have been born at St. Paul's Walden Bury, Hertfordshire.

7. Married (2) December 15, 1978 at Kensington, London, Lucy Mary Davies, born March 11, 1941 at Dublin, Ireland.

8. Succeeded to the earldom on the death of his father, October 6, 1929.

9. Married (2) March 14, 1973 at London, Jeremy Thorpe, born April 29, 1929, one time leader of the British Liberal Party.

10. The Hon. Alexander Lascelles is heir to the Earldom of Harewood after his father, Viscount Lascelles.

11. Married (1) March 6, 1973 at London (div.), John Porter.

12. Married (1) July 7, 1948, at Melbourne, Australia (div.), Athol Smith, born August 14, 1914 at Melbourne.

13. Following the death of The Duke of Gloucester in 1974, became known as HRH Princess Alice, Duchess of Gloucester.

14. Styled HRH Princess Richard of Gloucester until June 10, 1974. Now HRH The Duchess of Gloucester.

15. Princess Marina was a first cousin of Prince Philip, Duke of Edinburgh. Her father, Prince Nicholas of Greece and Denmark was a brother of King Constantine I of the Hellenes, who was married to Princess Sophie of Prussia and of Prince Andrew of Greece and Denmark, who was married to Princess Alice of Battenberg. Marina's mother, Grand Duchess Helen Vladimirovna of Russia was the sister of Grand Duke of Kirill Vladimirovitch, who was married to Princess Victoria Melita of Edinburgh, a granddaughter of Queen Victoria.

16. In June 1987, the Duke and Duchess of Kent announced the Earl of St. Andrew's engagement to <u>Sylvana</u> Palma Tomaselli, born May 28, 1957 at Placentia, New foundland, Canada, daughter of <u>Maximilian</u> Karl Tomaselli and Josiane Preschez. Sylvana Tomaselli was married (1) December 1977 at Vancouver, John Paul Jones (div. 1981.)

17. Because the Act of Settlement prohibits the marriage of a member of the British Royal Family with a Roman Catholic, Prince Michael of Kent was automatically excluded from the succession when he married. His children, however, retain their rights of succession as they are being brought up in the Anglican church. Vatican approval for the marriage was finally given in 1983 when Prince and Princess Michael of Kent were able to marry according to the rights of the Roman Catholic Church.

18. Married (1) September 15, 1971 at London (annulled 1978), Thomas Troubridge, born December 26, 1939 at London.

19. Succeeded his father as 6th Earl of Fife, August 7, 1879. He was created Duke of Fife and Marquess of Macduff two days after his marriage, and was further created Duke of Fife and Earl of Macduff, October 16, 1899 with a special remainder in default of male issue to his first and other daughters and their male issue.

20. Second daughter of William Hay, 18th Earl of Erroll and Lady Elizabeth FitzClarence, third natural daughter of King William IV and the actress Dorothy Jordan. Princess Louise and her husband were third cousins.

21. Usually referred to as HRH Princess Arthur of Connaught, although from 1912, she was Duchess of Fife in her own right.

22. Married (2) May 16, 1952 at Scone Palace, Perthshire, Evelyn Julia Williams-Freeman, born July 27, 1909 at Alton Pancras, Dorset, widow of Major Ion FitzGerald Campbell.

23. Married (2) November 7, 1980 at London, General Sir Richard Worsley, born May 23, 1923 at Ballywater, Co. Down, Northern Ireland.

24. Princess Maud and her husband were first cousins. Maud's mother and Carl's father were sister and brother.

25. Princess Märtha and King Olav were first cousins. Her mother, Princess Ingeborg of Denmark and his father, King Haakon VII were children of King Frederik VII of Denmark, who was a brother of Queen Alexandra.

26. Now styled as Princess Ragnhild, Mrs. Lorentzen, without the qualification of Royal Highness or Highness.

27. Now styled Princess Astrid, Mrs. Ferner, without the qualification of Royal Highness or Highness.

28. Married (1) 1951 (div. 1955) to Bitte Hesselberg-Meyer.

29. Although always referred as Prince Alexander in standard works such as H.M. Lane's <u>The Royal Daughters of England</u> (London 1911), when King George V's own son, Prince John was buried, he recorded in his diary, January 21, 1919 "dear little Johnnie was laid in the churchyard next to brother John.

THE EARL & COUNTESS MOUNTBATTEN of BURMA
(Lord Romsey)

CHAPTER XIV

THE DESCENDANTS OF PRINCESS ALICE OF GREAT BRITAIN AND
IRELAND, GRAND DUCHESS OF HESSE AND BY RHINE

HRH Princess <u>Alice</u> Maud Mary of Great Britain and Ireland, born April 25, 1843 at Buckingham Palace; died December 14, 1878 at Darmstadt. Married July 1, 1862 at Osborne, House, Isle of Wight, HRH <u>Ludwig VI</u> Karl, Grand Duke of Hesse and By Rhine.[1] Succeeded his uncle, Grand Duke Ludwig III, June 13, 1877. Born September 12, 1837 at Bessungen; died March 13, 1892 at Darmstadt, eldest son of HGDH Prince <u>Karl</u> Wilhelm Ludwig of Hesse and By Rhine and HRH Princess Marie <u>Elisabeth</u> Caroline Viktoria of Prussia.

A

HGDG Princess <u>Victoria</u> Albert Elisabeth Mathilde Marie of Hesse and by Rhine, born April 5, 1863 at Windsor Castle; died September 24, 1950 at Kensington Palace. Married April 30, 1884 at Darmstadt, HSH Prince <u>Louis</u> Alexander of Battenberg, 1st Marquess of Milford Haven, Earl of Medina and Viscount Alderney,[2] born May 24, 1854 at Graz, Austria, died September 11, 1921 at London, eldest son of HGDH Prince <u>Alexander</u> Ludwig Georg Friedrich Emil of Hesse and By Rhine and Countess <u>Julie</u> Therese von Hauke, who was created H Ill H Countess of Battenberg, November 5, 1851 and HSH Princess of Battenberg, December 26, 1858.

A1   HSH Princess Victoria <u>Alice</u> Elisabeth Julia Marie of Battenberg,[3] born February 15, 1885 at Windsor Castle; died December 5, 1969 at Buckingham Palace. Married October 7, 1903 at Darmstadt, HRH Prince Andrew of Greece and Denmark, born February 2, 1882 at Athens; died December 3, 1944 at Monte Carlo, Monaco, fourth son of HM GEORGE I, KING OF THE HELLENES[4] and HIH Grand Duchess Olga Constantinova of Russia.

1.   HRH Princess Margarita of Greece and Denmark, born April 18, 1905 at Athens; died April 24, 1981 at Bad Wiesse, West Germany. Married April 30, 1931 at Langenburg, HSH <u>Gottfried</u> Hermann Alfred Paul Maximilian Viktor, 8th Prince of Hohenlohe-Langenburg,* born March 24, 1897 at Langenburg; died May 11, 1960 at Langenburg, elder son of HSH <u>Ernst</u> Wilhelm Karl Maximilian, 7th Prince of Hohenlohe-Langenburg and HRH Princess <u>Alexandra</u> Louise Olga Victoria of Great Britain and Ireland, Princess of Saxe-Coburg and Gotha, Duchess of Saxony. (For issue, see Chapter XV.)

2.   HRH Princess Theodora of Greece and Denmark, born May 30, 1906 at Athens; died October 16, 1969 at Konstanz. Married August 17, 1931 at Baden-Baden, HRH Prince <u>Berthold</u> Friedrich Wilhelm Ernst August Karl of Baden, Margrave of Baden, Duke of Zähringen,[5] born February 24, 1906 at Karlsruhe; died October 27, 1963 at Spaichingen, Württemberg, only son of HRH Prince Maximilian (<u>Max</u>) Alexander Friedrich Wilhelm of Baden, Margrave of Baden and HRH Princess

Marie Louise Victoria Caroline Amalie Alexandra Auguste Friederike of Hanover, Princess of Great Britain and Ireland.

1) HGDH Princess Margarita Alice Thyra Viktoria Marie Louise Scholastica of Baden. Born July 14, 1932 at Schloss Salem, Baden. Married June 5 (civil) and June 6, 1957 (religious) at Schloss Salem (div. 1981), HRH Prince Tomislav of Yugoslavia,* born January 9, 1928 at Belgrade, second son of HM ALEXANDER I, KING OF YUGOSLAVIA and HRH Princess Marie of Roumania. (For issue, see Chapter XV.)

2) HRH Prince Maximilian Andreas Friedrich Gustav Ernst August Bernhard of Baden, Margrave of Baden, Duke of Zähringen, born July 3, 1933 at Schloss Salem. Married September 23 (civil) at Salem and September 30, 1966 (religious) at Schloss Persenbeug, Lower Austria, HI & RH Archduchess Valerie Isabella Maria Anne Alfonsa Thomasia Huberta Josepha Ignatia of Austria, Princess of Tuscany, born May 23, 1941 at Vienna, seventh daughter of HI & RH Archduke Hubert Salvator Rainer Maria Joseph Ignatius of Austria, Prince of Tuscany and HSH Princess Rosemary Friederike Isabella Eleonore Henriette Antonia of Salm-Salm.

    (1) HGDH Princess Marie Louise Elisabeth Mathilde Theodora Cecilie Sarah Charlotte of Baden, born July 3, 1969 at Schloss Salem

    (2) HRH Hereditary Prince Bernhard Max Friedrich August Gustav Louis Kraft of Baden, born May 27, 1970 at Schloss Salem

    (3) HGDH Prince Leopold Max Christian Ludwig Clemens Hubert of Baden, born October 1, 1971 at Schloss Salem

    (4) HGDH Prince Michael Max Andreas of Baden, born March 11, 1976 at Schloss Salem

3) HGDH Prince Ludwig Wilhelm Georg Ernst Christoph of Baden, born March 16, 1937 at Karlsruhe. Married September 21 (civil) at Salem and October 21, 1967 (religious) at Wald, Lower Austria, HSH Princess Maria Anna (Marianne) Henriette Eleonore Gobertina of Auersperg-Breunner, born December 15, 1943 at Zseliz, Kom. Bars, Hungary, youngest daughter of HSH Karl Alain August Gobertus, Prince of Auersperg-Breunner and Countess Marie Henriette Theresia Aloisa Benedikta von Meran.

    (1) HGDH Princess Sophie Thyra Josephine Georgine Henriette of Baden, born July 8, 1975 at Heidelberg

    (2) HGDH Prince Bernhard Ernst August Emich Rainer of Baden, born October 6, 1976 at Heidelberg

    (3) HGDH Princess Aglaë Margareta Tatiana Mary of Baden, born March 3, 1981 at Heidelberg

3. HRH Princess Cecilia of Greece and Denmark,[6] born June 22, 1911 at Tatoi, near Athens; died November 16, 1937 at Steene, Belgium in an air crash. Married February 2, 1931 at Darmstadt, HRH Hereditary Grand Duke Georg Donatus Wilhelm Nikolaus Eduard Heinrich Karl of Hesse and By Rhine,* born November 8, 1906 at Darmstadt; died November 16, 1937 at Steene, Belgium in an air crash, elder son of HRH Grand Duke Ernst Ludwig Karl Albert Wilhelm of Hesse and By Rhine and HSH Princess Eleonore Ernestine Marie of Solms-Hohensolms-Lich. (For issue, see Chapter XIV.)

4. HRH Princess Sophie of Greece and Denmark, born June 26, 1914 at Mon Repos, Corfu. Married (1) December 15, 1930 at Kronberg, HH Prince <u>Christoph</u> Ernst August of Hesse,* born May 14, 1901 at Frankfurt-am-Main; killed on active service October 7, 1943 in an air crash in the Appenines, youngest son of HRH Prince <u>Friedrich Karl</u> Ludwig Konstantin of Hesse, Landgrave of Hesse and HRH Princess <u>Margarete</u> Beatrice Feodora of Prussia. (For Issue, see Chapter XII.) Princess Sophie married (2) April 23 (civil) and April 24, 1946 (religious) at Salem HRH Prince <u>Georg Wihelm</u> Ernst August Friedrich Axel of Hanover,* born March 25, 1915 at Brunswick, second son of HRH Prince <u>Ernst August</u> Christian Georg of Hanover, Prince of Great Britain and Ireland, Duke of Brunswick and Lüneburg and HRH Princess <u>Viktoria Luise</u> Adelheid Mathilde Charlotte of Prussia. (For issue, see Chapter XII.)

5. HRH Prince Philip of Greece and Denmark, born June 10, 1921 at Mon Repos, Corfu. Married November 20, 1947 at Westminster Abbey, HM ELIZABETH II (Alexandra Mary), QUEEN OF GREAT BRITAIN AND NORTHERN IRELAND,* born April 21, 1926 at London, elder daughter of HM (Albert Frederick Arthur) GEORGE VI, KING OF GREAT BRITAIN AND NORTHERN IRELAND and Lady <u>Elizabeth</u> Angela Marguerite Bowes-Lyon. (For issue, see Chapter XIII.)

A2 HSH Princess <u>Louise</u> Alexandra Marie of Battenberg,[7] born July 13, 1889 at Schloss Heiligenberg, Jugenheim, near Darmstadt; died March 7, 1965 at Stockholm. Married November 3, 1923 at the Chapel Royal, St. James's Palace, HM (Oscar Frederik Vilhelm Olaf) GUSTAF VI ADOLF, KING OF SWEDEN. Succeeed to the throne on the death of his father, HM GUSTAV V, KING OF SWEDEN, October 29, 1950. Born November 11, 1882 at Stockholm; died September 15, 1973 at Helsingborg, eldest son of HM (Oscar) GUSTAV V (Adolf), KING OF SWEDEN and HRDH Princess Sophie Marie <u>Victoria</u> of Baden. (King Gustav VI Adolf was first married to Princess Margaret of Connaught, a granddaughter of Queen Victoria.)
1. A daughter, stillborn, May 30, 1925 at Stockholm

A3 HSH Prince <u>George</u> Louis Victor Henry Serge of Battenberg.[8] Succeeded his father as 2nd Marquess of Milford Haven, Earl of Medina and Viscount Alderney. Born November 6, 1892 at Darmstadt; died April 8, 1938 at London. Married November 15, 1916 at London, Countess Nadejda (<u>Nada</u>) Mikhailovna de Torby, born March 28, 1896 at Cannes; died January 22, 1963 at Cannes, younger daughter of HIH Grand Duke Mikhail Mikhailovitch of Russia and Countess Sophie von Merenberg.[9]
1. Lady <u>Tatiana</u> Elizabeth Mountbatten, born December 16, 1917 at Edinburgh

2. <u>David</u> Michael Mountbatten, 3rd Marquesss of Milford Haven, Earl of Medina and Viscount Alderney, born May 12, 1919 at Edinburgh; died April 14, 1970 at London. Married (1) February 4, 1950 at Washington D.C. (div. 1954 at Mexico; 1960 at England) <u>Romaine</u> Dalhgren Pierce,[10] born July 17, 1923 at Biltmore, North Carolina; died February 15, 1975 at New York City, only daughter of <u>Ulric</u> Dalhgren Pierce and Margaret Knickerbocker Clark. (No issue.) Lord Milford Haven married (2) November 17, 1960 at St. Andrew's Church, Frognal, London <u>Janet</u> Mercedes Bryce, born September 29, 1937 at Hamilton, Bermuda, daughter of Major Francis Bryce and <u>Gladys</u> Jean Mosley.

1) George Ivar Louis Mountbatten, 4th Marquess of Milford Haven, Earl of Medina and Viscount Alderney, born June 6, 1961 at London

2) Lord Ivar Alexander Michael Mountbatten, born March 9, 1963 at London

A4 HSH Prince Louis Francis Albert Victor Nicholas of Battenberg.[11] Created Viscount Mountbatten of Burma, August 23, 1946. Created Earl Mountbatten of Burma and Baron Romsey, October 28, 1947. Admiral of the Fleet, 1956. Born June 25, 1900 at Windsor Castle; died August 27, 1979 in an explosion off the coast of Ireland as the result of a bomb placed in his fishing boat by the Irish Republican Army.[12] Married July 18, 1922 at St. Margaret's Church, Westminster, London, Honourable Edwina Cynthia Annette Ashley, born November 28, 1901 at Broadlands, Romsey, Hampshire; died February 21, 1960 at Jesselton, British North Borneo, elder daughter of Wilfrid William Ashley, 1st (and last) Baron Mount Temple and Amalia Mary Maud Cassel.

1. Lady Patricia Edwina Victoria Mountbatten. Succeeded her father as 2nd Countess Mountbatten of Burma and Baroness Romsey. Born February 14, 1924 at London. Married October 26, 1946 at Romsey Abbey, Romsey, Hampshire, John Ulick Knatchbull, 7th Baron Brabourne and 16th Baronet, born November 9, 1924 at London, second son of Michael Herbert Rudolf Knatchbull, 5th Baron and 14th Baronet and Lady Doreen Geraldine Browne.

   1) Norton Louis Philip Knatchbull, Baron Romsey, born October 8, 1947 at London. Married October 20, 1979 at Romsey Abbey, Romsey, Penelope Meredith Eastwood, born April 16, 1953 at London, daughter of Reginald Wray Frank Eastwood and Marian Elizabeth Hood.

      (1) Honourable Nicholas Louis Charles Norton Knatchbull, born May 15, 1981 at London

      (2) Honourable Alexandra Victoria Edwina Diana Knatchbull, born December 5, 1982 at London

      (3) Honourable Leonora Louise Marie Elizabeth Knatchbull, born June 25, 1986 at London

   2) Honourable Michael-John Ulick Knatchbull, born May 24, 1950 at London. Married June 1, 1985 at Warwick, Melissa Clare Owen, born November 12, 1960 at Birmingham, daughter of Judge John Arthur Dalziel Owen, Q.C. and Valerie Ethell.

   3) A son, stillborn, April 6, 1952

   4) Lady Joanna Edwina Doreen Knatchbull, born March 5, 1955 at London. Married November 3, 1984 at Ashford, Kent, Baron Hubert Henry Francois Pernot du Breuil, born February 2, 1956 at Neuilly-sur-Seine, France, second son of Baron Bertrand Pernot du Breuil and Roselyne Beghin.

      (1) Baroness Eleuthera Roselyne Patricia Pernot du Breuil, born May 13, 1986 at New York City

   5) Lady Amanda Patricia Victoria Knatchbull, born June 26, 1957 at London. Married October 31, 1987 at Ashford, Kent, Charles Vincent Ellingworth, born February 7, 1957 at Leicester, son of William Vincent Ellingworth and Shirley Mary Roach.

   6) Honourable Philip Wyndham Ashley Knatchbull, born December 2, 1961 at London

   7) Honourable Timothy Nicholas Sean Knatchbull, born November 18, 1964 at London

8) Honourable <u>Nicholas</u> Timothy Charles Knatchbull, born November 18, 1964 at London; died August 27, 1979 in the same explosion that killed his grand-father, Lord Mountbatten

2. Lady <u>Pamela</u> Carmen Louise Mountbatten, born April 19, 1929 at Barcelona, Spain. Married January 13, 1960 at Romsey Abbey, Romsey, <u>David</u> Nightingale Hicks, born March 25, 1929 at Little Coggeshall, Essex, son of Herbert Hicks and <u>Iris</u> Elsie Platten.
    1) <u>Edwina</u> Victoria Louise Hicks, born December 24, 1961 at London. Married March 24, 1984 at Christ Church Cathedral, Oxford, <u>Jeremy</u> Alexander Rothwell Brudenell, born April 2, 1960 at London, son of <u>John</u> Michael Brudenell and Mollie Rothwell.
    2) <u>Ashley</u> Louis David Hicks, born July 18, 1963 at London
    3) <u>India</u> Amanda Caroline Hicks, born September 5, 1967 at London

B

HGDH Princess <u>Elisabeth</u> Alexandra Louise Alice of Hesse and By Rhine,[13] born November 1, 1864 at Bessungen; died July 17/18, 1918, killed by the Bolsheviks at Alapaievsk. Married June 15, 1884 at St. Petersburg, HIH Grand Duke Sergei Alexandrovitch of Russia,[14] born May 11, 1857 at Tsarkoie-Selo; died February 17, 1905, killed by an anarchist's bomb at Moscow, fifth son of HIM ALEXANDER II, TSAR OF ALL THE RUSSIAS and HGDH Princess Maximiliane Wilhelmine Auguste Sophie Marie of Hesse and By Rhine. (No Issue.)

C

HGDH Princess <u>Irene</u> Luise Maria Anna of Hesse and By Rhine, born July 11, 1866 at Darmstadt; died November 11, 1953 at Hemmelmark, near Eckernförde. Married May 24, 1888 at Charlottenburg, HRH Prince Albert Wilhelm <u>Heinrich</u> of Prussia,* born August 14, 1862 at Neues Palais, Potsdam; died April 20, 1929 at Hemmelmark, near Eckernförde, second son of HIM FRIEDRICH III (Wilhelm Nikolaus Karl), GERMAN EMPEROR AND KING OF PRUSSIA and HRH Princess <u>Victoria</u> Adelaide Mary Louisa of Great Britain and Ireland, Princess Royal. (For issue, see Chapter XII.)

D

HRH ERNST LUDWIG Albert Karl Wilhelm, Grand Duke of Hesse and By Rhine. Succeeded as Grand Duke of Hesse and By Rhine on the death of his father. Grand Duke Ernst Ludwig lost his throne on November 8, 1918, when Hesse was proclaimed a republic. Born November 25, 1868 at Darmstadt; died October 9, 1937 at Schloss Wolfsgarten, Langen. Married (1) April 19, 1894 at Coburg, (div. 1901) HRH Princess Victoria Melita of Great Britain and Ireland, Princess of Saxe-Coburg and Gotha, Duchess of Saxony,* born November 25, 1876 at the Palace of St. Antonio, Malta; died March 2, 1936 at Amorbach, second daughter of HRH Prince <u>Alfred</u> Ernest Albert of Great Britain and Ireland, Duke of Edinburgh, Earl of Ulster and Earl of Kent, Duke of Saxe-Coburg and Gotha and HIH Grand Duchess Marie Alexandrovna of Russia.

D1 HGDH Princess <u>Elisabeth</u> Marie Alice Victoria of Hesse and By Rhine, born March 11, 1895 at Darmstadt; died November 16, 1903 at Skierniewice, Poland.

D2 A son, stillborn, May 25, 1900 at Schloss Wolfsgarten, Langen.

Grand Duke Ernst Ludwig married (2) February 2, 1905 at Darmstadt, HSH Princess
Eleonore Ernestine Marie of Solms-Hohensolms-Lich, born September 17, 1871 at Lich;
died November 16, 1937 at Steene, Belgium in an air crash, second daughter of HSH
Hermann Adolf, 5th Prince of Solms-Hohensolms-Lich and H Ill H Countess Agnes of
Stolberg-Wernigerode.

D3 HRH Hereditary Grand Duke Georg Donatus Wilhelm Nikolaus Eduard Heinrich Karl of
Hesse and By Rhine, born November 8, 1906 at Darmstadt; died November 16, 1937 at
Steene, Belgium in an air crash. Married February 2, 1931 at Darmstadt, HRH
Princess Cecilia of Greece and Denmark,*[15] born June 22, 1911 at Tatoi, near
Athens; died November 16, 1937 at Steene, Beligum in an air crash, third daughter of
HRH Prince Andrew of Greece and Denmark and HSH Princess Victoria Alice
Elisabeth Julia Marie of Battenberg.
1. HRH Prince Ludwig Ernst Andreas of Hesse and By Rhine, born October 25, 1931
    at Darmstadt; died November 16, 1937 at Steene, Beligum in an air crash
2. HGDH Prince Alexander Georg Karl Heinrich of Hesse and By Rhine, born April
    14, 1933 at Darmstadt; died November 16, 1937 at Steene, Belgium in an air crash
3. HGDH Princess Johanna Marina Eleonore of Hesse and By Rhine,[16] born Sep-
    tember 20, 1936 at Schloss Wolfsgarten, Langen; died June 14, 1939 at Darmstadt
4. A child, stillborn, November 16, 1937 at Steene, Belgium

D4 HRH Prince Ludwig Hermann Alexander Chlodwig of Hesse and By Rhine,[17] born
November 20, 1908 at Darmstadt; died May 30, 1968 at Frankfurt-am-Main. Married
November 17, 1937 at London, Honourable Margaret Campbell Geddes, born March 18,
1913 at Dublin, only daughter of Auckland Campbell Geddes, 1st Baron Geddes and
Isabella Gamble Ross. (No Issue.)

E
HGDH Prince Friedrich Wilhelm August Viktor Leopold Ludwig of Hesse and By Rhine.
Born October 7, 1870 at Darmstadt; died May 29, 1873 at Darmstadt, of hemophilia as a
result of a fall from a window.

F
HGDH Princess Victoria Alix Helena Louise Beatrice of Hesse and By Rhine,[18] born June
6, 1872 at Darmstadt; died July 16/17, 1918, killed by the Bolsheviks at Ekaterinburg.
Married November 26, 1894 at St. Petersburg, HIM NICHOLAS II, TSAR OF ALL THE
RUSSIAS.[19] Succeeded his father, November 2, 1894. Abdicated for himself and for his
son, March 28, 1917. Born May 18, 1868 at St. Petersburg; died July 16/17, 1918, killed
by the Bolsheviks at Ekaterinburg, second son of HIM ALEXANDER III, TSAR OF ALL
THE RUSSIAS and HRH Princess Marie Friederikke Dagmar of Denmark.[20]

F1 HIH Grand Duchess Olga Nicolaievna of Russia, born November 15, 1895 at Tsarskoie-
    Selo, St. Peterburg; died July 16/17, 1918 at Ekaterinburg.
F2 HIH Grand Duchess Tatiana Nicolaievna of Russia, born June 10, 1897 at Peterhof;
    died July 16/17, 1918 at Ekaterinburg.

F3 HIH Grand Duchess Marie Nicolaievna of Russia, born June 26, 1899 at Peterhof; died July 16/17, 1918 at Ekaterinburg.

F4 HIH Grand Duchess Anastasia Nicolaievna of Russia,[21] born June 18,1901 at Peterhof; died July 16/17, 1918 at Ekaterinburg.

F5 HIH Tsarevitch Alexis Nicolaievitch of Russia, born August 12, 1904 at Peterhof; died July 16/17, 1918 at Ekaterinburg.

G

HGDH Princess <u>Marie</u> Victoria Feodore Leopoldine of Hesse and By Rhine, born May 24, 1874 at Darmstadt; died November 16, 1878 at Darmstadt.

ENDNOTES

1. Married (2) morganatically, April 30, 1884, Countess Alexandrine von Hutten-Czapska, born September 3, 1854 at Warsaw; died May 8, 1941 at Vevey, Switzerland, daughter of Count Adam von Hutten-Czapski and Countess Marianne Rzewuska. She was created Countess von Romrod, May 31, 1884, but following family opposition, not least from Queen Victoria, the marriage was dissolved by divorce July 9, 1884. Alexandrine first married February 2, 1873 Alexander von Kolemine, Russian Chargé d'Affaires at Darmstadt, but they were separated in March 1884. He died March 1894 in Trieste. She married (3) Basil von Bacheracht, who died October 18, 1916 at Berne.
2. At the request of George V, Prince Louis relinquished the style and title of Serene Highness, Prince of Battenberg, July 14, 1917 and took the surname Mountbatten. On July 17, 1917, he was created Marquess of Milford Haven, Earl of Medina and Viscount Alderney. He and his wife were first cousins once removed, his father-in-law was his own first cousin.
3. Known as HRH Princess Andrew of Greece and Denmark.
4. Born HRH Prince Christian <u>Vilhelm</u> Ferdinand Adolf Georg of Denmark, second son of King Christian IX and Princess Louise of Hesse-Cassel.
5. Younger brother of HGDH Princess Marie Alexandra of Baden, who married HH Prince Wolfgang of Hesse.
6. Princess Cecilia and Hereditary Grand Duke Georg were first cousins once removed. Her mother, Princess Alice, was Georg's first cousin.
7. Known as Lady Louise Mountbatten from 1917 until her marriage.
8. From 1917 until he succeeded his father as 2nd Marquess of Milford Haven, he was styled George Louis Victor Henry Serge Mountbatten, Earl of Medina.
9. Daughter of HH Prince <u>Nikolaus</u> Wilhelm of Nassau and his morganatic wife, Natalia Alexandrovna Pushkin, daughter of the Russian poet Alexander Pushkin. Natalia was created Countess von Merenberg by HSH Georg Viktor, Prince of Waldeck and Pyrmont, July 29, 1868. Sophie was created Countess de Torby by HRH Grand Duke Adolf of Luxembourg in 1891. Countess Nada's elder sister, Anastasia (<u>Zia</u>) married Sir Harold Werhner, 3rd Baronet, and was known as Lady Zia Werhner, having been granted the style and precedence of the daughter of an Earl by Royal Warrant, September 1, 1917.
10. Married (1) May 23, 1946 at New York City (div. 1948), William Simpson, born February 22, 1911 at Chicago. (Articles in <u>The New York Times</u> and the Washington D.C. <u>Evening News</u>, say that the marriage took place in New Jersey.) Married (3) July 10, 1964 at New York City, James B. Orthwein, born March 13, 1924 at St. Louis, Missouri.
11. Known from 1917 until 1946 as Lord Louis Mountbatten.
12. Lord and Lady Brabourne, the Hon. Timothy Knatchbull, the Dowager Lady Brabourne and Paul Maxwell, 15, were also on board the fishing boat, Shadow V. Paul Maxwell was killed instantly with Lord Mountbatten and the Hon. Nicholas Knatchbull. The Dowager Lady Brabourne died the following day.

13. Received into the Orthodox faith and took the name Elisabeth Feodorovna.
14. Another first cousin once removed marriage. Grand Duke Serge was a first cousin of Grand Duke Ludwig IV and Prince Louis of Battenberg
15. Hereditary Grand Duke Georg, his wife, mother and two sons were en route to London for the wedding of his brother to the Hon. Margaret Geddes when their plane crashed in fog having hit a brickworks chimney. Eleven people were killed in the crash. Also lost in the wreckage were the Hessian pearls and Princess Alice's wedding veil, which was worn by other Hessian brides.
16. Princess Johanna was adopted by her uncle Prince Ludwig, but died of meningitis.
17. Upon the death of Prince Ludwig in 1968, the male line of the Rhine branch of the House of Hesse (apart from the morganatic branch of Battenberg, now Mountbatten) became extinct and HRH Landgrave Moritz of Hesse became Head of all the House of Hesse. He was adopted by Prince Ludwig, December 24, 1960, which was ratified at Langen, Hesse, December 4, 1961.
18. Received into the Orthodox faith and took the name Alexandra Feodorovna.
19. Alix and Nicholas were second cousins. Nicholas's grandmother, Tsarina Marie, was Alix's great aunt.
20. Sister of Queen Alexandra, wife of Edward VII, and of King George I of the Hellenes.
21. According to most accounts, Tsar Nicholas II, the Tsarina, their five children and several servants were executed by the Bolsheviks at Ekaterinburg in the Urals in the night of July 16/17, 1918. But because there has never been sufficient evidence to substantiate the mass murder, it cannot be fully determined that the Imperial Family were killed that night. Unlike other members of the Imperial Family, who were killed by the Bolsheviks, including the Tsarina's sister, Grand Duchess Elisabeth and the Tsar's younger brother, Tsar Michael, the bodies of the Tsar and his immediate family were never found.

There is evidence to believe that only Nicholas and his son were executed that night and that the Tsarina and the four Grand Duchesses were removed to another place (probably Perm) where they were executed later in the year. But according to several accounts, one Grand Duchess (probably Anastasia) escaped. In February 1921, a young, distraught woman plunged into the Landwehr Canal in Berlin. She was pulled out and brought to a hospital. Soon afterwards, the woman, later known as Anna Anderson, became one of the first to claim that she was Anastasia. Her claim lasted for more than sixty years and was never proved or disproved. Several members of the family came to Anna Anderson's defense; others dismissed her claim as nonsense. Most of the legal battles occured in West Germany where in 1970, a court said it could not decide either way, and the case was closed.

Anna Anderson married December 23, 1968 at Charlottesville, Virginia, John Eacott Manahan (born December 11, 1919), son of John Levi Manahan and Lucile Becker. Anderson died February 13, 1984 at Charlottesville. In June 1984, her ashes were brought to West Germany and were buried near a lake at Seeon in the Bavarian Alps.

CHAPTER XV

THE DESCENDANTS OF PRINCE ALFRED OF GREAT BRITAIN AND IRELAND, DUKE OF EDINBURGH, DUKE OF SAXE-COBURG AND GOTHA

HRH Prince <u>Alfred</u> Ernest Albert of Great Britain and Ireland. Created Duke of Edinburgh and Strathearn, Earl of Ulster and Earl of Kent, May 24, 1866. Succeeded his paternal uncle HH Ernst II, Duke of Saxe-Coburg and Gotha, as HRH Alfred, Duke of Saxe-Coburg and Gotha, August 22, 1893. Born August 6, 1844 at Windsor Castle; died July 30, 1900 at Schloss Rosenau, near Coburg. Married January 23, 1874 at St. Petersburg, HIH Grand Duchess Marie Alexandrovna of Russia, born October 17, 1853 at Tsarskoie-Selo; died October 24, 1920 at Zurich, second daughter of HIM ALEXANDER II, TSAR OF ALL THE RUSSIAS and HGDH Princess Maximiliane Wilhelmine Auguste Sophie <u>Marie</u> of Hesse and By Rhine.

A

HRH Prince <u>Alfred</u> Alexander William Ernest Albert of Edinburgh, Hereditary Prince of Saxe-Coburg and Gotha, Duke of Saxony[1], born October 15, 1874 at Buckingham Palace; died February 6, 1899 at Meran.

B

HRH Princess <u>Marie</u> Alexandra Victoria of Edinburgh, Princess of Saxe-Coburg and Gotha, Duchess of Saxony, born October 29, 1875 at Eastwell Park, Kent; died July 10, 1938 at Sinaia, Roumania. Married January 10, 1893 at Sigmaringen, HSH Prince <u>Ferdinand</u> Viktor Albert Meinrad of Hohenzollern. Succeeded his uncle, HM King Carol I of Roumania as HM KING FERDINAND OF ROUMANIA, October 10, 1914; born August 25, 1865 at Sigmaringen; died July 20, 1927 at Sinaia, second son of HSH <u>Leopold</u> Stephan Karl Anton Gustav Eduard Tassilo, Prince of Hohenzollern and HRH Infanta <u>Antonia</u> Maria Fernanda Micaela Gabriela Rafaela Francesca de Assis Ana Gonzaga Silvina Julia Augusta of Portugal.

B1 HM KING CAROL II OF ROUMANIA.[2] Reigned from June 8, 1930 until his abdication in favor of his son, Michael, September 6, 1940; born October 15, 1893 at Castle Pelesch, Sinaia[3]; died April 4, 1953 at Estorial, Portugal. Married (1) August 31, 1918 at Odessa (annulled 1919), Joana Marie Valentina (<u>Zizi</u>) Lambrino, born October 3, 1898 at Roman, Roumania; died March 11, 1953 at Paris, daughter of Colonel Constantin Lambrino and Euphrosine Alcaz.
   1. Mircea Gregor <u>Carol</u> Hohenzollern,[4] born January 8,1920 at Bucharest. Married (1) March 22, 1944 at Paris (Div. 1960), <u>Hélène</u> Henriette Nagavitzine,[5] born May 26, 1925 at Paris, daughter of Paul Nagavitzine and Marguerite Brissot.
      1) Paul Philippe Hohenzollern, born August 3, 1948 at Paris

Carol married (2) December 20, 1960 at Paris (div. 1977), <u>Thelma</u> Jeanne Williams, born November 15, 1930 at Nashville, Tennessee, daughter of Richard Williams and Josephine Owens.

2) Ion George Nicolas <u>Alexander</u> Hohenzollern, born September 1, 1961 at Poole, Dorset

Carol married (3) June 27, 1984 at Fulham Town Hall, London, Antonia Colville[6], born May 29, 1939 at Bracken, Church Crookham, Hampshire, younger daughter of Major General <u>Edward</u> Charles Colville and <u>Barbara</u> Joan Denny.

King Carol II married (2) March 10, 1921 at Athens (div. 1928), HRH Princess Helen of Greece and Denmark*[7], born May 3, 1896 at Athens; died November 28, 1982 at Lausanne, elder daughter of HM CONSTANTINE I, KING OF THE HELLENES and HRH Princess <u>Sophie</u> Dorothea Ulrike Alice of Prussia.

2. HM MICHAEL I, KING OF ROUMANIA,[8] born October 25, 1921 at Castle Pelesch, Sinaia. Married June 10, 1948 at Athens, HRH Princess <u>Anne</u> Antoinette Francoise Charlotte of Bourbon-Parma, born September 18, 1923 at Paris, only daughter of HRH Prince <u>René</u> Charles Marie Joseph of Bourbon-Parma and HRH Princess <u>Margrethe</u> Francoise Louise Marie Hélène of Denmark.

1) HRH Princess Margarita of Roumania, born March 26, 1949 at Lausanne
2) HRH Princess Helen of Roumania, born November 15, 1950 at Lausanne. Married July 20 (civil) at Durham, England and September 24, 1983 (religious) at Lausanne, Leslie <u>Robin</u> Medforth-Mills, born December 8, 1942 at Sproatley, Yorkshire, son of Cyril Mills and Nora Medforth
   (1) <u>Nicholas</u> Michael de Roumanie Medforth-Mills, born April 1, 1985 at Meyran, Geneva
3) HRH Princess Irina of Roumania, born February 28, 1953 at Lausanne. Married December 10, 1983 (civil) at Lausanne and February 11, 1984 (religious) at Phoenix, Arizona, John Kreuger[9], born August 3, 1945 at Solna, Sweden, son of Torsten Kreuger and <u>Diana</u> Blanchfleur Beve
   (1) <u>Michael</u> Torsten de Roumanie Kreuger, born February 25, 1985 at Coos Bay, Oregon
   (2) <u>Angelica</u> Margareta Bianca Kreuger, born December 29, 1986 at Coos Bay, Oregon
4) HRH Princess Sophie of Roumania, born October 29, 1957 at Tatoi, near Athens
5) HRH Princess Maria of Roumania, born July 13, 1964 at Hellerup, Denmark

King Carol II married (3) June 3, 1947 (civil) at Rio de Janeiro, Brazil and August 19, 1949 (religious) at Lisbon, Elena Lupescu[10], born September 15, 1895 or 1896 at Hertza, Moldavia; died June 29, 1977 at Estoril, Portugal, daughter of Nicolas Wolf[11] and Elisabeth N.

B2 HRH Princess Elisabeth Charlotte Josephine Alexandra Victoria of Roumania, Princess of Hohenzollern, born October 12, 1894 at Castle Pelesch, Sinaia; died November 15, 1956 at Cannes. Married February 27, 1921 at Bucharest (div. 1935), HM GEORGE II, KING OF THE HELLENES*, born July 19, 1890 at Tatoi, near Athens; died April 1, 1947 at Athens, eldest son of HM KING CONSTANTINE I OF THE HELLENES and HRH Princess Sophie Dorothea Ulrike Alice of Prussia. (No Issue.)

B3 HRH Princess Marie of Roumania, Princess of Hohenzollern, born January 9, 1900 at Gotha; died June 22, 1961 at London. Married June 8, 1922 at Belgrade, HM ALEXANDER I, KING OF YUGOSLAVIA[12], born December 16, 1888 at Cetinje, Montenegro; died October 9, 1934, assassinated at Marseilles while on a state visit, second son of HM PETER I, KING OF THE SERBS, CROATS AND SLOVENES and HH Princess Zorka Ljubica of Montenegro.

1. HM PETER II, KING OF YUGOSLAVIA[13], born September 6, 1923 at Belgrade; died November 3, 1970 at Denver, Colorado. Married March 20, 1944 at the Yugoslav Embassy, London, HRH Princess Alexandra of Greece*, born March 25, 1921 at Athens, only daughter of HM ALEXANDER I, KING OF THE HELLENES and Aspasia Manos.

   1) HRH Crown Prince Alexander of Yugoslavia, born July 17, 1945 at London. Married (1) July 1, 1972 at Villamanrique de la Condesa, Seville, Spain (div. 1985), HRH Princess Maria da Glória Henriqueta Dolores Lúcia Miguela Rafaela Gabriela Gonzaga of Orléans and Braganca[14], born December 13, 1946 at Petropolis, Brazil, elder daughter of HRH Prince Pedro de Alcántra Gastáo João Maria Felipe Lourenco Humberto Miguel Gabriel Rafael Gonzaga of Orléans and Branganca and HRH Princess Maria de la Esperanza Amalia Raniera Maria do Rosario Luisa Gonzaga of the Two Sicilies, Infanta of Spain[15]

      (1) HRH Prince Peter of Yugoslavia, born February 5,1980 at Chicago, Illinois

      (2) HRH Prince Philip of Yugoslavia, born January 15, 1982 at Falls Church, Virginia

      (3) HRH Prince Alexander of Yugoslavia, born January 15, 1982 at Falls Church, Virginia (twin of Prince Philip)

      Crown Prince Alexander married (2) September 20 (civil) and September 21, 1985 (religious) at London, Katherine Clairy Batis[16], November 13, 1943 at Athens, daughter of Robert Batis and Anna Dosti.

2. HRH Prince Tomislav of Yugoslavia, born January 9, 1928 at Belgrade. Married (1) June 5 (civil) and June 6, 1957 (religious) at Salem, Baden (div. 1981), HGDH Princess Margarita Alice Thyra Viktoria Marie Louise Scholastica of Baden*, born July 14, 1932 at Schloss Salem, Baden, only daughter of HRH Prince Berthold Friedrich Wilhelm Ernst August Karl of Baden, Margrave of Baden and HRH Princess Theodora of Greece and Denmark.

   1) HRH Prince Nikolas of Yugoslavia, born March 15, 1958 at London

   2) HRH Princess Katarina of Yugoslavia, born November 28, 1959 at London
      Prince Tomislav married (2) October 16, 1982 at Bournville, near Birmingham, Linda Mary Bonney, born June 22, 1949 at London, daughter of Holbrook Van Dyke Bonney and Joan Evans.

3) HRH Prince George of Yugoslavia, born May 25, 1984 at London

4) HRH Prince Michael of Yugoslavia, born December 15, 1985 at London

3. HRH Prince Andrej of Yugoslavia, born June 28, 1929 at Bled. Married (1) August 1 (civil) and August 2, 1956 (religious) at Kronberg (div. 1962), HH Princess Christina Margarethe of Hesse*, born January 10, 1933 at Kronberg, eldest daughter of HH Prince Christoph Ernst August of Hesse and HRH Princess Sophie of Greece and Denmark.

1) HRH Princess Maria Tatiana of Yugoslavia, born July 18, 1957 at London

2) HRH Prince Christopher of Yugoslavia, born February 4,1960 at London Prince Andrej married (2) September 18 (civil) at Langton Green, Kent and October 12, 1963 (religious) at Amorbach (div. 1972) HSH Princess Kira Melita Feodora Marie Viktoria Alexandra of Leiningen*, born July 18, 1930 at Coburg, eldest daughter of HSH Friedrich Karl Eduard Erwin, 6th Prince of Leiningen and HH Princess Maria Kirillovna of Russia.

3) HRH Prince Karl Wladimir Cyril Andrej of Yugoslavia, born March 11, 1964 at London

4) HRH Prince Dimitri Ivan Mihailo of Yugoslavia, born April 21, 1965 at London

Prince Andrej married (3) March 30, 1974 at Palm Springs, California, Eva Maria Andjelkovich[17], born August 26, 1926 at Vrnjacka-Banja, Serbia, daughter of Milan T. Andjelkovich and Eva Jovanovich.

B4 HRH Prince Nicolas of Roumania, Prince of Hohenzollern[18], born August 18, 1903 at Castle Pelesch, Sinaia; died June 9, 1978 at Madrid. Married (1) October 24, 1931 at Tohani, Roumania, Joana Lucia Dumitrescu-Doletti[19], born September 24, 1902 at Bucharest; died February 19, 1963 at Lausanne, daughter of Ion Dumitrescu-Doletti and Nella Theodoru (No Issue.) Married (2) July 13, 1967, at Lausanne Thereza Lisboa Figueira de Mello[20], born June 10, 1913 at Rome, daughter of Jerónymo de Avellar Figueria de Mello and Candida Riberia Lisboa (No Issue.)

B5 HRH Princess Ileana of Roumania, Princess of Hohenzollern[21], born January 5, 1909 at Bucharest. Married (1) July 26, 1931 at Sinaia (div. 1954), HI & RH Archduke Anton Maria Franz Leopold Blanka Karl Joseph Ignaz Raphael Michael Margareta Nicetas of Austria, Prince of Tuscany, born March 20, 1901 at Vienna, third son of HI & RH Archduke Leopold Salvator Maria Joseph Ferdinand Franz von Assisi Karl Anton von Padua Johann Baptist Januarius Aloys Gonzaga Rainer Wenzel Gallus of Austria, Prince of Tuscany and HRH Infanta Blanca de Castilla Maria de la Concepción Teresa Francisca de Asis Margareta Juana Beatriz Carlota Aloysia Fernanda Adelgunda Elvira Ildefonsa Regina Josefina Micaela Gabriela Raquela of Spain.

1. HI & RH Archduke Stefan of Austria, Prince of Tuscany[22], born August 15, 1932 at Mödling, Austria. Married August 28, 1954 at Milton, Massachusetts, Mary Jerrine Soper, born June 19, 1931 at Boston, Massachusetts, daughter of Charles Soper and Agnes McNeil.

1) Christopher Habsburg-Lothringen, born January 26, 1957 at Boston. Married May 2, 1987 at Mt. Tamalpais, California, Elizabeth Ann Blanchette, born January 22, 1967 at Peoria, Illinois, daughter of Larry Lee Popejoy and Regina Irene Keller.

2) Ileana Habsburg-Lothringen, born January 4, 1958 at Detroit, Michigan. Married June 23, 1979 at Farmington Hills, Michigan, David Scott Snyder, born November 18, 1956 at Pontiac, Michigan, son of Loyce Daniel Snyder and Laura Ann Hutton.

    (1) Alexandra Marie Snyder, born August 18, 1984 at Southfield, Michigan

    (2) Nicholas David Snyder, born February 27, 1986 at Southfield, Michigan

3) Peter Habsburg-Lothringen, born February 19, 1959 at Detroit. Married June 27, 1981 at Farmington Hills, Michigan (div. 1985), Shari Suzanne Reid, born September 11, 1960 at Highland Park, Michigan, daughter of William Marshall Reid and Barbara Lou Miller (No Issue.)

4) Constantza (Tantzi) Habsburg-Lothringen, born October 2, 1960 at Detroit. Married January 16, 1987 at Franklin, Michigan, Mark Lee Matheson[23], born February 15, 1958 at Grosse Pointe, Michigan, son of Robert Kenneth Matheson and Lois Dove.

5) Anton Habsburg-Lothringen, born November 7, 1964 at Detroit.

2. HI & RH Archduchess Maria Ileana of Austria, Princess of Tuscany, born December 18, 1933 at Mödling, Austria; died January 11, 1959 in an air crash at Rio de Janeiro. Married December 7, 1957 at Vienna, Count Jaroslav Franz Josef Ignaz Maria Kottulinsky, Baron Kottulin, Krzizkowitz and Dobrenzenicz, born January 3, 1917 at Graz, Austria; died January 11, 1959 in an air crash at Rio de Janeiro, third son of Count Karl Kunata Kottulinsky, Baron Kottulin, Krziz-kowitz and Dobrenzenicz and Countess Maria Theresia Johanna Anna Franziska Ignazia Huberta von Meran.

1) Countess Maria Ileana Kottulinsky, Baroness Kottulin, Krzizkowitz and Dob-renzenicz, born August 25, 1958 at Klagenfurt

3. HI & RH Archduchess Alexandra of Austria, Princess of Tuscany, born May 21, 1935 at Sonnberg, Lower Austria. Married (1) August 31 (civil) at Mondsee and September3, 1962 (religious) at Salzburg (annulled 1972; div. 1973), HRH Duke Eugen Eberhard Albrecht Maria Joseph Ivan Rilsky Robert Ulrich Philipp Odo Carl Hubert of Württemberg, born November 2, 1930 at Carlsruhe, Silesia, second son of HRH Duke Albrecht Eugen Maria Philipp Carl Joseph Fortunatus of Württemberg and HRH Princess Nadejda Klementine Maria Pia Majella of Bulgaria (No Issue.) Married (2) August 22 (civil) at Mondsee and December 29, 1973 (religious) at Salzburg, Baron Victor Franz Clemens Raoul Emil Wilhelm von Baillou, born June 27, 1931 at Vienna, elder son of Baron Clemens Otto Johann Hermann Julia Maria von Baillou and Magdalene Merck.

1) A child, stillborn, March 24, 1976 at Darmstadt.

4. HI & RH Archduke Dominic of Austria, Prince of Tuscany, born July 4, 1937 at Sonnberg, Lower Austria. Married June 11, 1960, at Houston, Texas Engel von Voss, born March 31, 1937 at Houston, Texas, daughter of Friedrich Ditlev von Voss and Mildred McKibben.

1) Sandor Habsburg-Lothringen, born February 13, 1965 at Vienna

2) Gregor Habsburg-Lothringen, born November 20, 1968 at Vienna

5. HI & RH Archduchess Maria Magdalena of Austria, Princess of Tuscany, born October 2, 1939 at Sonnberg, Lower Austria. Married August 27 (civil) and August 29, 1959 (religious) at Mondsee, Austria, Baron <u>Hans</u> Ulrich von Holzhausen, born September 1, 1929 at Windischgarsten, Austria, only son of Baron <u>Kurt</u> Ludwig Hermann von Holzhausen and Mary Heyssler.

1) Baron <u>Johann</u> Friedrich Anton von Holzhausen, born July 29, 1960 at Salzburg

2) Baron <u>Georg</u> Ferdinand von Holzhausen, born February 16, 1962 at Salzburg

3) Baroness <u>Alexandra</u> Maria von Holzhausen, born January 22, 1963 at Salzburg. Married July 2 (civil) at Salzburg and July 7, 1985 (religious) at Kirchberg, Austria, Christian Ferch, born August 4, 1959 at Salzburg, son of <u>Rudolf</u> Maria Ferch and Countess <u>Elisabeth</u> Alexandra Marianne Paula Coreth zu Coredo.

(1) <u>Ferdinand</u> Georg Botho Ferch, born October 17, 1986 at Salzburg

6. HI & RH Archduchess Elisabeth of Austria, Princess of Tuscany, born January 15, 1942 at Sonnberg. Married August 3, 1964 at Mondsee, Dr. <u>Friederich</u> Josef Sandhofer, born August 1, 1934 at Salzburg, son of Joseph Sandhofer and Emma Waldeck.

1) <u>Anton</u> Dominic Sandhofer, born October 26, 1966 at Salzburg

2) <u>Margareta</u> Elisabeth Sandhofer, born September 10, 1968 at Innsbruck

3) <u>Andrea</u> Alexandra Sandhofer, born December, 13,1969 at Innsbruck

4) <u>Elisabeth</u> Victoria Magdalena Sandhofer, born November 16, 1971 at Innsbruck

HRH Princess Ileana married (2) June 19, 1954 at Newton, Massachusetts (div. 1965), <u>Stefan</u> Virgil Issarescu, born October 5, 1906 at Turnu-Severin, Roumania, son of Ionn Issarescu and Virginia Popescu (No Issue.)

B6 HRH Prince Mircea of Roumania, Prince of Hohenzollern, born January 3, 1913 at Bucharest; died November 2, 1916 at Buftea.

C

HRH Princess Victoria Melita of Edinburgh, Princess of Saxe-Coburg and Gotha, Duchess of Saxony[24], born November 25, 1876 at the Palace of St. Antonio, Malta; died March 2, 1936 at Amorbach. Married (1) April 19, 1894 at Coburg (div 1901)[25], HRH <u>Ernst Ludwig</u> Karl Albert Wilhelm, Grand Duke of Hesse and By Rhine,* born November 25, 1868 at Darmstadt; died October 9, 1937 at Schloss Wolfsgarten, Langen, eldest son of HRH <u>Ludwig IV</u> Karl, Grand Duke of Hesse and By Rhine and HRH Princess <u>Alice</u> Maud Mary of Great Britain and Ireland (For issue, see Chapter XIV.) Princess Victoria Melita married (2) October 8, 1905 at Tegernsee[26], HIH Grand Duke Kirill Vladimirovitch of Russia[27], born September 30, 1876 at Tsarskoie-Selo; died October 13, 1898 at Neuilly-sur-Seine, second son of HIH Grand Duke Vladimir Alexandrovitch of Russia and HH Duchess <u>Marie</u> Alexandrine Elisabeth Eleonore of Mecklenburg-Schwerin.[28]

C1 HH Princess Maria Kirillovna of Russia, born February 2, 1907 at Coburg; died October 27, 1951 at Madrid. Married November 25, 1925 at Coburg, HSH Friedrich Karl Eduard Erwin, 6th Prince of Leiningen, born February 13, 1898 at Strassburg; died August 2, 1946 as a Russian prisoner-of-war at Saransk, U.S.S.R., eldest son of HSH Emich Eduard Karl, 5th Prince of Leiningen[29] and HSH Princess Feodora Viktoria Alberta of Hohenlohe-Langenburg.

1. HSH Emich Cyrill Ferdinand Hermann, 7th Prince of Leiningen, born October 18, 1926 at Coburg. Married August 10, 1950 at Rastede, Lower Saxony, HH Duchess Eilika Stephanie Elisabeth Thekla Juliana of Oldenburg[30], born February 2, 1928 at Lensahn, Lower Saxony, second daughter of HRH Hereditary Grand Duke Nikolaus Friedrich Wilhelm of Oldenburg[31] and HSH Princess Helene Bathildis Charlotte Maria Friederike of Waldeck and Pyrmont.[32]

   1) HSH Princess Melita Elisabeth Bathildis Helene Margarita of Leiningen, born June 10, 1951 at Amorbach

   2) HSH Hereditary Prince Karl-Emich Nikolaus Friedrich Hermann of Leiningen, born June 12, 1952 at Amorbach. Married June 8 (civil) at Amorbach and June 16, 1984 (religious) at Neuenstein, Württemberg, HSH Princess Margarita Katharina Elisabeth of Hohenlohe-Öhringen, born April 28, 1960 at Munich, elder daughter of HSH Kraft Hans Konrad, 8th Prince of Hohenlohe-Öhringen, 5th Duke of Ujest and Katharina von Siemens.

   3) HSH Prince Andreas of Leiningen, born November 27, 1955 at Frankfurt-am-Main. Married October 5 (civil) at Amorbach and October 11, 1981 (religious) at Gmünden, HRH Princess Alexandra Irene Margaretha Elisabeth Bathildis of Hanover*, born February 18, 1959 at Hanover, youngest daughter of HRH Prince Ernst August Georg Wilhelm Christian Ludwig Franz Joseph Nikolaus of Hanover, Duke of Brunswick-Lüneburg and HH Princess Ortrud Bertha Adelheid Hedwig of Schleswig-Holstein-Sonderburg-Glücksburg.

      (1) HSH Prince Ferdinand Heinrich Emich Christian Karl of Leiningen, born August 8, 1982 at Frankfurt-am-Main

      (2) HSH Princess Olga Margarita Valerie Elisabeth Stephanie Alexandra of Leiningen, born October 23, 1984 at Frankfurt-am-Main

   4) HSH Princess Stephanie of Leiningen, born October 1, 1958 at Frankfurt-am-Main

2. HSH Prince Karl Wladimir Ernst Heinrich of Leiningen, born January 2, 1928 at Coburg. Married February 14 (civil) at Amorbach and February 20, 1957 (religious) at Cannes (div. 1968), HRH Princess Marie Louise of Bulgaria,[33] born January 13, 1933 at Sofia, Bulgaria, only daughter of HM BORIS III (Clemens Robert Maria Pius Ludwig Stanislaus Xaver), KING OF BULGARIA and HRH Princess Giovanna Elisabetta Antonia Romana Maria of Savoy.

   1) HSH Prince Karl Boris Frank Markwart of Leingen, born April 17, 1960 at Toronto, Ontario. Married February 14, 1987 at Westfield, New Jersey, Millena Manov, born August 22, 1962 at Sofia, Bulgaria, daughter of Wladimir Manov and Elly Nedeva.

   2) HSH Prince Hermann Friedrich Roland Fernando of Leiningen, born April 16, 1963 at Toronto, Ontario. Married May 16, 1987 at Oakville, Ontario, Deborah Culley, born December 2, 1961 at Belfast, Northern Ireland, daughter of Robert Culley and Myrna Ruth.

3. HSH Princess <u>Kira</u>-Melita Feodora Marie Viktoria Alexandra of Leiningen, born July 18, 1930 at Coburg. Married September 18 (civil) at Langton Green, Kent and October 12, 1963 (religious) at Amorbach (div. 1972), HRH Prince Andrej of Yugoslavia,* born June 28, 1929 at Bled, youngest son of HM ALEXANDER I, KING OF YUGOSLAVIA and HRH Princess Marie of Roumania. (For issue, see Chapter XV.) Princess Kira has a natural daughter:
   1) <u>Lavinia</u> Maria Lane,[34] born October 18, 1961 at London

4. HSH Princess <u>Margarita</u> Ileana Viktoria of Leiningen, born May 9, 1932 at Coburg. Married January 5 (civil) at Sigmaringen and February 3, 1951 (religious) at Amorbach, HH <u>Friedrich Wilhelm</u> Ferdinand Joseph Maria Manuel Georg Meinrad Fidelis Benedikt Michael Hubert, Prince of Hohenzollern,[35] born February 3, 1924 at Umkirch, eldest son of of HH <u>Friedrich</u> Viktor Pius Alexander Leopold Karl Theodor Ferdinand, Prince of Hohenzollern and HRH Princess <u>Margarete</u> Karola Wilhelmine Viktoria Adelheid Albertina Petrusa Bertram Paula of Saxony.
   1) HSH Hereditary Prince <u>Karl Friedrich</u> Emich Meinrad Benedikt Fidelis Maria Michael Gerold of Hohenzollern, born April 20, 1952 at Sigmaringen. Married May 17 (civil) at Sigmaringen and June 15, 1985 (religious) at Beuron, near Sigmaringen, Countess <u>Alexandra</u> Petra Sofie Schenk von Stauffenberg, born May 25, 1960 at Detmold, eldest daughter of Count <u>Clemens</u> Anton Maria Friedrich Schenk von Stauffenberg and Countess <u>Clementine</u> Elisabeth Franziska Adelheid Maria Apollonia von Wolff-Metternich.
      (1) HSH Prince <u>Alexander</u> Friedrich Antonius Johannes of Hohenzollern, born March 16, 1987 at New York City
   2) HSH Prince <u>Albrecht</u> Johannes Hermann Meinrad Hubertus Michael Stephan of Hohenzollern, born August 3, 1954 at Umkirch.
   3) HSH Prince <u>Ferdinand</u> Maria Fidelis Leopold Meinrad Valentin of Hohenzollern, born February 14, 1960 at Sigmaringen.

5. HSH Princess <u>Mechtilde</u> Alexandra of Leiningen, born January 2, 1936 at Würzburg. Married November 25, 1961 at Amorbach <u>Karl</u> Anton Bauscher, born August 26, 1931 at Grafenwöhr, son of Rudolf Schöll and Hedwig Fischer.
   1) <u>Ulf</u> Heiz Stephan Bauscher, born February 20, 1963 at Frankfurt-am-Main
   2) <u>Berthold</u> Alexander Eric Bauscher, born October 31, 1965 at Bamberg
   3) <u>Johann</u> Karl Joachim Fritz Markwart Bauscher, born February 2, 1971 at Bamberg

6. HSH Prince <u>Friedrich Wilhelm</u> Berthold of Leiningen, born June 18, 1938 at Würzburg. Married (1) July 9, 1960 at Würzburg (div. 1962), <u>Karin</u> Evelyne Göss, born May 27, 1942 at Nuremberg, daughter of N.N. and N.N. (No Issue.) Married (2) August 23, 1971 at at Gmünden-am-Traunsee, Austria, Helga Eschenbacher, born January 5, 1940 at Gmünden, daughter of Hans Eschenbacher and Sofie Theobold.

7. HSH Prince <u>Peter</u> Viktor of Leiningen, born December 23, 1942 at Würzburg; died January 12, 1943 at Würzburg.

C2 HH Princess Kira Kirillovna of Russia, born May 9, 1909 at Paris; died September 8, 1967 at St. Briac-sur-Mer, France. Married May 2 (civil and Orthodox) at Potsdam and May 4, 1938 (Lutheran) at Haus Doorn, The Netherlands, HI & RH Prince <u>Louis Ferdinand</u> Viktor Albert Michael Hubertus of Prussia,* born November 9, 1907 at Marmorpalais, Potsdam, second son of HI & RH Friedrich <u>Wilhelm</u> Viktor August Ernst Crown Prince of the German Empire, Crown Prince of Prussia and HH Duchess <u>Cecilie</u> Auguste Marie of Mecklenburg-Schwerin. (For issue, see Chapter XII

C3 HH Prince Wladimir Kirillovitch of Russia,[36] born August 13, 1917 at Borga, Finland. Married August 13, 1948 at Lausanne, Princess Leonida Georgievna Bagration-Moukhransky,[37] born September 23, 1914 at Tilfis, Georgia, second daughter of Prince Georgi Alexandrovitch Bagration-Moukhranksy and Elena Zlotnicka.
  1. HSH Princess Maria Wladimirovna of Russia,[38] born December 23, 1953 at Madrid. Married September 4 (civil) at Dinard, France and September 22, 1976 (religious) (div. 198?) at Madrid, HRH Prince <u>Franz Wilhelm</u> Viktor Christoph Stephan of Prussia,* born September 3, 1943 at Grünberg, Silesia, eldest son of HRH Prince <u>Karl Franz Joseph</u> Wilhelm Friedrich Eduard Paul of Prussia and HSH Princess <u>Henriette</u> Hermine Wanda Ida Luise of Schönaich-Carolath. (For issue, see Chapter XII)

D
HRH Princess <u>Alexandra</u> Louise Olga Victoria of Edinburgh, Princess of Saxe-Coburg and Gotha, Duchess of Saxony, born September 1, 1878 at Coburg; died April 16 1942 at Schwäbisch Hall. Married April 20, 1896 at Coburg, HSH <u>Ernst</u> Wilhelm Friedrich Karl Maximilian, 7th Prince of Hohenlohe-Langenburg, born September 13, 1863 at Langenburg; died December 11, 1950 at Langenburg, only son of HSH Prince <u>Hermann</u> Ernst Bernhard, 6th Prince of Hohenlohe-Langenburg[39] and HGDH Princess <u>Leopoldine</u> Wilhelmine Pauline Amalie Maximiliane of Baden.

D1 HSH <u>Gottfried</u> Hermann Alfred Paul Maximilian Viktor, 8th Prince of Hohenlohe-Langenburg, born March 4, 1897 at Langenburg; died May 11, 1960 at Langenburg. Married April 20, 1931 at Langenburg, HRH Princess Margarita of Greece and Denmark,* born April 18, 1905 at Athens; died April 24, 1981 at Bad Weisse, West Germany, eldest daughter of HRH Prince Andrew of Greece and Denmark and HSH Princess Victoria <u>Alice</u> Elisabeth Julia Marie of Battenberg.
  1. A daughter, stillborn, December 3, 1933 at Schwäbisch Hall, Württemberg.

  2. HSH <u>Kraft</u> Alexander Ernst Ludwig Georg Emich, 9th Prince of Hohenlohe-Langenburg, born June 25, 1935 at Schwäbisch Hall. Married June 5 (civil) at Langenburg and July 16, 1965 (religious) at Zwingenburg, HSH Princess <u>Charlotte</u> Alexandra Marie Clotilde of Croÿ, born December 31, 1938 at London, elder daughter of HSH Prince <u>Alexander</u> Georg Maria Josef Ignatius of Croÿ and <u>Anne</u> Elspeth Campbell.

1) HSH Princess <u>Cecile</u> Marita Dorothea of Hohenlohe-Langenburg, born December 16, 1967 at Crailsheim, Württemberg

2) HSH Hereditary Prince <u>Philipp</u> Gottfried Alexander of Hohenlohe-Langenburg, born January 20, 1970 at Crailsheim

3) HSH Princess <u>Xenia</u> Margarita Anne of Hohenlohe-Langenburg, born July 8, 1972 at Crailsheim

3. HSH Princess <u>Beatrix</u> Alice Marie Melita Margarete of Hohenlohe-Langenburg, born July 10, 1936 at Schwäbisch Hall

4. HSH Prince Georg <u>Andreas</u> Heinrich of Hohenlohe-Langenburg, born November 24, 1938 at Schwäbisch Hall. Married September 9, 1969 at Burghausen-an-der-Inn, Austria, HSH Princess <u>Luise</u> Pauline Amelie Vibeke Beatrix of Schönburg-Waldenburg, born October 12, 1943 at Frankfurt-am-der Oder, youngest daughter of HSH Prince <u>Georg</u> Ulrich of Schönburg-Waldenburg and H Ill H Countess <u>Pauline</u> Emma Amalie Gertrud Elisabeth Madeleine of Castell-Castell.

1) HSH Princess <u>Katarina</u> Clementine Beatrix of Hohenlohe-Langenburg, born November 21, 1972 at Munich

2) HSH Princess <u>Tatiana</u> Luise of Hohenlohe-Langenburg, born February 10, 1975 at Munich

5. HSH Prince <u>Ruprecht</u> Sigismund Philipp Ernst of Hohenlohe-Langenburg, born April 7, 1944 at Langenburg; died April 8, 1978 at Munich.

6. HSH Prince <u>Albrecht</u> Wolfgang Christof of Hohenlohe-Langenburg, born April 7, 1944 at Langenburg (twin of Prince Ruprecht). Married January 23, 1976 at Berlin-Zehlendorf, <u>Maria</u>-Hildegard Fischer, born November 30, 1933 at Freiberg, Saxony, daughter of <u>Max</u> Willy Fischer and <u>Johanna</u> Maria Berta Fiedler.

1) Ludwig Prinz zu Hohenlohe-Langenburg, born April 21, 1976 at Berlin-Neuköln

D2 HSH Princess <u>Marie Melita</u> Leopoldine Viktoria Feodora Alexandra of Hohenlohe-Langenburg, born January 18, 1899 at Langenburg; died November 8, 1967 at Munich. Married February 15, 1916 at Coburg, HH Wilhelm <u>Friedrich</u> Christian Günther Albert Adolf Georg, Duke of Schleswig-Holstein-Sonderburg-Glücksburg, born August 23, 1891 at Grünholz; died February 10, 1965 at Grünholz, only son of HH <u>Friedrich Ferdinand</u> Georg Christian Karl Wilhelm, Duke of Schleswig-Holstein-Sonderburg-Glücksburg and HH Princess Viktoria Friederike Auguste Marie <u>Caroline Mathilde</u> of Schleswig-Holstein-Sonderburg-Augustenburg.[40]

1. HH Prince <u>Hans</u> Albert Viktor Alexander Friedrich Ernst Gottfried August Heinrich Waldemar of Schleswig-Holstein-Sonderburg-Glücksburg, born May 12, 1917 at Schloss Louisenlund, near Schleswig; killed in action August 10, 1944 at Zedlinsk, Poland.

2. HH Prince <u>Wilhelm</u> Alfred Ferdinand of Schleswig-Holstein-Sonderburg-Glücksburg, born September 24, 1919 at Schloss Louisenlund; died June 17, 1926 at Kiel.

3. HH Friedrich Ernst <u>Peter</u>, Duke of Schleswig-Holstein-Sonderburg-Glücksburg,

born April 30,1922 at Schloss Louisenlund; died September 30, 1980 at Bienebek.
Married October 9, 1947 at Glücksburg, HSH Princess Marie-Alix of Schaumburg-
Lippe, born April 2, 1923 at Bückeburg, only daughter of HSH Prince Stephan
Alexander Viktor of Schaumburg-Lippe and HH Duchess Ingeborg Alix of Olden-
burg.[41]

1) HH Princess Marita of Schleswig-Holstein-Sonderburg-Glücksburg, born
September 5, 1948 at Schloss Louisenlund. Married May 23, 1975 at Glücksburg, Baron Wilfrid Eberhard Manfred von Plotho, born August 10, 1942 at
Bliestorf, only son of Baron Manfred Gebhard Adalbert Wedigo von Plotho
and Baroness Ingrid Julinka von Schröder.

(1) Baron Christoph von Plotho, born March 14, 1976 at Eckernförde
(2) Baroness Irina von Plotho, born January 28, 1978 at Eckernförde

2) HH Christoph, Duke of Schleswig-Holstein-Sonderburg-Glücksburg, born
August 22, 1949 at Schloss Louisenlund. Married September 23, (civil) at
Damp, Amt Schwansen and October 3, 1981 (religious) at Glücksburg, HSH
Princess Elisabeth of Lippe-Weissenfeld, born July 28, 1957 at Munich, second
daughter of HSH Prince Alfred Karl Friedrich Georg Franz of Lippe-Weissen-
feld and Baroness Irmgard Julinka Wagner von Wehrborn.

(1) HH Princess Sophie of Schleswig-Holstein-Sonderburg-Glücksburg, born
October 9, 1983 at Eckernförde
(2) HH Prince Friedrich-Ferdinand of Schleswig-Holstein-Sonderburg-Glücksburg, born July 19, 1985 at Eckernförde
(3) HH Prince Constantin of Schleswig-Holstein-Sonderburg-Glücksburg, born
July 14, 1986 at Eckernförde

3) HH Prince Alexander of Schleswig-Holstein-Sonderburg-Glücksburg, born July
9, 1953 at Bienebek

4) HH Princess Ingeborg of Schleswig-Holstein-Sonderburg-Glücksburg, born July
9, 1956 at Bienebek

4. HH Princess Marie Alexandra Caroline Mathilde Viktoria Irene of Schleswig-
Holstein-Sonderburg-Glücksburg, born July 9, 1927 at Schloss Louisenlund.
Married July 22, 1970 at Grünholz Douglas Barton Miller, born December 8, 1929
at San Francisco, California, son of Douglas Barton Miller and Harriet Maxine
Deter.

D3 HSH Princess Alexandra Beatrice Leopoldine of Hohenlohe-Langenburg, born April 2,
1901 at Langenburg; died October 26, 1963 at Langenburg.

D4 HSH Princess Irma Helene of Hohenlohe-Langenburg, born July 4, 1902 at Langenburg;
died March 8, 1986 at Heilbronn, Württemberg.

D5 HSH Prince Alfred of Hohenlohe-Langenburg, born April 16, 1911 at Langenburg; died
April 18, 1911 at Langenburg.

E
A son, stillborn, October 13, 1879 at Eastwell Park, Kent[42].

F

HRH Princess <u>Beatrice</u> Leopoldine Victoria of Edinburgh, Princess of Saxe-Coburg and Gotha, Duchess of Saxony, born April 20, 1884 at Eastwell Park, Kent; died July 13, 1966 at Sanlucar de Barrameda, Spain. Married July 15, 1909 at Schloss Rosenau, near Coburg, HRH Prince <u>Alfonso</u> Maria Francisco Diego de Orleans y de Borbón, Infante of Spain, 5th Duke of Galliera[43], born November 12, 1886 at Madrid; died August 10, 1975 at Sanlucar de Barrameda, Spain, elder son of HRH Prince <u>Antonio</u> Maria Luis Felipe Juan Florencio de Orleans y de Borbón, Infante of Spain, 4th Duke of Galliera and HRH Infanta Maria <u>Eulalia</u> Francisca de Asis Margarita Roberta Isabel Francisca de Paula Cristina Maria de la Piedad of Spain.

F1　HRH Prince <u>Alvaro</u> Antonio Fernando Carlos Felipe of Orleans-Borbón y Sajonia-Coburgo-Gotha, 6th Duke of Galliera,[44] born April 20, 1910 at Coburg. Married July 10, 1937 at Rome, Carla Parodi Delfino, born December 13, 1909 at Milan, daughter of Leopoldo Girolamo Parodi Delfino and Lucia Henny.

1. Princess Gerarda de Orleans-Borbón y Parodi Delfino, born August 25, 1939 at Rome. Married July 26, 1963 at New York City (div. 1977), <u>Harry</u> Freeman Saint, born February 13, 1941 at New York City, son of <u>Ellis</u> Chandler Saint and Rachel Freeman.
   1) Carla d'Orleans-Borbón Saint, born May 22, 1967 at New York City
   2) Marc d'Orleans-Borbón Saint, born March 20, 1969 at New York City

2. Prince Alvaro de Orleans-Borbón y Parodi Delfino, born August 23, 1941 at Rome; died September 6, 1975 at Houston, Texas. Married January 12, 1966 at Naples, Donna Emilia Ferrara-Pignatelli dei Principi di Strongoli, born April 6, 1940 at Naples, eldest daughter of Don Vincenzo Ferrara-Pignatelli, Principi di Strongoli, Conte di Melissa, Barone di Silvie e Castiglione and Nobile Francesca Pulci-Doria.
   1) Don Alfonso de Orleans-Borbón y Ferrara-Pignatelli, born January 2, 1968 at Santa Cruz de Teneriffe
   2) Don Alvaro de Orleans-Borbón y Ferrara-Pignatelli, born October 4, 1969 at Santa Cruz de Teneriffe

3. Princess Beatriz de Orleans-Borbón y Parodi Delfino, born April 27, 1943 at Seville, Spain. Married April 25, 1964 at Rome, Tomaso dei Conti Farini, born September 16, 1938 at Turin, Italy, only son of Count <u>Antonio</u> Maria Farini and Silvia Bellia.
   1) Gerardo dei Conti Farini, born November 23, 1967 at Bologna
   2) Elena dei Conti Farini, born October 27, 1969 at Rome

4. Prince Alvaro-Jaime de Orleans-Borbón y Parodi Delfino, born March 1, 1947 at Rome. Married May 24, 1974 at Campiglione, Italy, Giovanna San Martino d'Aglie dei Marchesi di San Germano, born April 10, 1945 at Campiglione, third daughter of Casimiro San Martino di San Germano d'Aglie, Marchese di San Germano amd Donna Maria Cristina Ruffo di Calabria dei duchi Guarda Lombarda.[45]
   1) Pilar de Orleans-Borbón, born May 27, 1975 at Rome
   2) Andrés de Orleans-Borbón, born July 7, 1976 at Rome
   3) Alois de Orleans-Borbón, born March 24, 1979 at Rome

F2 HRH Prince Alonso Maria Cristino Justo de Orleans-Borbón y Sajonia-Coburgo-Gotha, born May 28, 1912 at Madrid; died November 18, 1936 in action in the Spanish civil war outside Madrid.

F3 HRH Prince Ataulfo Alejandro Isabelo Carlos de Orleans-Borbón y Sajonia-Coburgo-Gotha, born October 20, 1913 at Madrid; died October 4, 1974 at Malaga.

ENDNOTES

1. A recent biography on Queen Victoria's second son, Prince Alfred, entitled Dearest Affie by John van der Kiste and Bee Jordaan repeats suggestions that Prince Alfred of Saxe-Coburg and Gotha was married to Mabel FitzGerald (daughter of Colonel Sir Charles FitzGerald and Lady Alice FitzGerald, daughter of the 4th Duke of Leinister,) by whom he had a daughter Irene Victoria Alexandra Louise Isabel, born February 24, 1899 at Carton, Maynooth, Co. Kildare; died September 30, 1981 at Opa-Locka, Florida, who married September 21, 1914 at Elmira, New York, Frank Bush.

    Prince Alfred and Mabel FitzGerald were alleged to have been married at Potsdam on May 15, 1898 in a civil ceremony followed by Lutheran and Anglican services, all on the same day, but a check of vital records easily invalidates these claims. No record exists in Potsdam of any such marriage and no record of Irene's baptism, said to have taken place at Carton on the Leinster estate can be found, or in the records at Dublin. According to the certificate of Irene's marriage to Frank Bush, she was born at Cortland, New York and her parents were Arthur Hollenbeck and Ella Hollenbeck, née Armstrong.

    According to her birth certificate, Mabel FitzGerald was born May 17, 1884 at Carton; she would therefore have been two days short of her 14th birthday when said to have married Prince Alfred, and only 14 years 9 months old when he died on February 6, 1899. It can hardly be conjectured when still so much under age, she went through three marriage ceremonies and within eighteen days of Prince Alfred's death, gave birth to a daughter. Mabel FitzGerald married March 12, 1910 at Eastbourne, Sussex, William Clarke Hadoke and is described on her marriage certificate as 'spinster.' Their surviving son Gerald Hadoke and the present Duke of Leinster confirm they have no knowledge of any such union. Suggestions by Irene's son, also named Frank Bush, that his mother was created a Princess of the United Kingdom by King Edward VII in 1905 only serve to further discredit such claims and confirm them as fabrications.

2. As Crown Prince of Roumania, Carol renounced his rights of succession on December 25, 1925, A law enacting the renouncement was passed by January 4, 1926. Carol returned to Roumania and reclaimed his rights June 6, 1930.

3. Most genealogical sources give October 16, 1893 as King Carol's date of birth. According to his mother and two entries in the Court Circular of The Times, he was born October 15, 1893. The first announcement of his birth in The Times on October 16 reads "a telegram from Sinaia announces that the Princess of Roumania gave birth to a son yesterday. The following bulletin has been issued...." On October 17, a further announcement in The Court Circular informs readers that the new Roumanian prince had been born on the anniversary of his uncle, the Hereditary Prince of Saxe-Coburg and Gotha (October 15) and commented that it was also the anniversary of Queen Victoria's bethrothal to Prince Albert.

4. Until his father's death, Carol used the surname Lambrino. His legitimacy was recognized by a French court, December 17, 1955 at Paris. Although Carol has assumed the style and title of HRH Prince of Roumania for himself and for his two sons, he and his descendants are only entitled to the surname of Hohenzollern without the style and title of HRH Prince of Roumania or Prince of Hohenzollern.

5. Married (2) November 16, 1969 at New York City, Michael Rainer.

6. Married (1) March 20, 1962 at London, Garry Lacon Jack Ropner, born October 7, 1937 at Kingston, Ontario.

7. Although divorced from King Carol before he became King, Princess Helen on her return to Roumania in 1940 was accorded the style and dignity of HM Queen Helen, Queen Mother of Roumania by an Act of Parliament.

8. Succeeded to the throne on the death of his grandfather, July 20, 1927. Reigned under a regency headed by his uncle Prince Nicolas until June 8, 1930 when his father returned to Roumania and was proclaimed King. Following his father's abdication on September 6, 1940, King Michael began his second reign which ended when the Communists forced his own abdication, December 30, 1947.

9. Married (1) (div.) Estelle N.

10. Granted the style and title of HRH Princess Elena of Hohenzollern by HRH The Prince of Hohenzollern. Married (1) February 17, 1919 at Jassy, Ion Tampeanu.

11. Lupescu is the Roumanian form of Wolf.

12. Succeeded his father, King Peter I (King of Serbia from June 15, 1903 until November 24, 1918, when he was proclaimed King of the Serbs, Croats and Slovenes,) on August 16, 1921. Alexander adopted the title King of Yugoslavia, October 3, 1929.

13. Succeeded on his father's assassination. Reigned under a regency headed by his father's first cousin, Prince Paul of Yugoslavia until March 27, 1941 when he assumed power. He left Yugoslavia following the German invasion and headed the government in exile until the monarchy was abolished November 29, 1945.

14. Remarried October 24, 1985 at Seville, Spain, Don Ignacio Medina y Fernandez de Cordoba, 21st Duke of Segorbe and 9th Count of Moriana. Son of Rafael de Medina y Villalonga and Doña Victoria Eugenia Fernandez de Cordoba de Henestrosa, Duchess of Medinacelli (and 38 other titles) and a Grandee of Spain.

15. Younger sister of HRH Princess Maria de las Mercedes of the Two-Sicilies, Infanta of Spain, who is the wife of HRH Infante Don Juan of Spain, Count of Barcelona.

16 Married (1) (div.) Jack W. Andrews.

17. Married (1) N.N. Married (2) (div.1973), Dr. Frank Lowe.

18. Deprived of his royal rank by decision of the Crown Council, April 9, 1937. Prince Nicolas then assumed the surname Brana. On June 10, 1942, he assumed the surname Hohenzollern and with the approval of HRH The Prince of Hohenzollern, he assumed the style and title of HRH Prince Nicolas of Hohenzollern, January 15, 1947.

19. Married (1) December 11, 1924 (div. 1928), Radu Savianu.

20. Married (1) July 2, 1936 at Caracas, Venezuela (div. 1956), Andrès Bolton Pietri.

21. Became an Orthodox nun. Now Mother Alexandra of the Monastery of the Transfiguration, Ellwood City, Pennsylvania. Retired as Mother Abbess, 1983.

22. Archduke Stefan Habsburg became an American citizen and uses the surname Habsburg-Lothringen.

23. Married (1) (div.; annulled 1986), Debra Kalita.

24. Following her marriage she was styled HIH Grand Duchess Victoria Feodorovna of Russia.

25. Victoria Melita and Ernst Ludwig were first cousins, her father and his mother both being children of Queen Victoria.

26. Also a first cousin marriage. Victoria Melita's mother, Grand Duchess Marie Alexandrovna and Kirill's father, Grand Duke Vladimir Alexandrovitch, were both children of Alexander II, Tsar of all the Russias.

27. After the assassination of the Imperial Family and the murder of the other members of the House of Romanov, Grand Duke Kirill Vladimirovitch, as senior surviving member of the Imperial Family who had not married morganatically, assumed the position of the Head of the Imperial House. He proclaimed himself Head of the Imperial House and Guardian of the Throne at St. Briac, August 8, 1922 and Emperor and Autocrat of all the Russias, August 31, 1924 when his three children assumed the style and title of Imperial Highness and Grand Duke and Grand Duchess of Russia. Upon the death of Grand Duke Kirill, his son Wladimir proclaimed himself Head of the House, October 31, 1938. Dispute exists, however, about his Headship of the House because neither Wladimir's mother, Victoria Melita, or his grandmother, born a Duchess of Mecklenburg-Schwerin were converted to the Orthodox faith until after their marriages. Furthermore, since 1948 there has been dissent as to whether the Moukhransky branch of the Bagration family, cadets of the Kings of Kartli and Sovereign Princes of Moukhrani until 1800 when the principality was annexed by Russia, are of equal rank.

    In April 1970, the representatives of three lines of the Imperial House, Prince Vsevelode, Prince Roman and Prince Andrew of Prussia protested that they did not recognize the right of Wladimir's wife or daughter to the title of Grand Duchess or recognize his daughter as the future Guardian of the Throne. The protest was reasserted on March 25, 1981 when Prince Vassili Alexandrovitch on behalf of the Romanov Family Association refused to recognize the title of Grand Duke granted to Prince Franz Wilhelm of Prussia and to his newborn son. See also La Succession au Trone Imperial de Russie, published under direction of Monseigneur Antoine, Archsbishop of Los Angeles.

28. Following her marriage, she was styled HIH Grand Duchess Marie Pavlovna of Russia.

29. Grandson of Carl, 3rd Prince of Leiningen and Countess Marie von Klebelsberg.

30. Elder sister of Friedrich August, Duke of Oldenburg, husband of Princess Marie Cecile of Prussia.
31. Younger half-brother of Duchess Sophie Charlotte of Oldenburg, who was married to Prince Eitel-Friedrich of Prussia.
32. Niece of HRH The Duchess of Albany (Princess Helene of Waldeck and Pyrmont), wife of Victoria's youngest son Prince Leopold.
33. Married (2) November 16, 1969 at Toronto, Ontario, Bronsilaw Chrobok, born August 27, 1933 at Kattowitz,
34. Lavinia Maria Lane was born at 16 Avenue Road, St. John's Wood, London. No father's name appears on her birth certificate, but her mother's name is given as Kira Lane. She was adopted by her natural mother and HRH Prince Andrej of Yugoslavia, November 15, 1965. On Prince Dimitri of Yugoslavia's birth certificate, his mother's name is given as Kira Karageorgevich, late Lane, formerly Leiningen. Both Dimitri and Lavinia were born at 16 Avenue Road, while Prince Wladimir was born at the Royal Northern Hospital, Islington. HRH Crown Prince Alexander of Yugoslavia, as Head of the Family, as confirmed that Lavinia Marie (the middle name was changed from Maria to Marie in the adoption) is entitled to the style and title of HRH Princess of Yugoslavia.
35. Eldest brother of Prince Johann Georg of Hohenzollern, husband of Princess Birgitta of Sweden, who is a descendant of Queen Victoria.
36. See note 27.
37. Married (1) November 6, 1934 at Nice, France (div. 1937), Sumner Moore Kirby, born September 5, 1895 at Wilkes-Barre, Pennsylvania; died April 7, 1945 in a concentration camp at Leau, near Bernberg.
38. See note 27.
39. Second son of Ernst, 4th Prince of Hohenlohe-Langenburg and of Queen Victoria's half-sister, Princess Feodora of Leiningen.
40. Younger sister of Princess Auguste Viktoria of Schleswig-Holstein-Sonderburg-Augustenberg, who was the first wife of Kaiser Wilhelm II.
41. Younger half-sister of Duchess Sophie of Oldenburg, wife of Prince Eitel-Friedrich of Prussia.
42. Burke's Royal Families of the World (Vol 1.) states that the Duchess of Edinburgh was delivered of a stillborn daughter, October, 14, 1879. However, Queen Victoria, writing to her granddaughter, Princess Victoria of Hesse and By Rhine, October 15, 1879, says that the child was a boy. "Poor Aunt Marie E has had a little boy who died at once. . . ."
43. His parents were first cousins. The Infante Antonio's mother, the Infanta Luisa, was the younger sister of the Infanta Eulalia's mother, Queen Isabel II of Spain.
44. Succeeded to the title of Duke of Galliera upon his father's resignation, July 14, 1937.
45. Eldest sister of Donna Paola Ruffo di Calabria, now HRH The Princess of Liege, wife of HRH Prince Albert, Prince of Liege, younger brother of HM KIng Baudouin of the Belgians.

CHAPTER XVI

THE DESCENDANTS OF PRINCESS HELENA OF GREAT BRITAIN AND IRELAND,
PRINCESS CHRISTIAN OF SCHLESWIG-HOLSTEIN-SONDERBURG-AUGUSTENBERG

HRH Princess <u>Helena</u> Augusta Victoria of Great Britain and Ireland, born May 25, 1846 at Buckingham Palace; died June 9, 1923 at Schomberg House, London. Married July 5, 1866 at the Private Chapel, Windsor Castle, HH Prince Friedrich <u>Christian</u> Karl August of Schleswig-Holstein-Sonderburg-Augustenberg. Granted the qualification of Royal Highness, 1866 by Queen Victoria. Born January 22, 1831 at Augustenberg; died October 28, 1917 at Schomberg House, third son of HH <u>Christian</u> Karl Friedrich August, Duke of Schleswig-Holstein-Sonderburg-Augustenberg and Countess <u>Luise</u> Sophie of Danneskjold-Samoe.

A

HH Prince <u>Christian Victor</u> Albert Ernst Anton of Schleswig-Holstein-Sonderburg-Augustenberg,[1] born August 14, 1867 at Windsor Castle; died October 29, 1900 at Pretoria, South Africa.

B

HH <u>Albert</u> John Charles Frederick Arthur George, Duke of Schleswig-Holstein-Sonderburg-Augustenberg,[2] born February 28, 1869 at Frogmore House, Windsor; died March 13, 1931 at Berlin. Duke Albert was unmarried but had one natural daughter.

B1 Valerie Marie zu Schleswig-Holstein,[3] born April 3, 1900 at Liptovsky-Svaty Mikulas, Hungary; died August 14, 1953 at Mont-Boron, France. Married (1) June 28, 1935 at Vienna (div. 1938; annulled 1940), <u>Ernst</u> Johann Wagner, dr. jur., born January 10, 1896 at Vienna, son of Johann Wagner and Josephine (Josefa) Nimecsek. (No Issue.) Married (2) June 15, 1939 (civil) at Berlin-Charlottenburg and October 9, 1940 (religious) at Münster, Westphalia, HSH <u>Engelbert-Charles</u> Marie Henri Antoine Francois Prosper Ernest Gaspard, 10th Duke of Arenberg, Duke of Aerschot and Croy, Duke of Neppen, Prince of Recklinghausen, Count von der Marck,[4] born April 20, 1899 at Chateau d'Héverlé, Belgium; died April 20, 1899 at Monte Carlo, Monaco, elder son of HSH <u>Engelbert</u> Prosper Ernest Marie Joseph Jules Balthasar Benoit Antoine Eléonore Laurent, 9th Duke of Arenberg and HSH Princess <u>Hedwige</u> Marie Gabrielle de Ligne. (No Issue.)

C

HH Princess Victoria Louise Sophia Augusta Amelia Helena (<u>Helena Victoria</u>) of Schleswig-Holstein-Sonderburg-Augustenberg,[5] born May 3, 1870 at Frogmore House, Windsor; died March 13, 1948 at London.

D

HH Princess Franziska Josepha Louise Augusta Marie Christina Helena (<u>Marie Louise</u>) of Schleswig-Holstein-Sonderburg-Augustenberg, born August 12, 1872 at Cumberland Lodge, Windsor; died December 8, 1957 at London. Married July 6, 1891 at Windsor Castle (Div. 1900), HH Prince <u>Aribert</u> Joseph Alexander of Anhalt, born June 18, 1864 at Wörlitz; died December 24, 1933 at Munich, fourth son of HH <u>Leopold</u> Friedrich Franz Nikolaus, Duke of Anhalt and HH Princess <u>Antoinette</u> Charlotte Marie Josephine Karoline Frida of Saxe-Altenburg, Duchess of Saxony. (No Issue.)

E

HH Prince Frederick Christian Augustus Leopold Edward <u>Harald</u> of Schleswig-Holstein-Sonderburg-Augustenberg, born May 12, 1876 at Cumberland Lodge, Windsor; died May 20, 1876 at Cumberland Lodge.

F   A son, stillborn, May 7, 1877 at Cumberland Lodge.

ENDNOTES

1. Prince Christian Victor died of enteric fecer while serving with the British Army in the Boer War.
2. Succeeded his first cousin Ernst Günther in 1921 as Duke of Schleswig-Holstein-Sonderburg-Augustenberg. Upon Albert's death in 1931, the Augustenberg line of the Ducal House became extinct.
3. The name of Valerie's mother is unkown. On April 15, 1931, Duke Albert wrote to his daughter to inform her that he was her natural father. He, however, chose to keep the name of Valerie's mother a secret. Valerie was raised by a Jewish family named Schwalb. Her birth was registered under the name Schwalb, but this was changed on May 12, 1931 when she acquired by registration the surname zu Schleswig-Holstein. She was officially acknowledged by her aunts, Helena Victoria and Marie Louise, on July 26, 1938. She also is mentioned in Marie Louise's memoirs, <u>My Memories of Six Reigns.</u>

    Information on Valerie Marie was provided through a number of sources including HH Prince Friedrich Ferdinand of Schleswig-Holstein-Sonderburg-Glücksburg, who has control of the family's archives at Ostsee, West Germany; the University of Vienna's Medical School, where I located information on Johann Wagner (who received a law degree from the University of Vienna in 1931), several registry offices in Vienna were I was able to locate Wagner's birth registration as well as his marriage to Valerie Marie; and the Arenberg family archivist, who provided me with other information as well as several photos.
4. Married (2) May 23, 1955 at Berchem, Prov. Antwerp, Mathild Cally, born February 28, 1913 at Hemiksen, Belgium.
5. Princess Helena Victoria and Princess Marie Louise relinquished their German titles in 1917 and were known simply as HH Princess Helena Victoria and HH Princess Marie Louise.

CHAPTER XVII

HRH PRINCESS LOUISE OF GREAT BRITAIN AND IRELAND
DUCHESS OF ARGYLL

HRH Princess <u>Louise</u> Caroline Alberta of Great Britain and Ireland, born March 18, 1848 at Buckingham Palace; died December 3, 1939 at Kensington Palace. Married March 21, 1871 at St. George's Chapel, Windsor Castle to <u>John</u> George Edward Henry Douglas Sutherland Campbell, 9th Duke of Argyll, Marquess of Lorne, Earl of Campbell and Viscount Lochow. Succeeded his father as 9th Duke of Argyll, April 24, 1900. Born August 6, 1845 at London; died May 2, 1914 at Kent House, Cowes, Isle of Wight; Eldest son of <u>George</u> Douglas Campbell, 8th Duke of Argyll, etc., and Lady <u>Elizabeth</u> Georgiana Leveson-Gower. (No Issue.)

Count Sigvard Bernadotte af Wisborg and his wife, Marianne (Count Sigvard Bernadotte af Wisborg.)

CHAPTER XVIII

THE DESCENDANTS OF PRINCE ARTHUR OF GREAT BRITAIN
AND IRELAND, DUKE OF CONNAUGHT AND STRATHEARN

HRH Prince <u>Arthur</u> William Patrick Albert of Great Britain and Ireland. Created Duke of Connaught and Strathearn and Earl of Sussex, May 24, 1874. Born May 1, 1850 at Buckingham Palace; died January 16, 1942 at Bagshot Park, Surrey. Married March 13, 1879 at St. George's Chapel, Windsor Castle, HRH Princess <u>Luise Margarete</u> Alexandra Viktoria Agnes of Prussia, born June 25, 1860 at Marmorpalais, Potsdam; died March 14, 1917 at Clarence House, St. James's Palace, fourth daughter of HRH Prince <u>Friedrich Karl</u> Nikolaus of Prussia and HH Princess Maria Anna of Anhalt.

A

HRH Princess <u>Margaret</u> Victoria Charlotte Augusta Norah of Connaught,[1] born January 15, 1882 at Bagshot Park, Surrey; died May 1, 1920 at Stockholm. Married June 15, 1905 at St. George's Chapel, Windsor Castle, HRH Crown Prince Oscar Frederik Vilhelm Olaf <u>Gustaf Adolf</u> of Sweden, who succeeded to the throne on the death of his father, October 29, 1950 as HM GUSTAF VI ADOLF, KING OF SWEDEN. Born November 11, 1882 at Stockholm; died September 15, 1973 Helsingborg, eldest son of HM (Oscar) GUSTAF V (Adolf), KING OF SWEDEN and HGDH Princess Sophie Marie <u>Victoria</u> of Baden. Crown Prince Gustaf Adolf married (2) November 23, 1923 to Lady <u>Louise</u> Alexandra Marie Irene Mountbatten (See Chapter XIV.)

A1 HSH Hereditary Prince <u>Gustaf Adolf</u> Oscar Frederik Arthur Edmund of Sweden, Duke of Västerbotten, born April 22, 1906 at Stockholm; died January 26, 1947 in an air accident at Kastrup, Denmark. Married October 19 (civil) and October 20, 1932 (religious) at Coburg, HH Princess <u>Sibylla</u> Calma Marie Alice Bathildis Feodora of Saxe-Coburg and Gotha, Duchess of Saxony,*[2] born January 18, 1908 at Schloss Friedenstein, Gotha; died November 28, 1972 at Stockholm, elder daughter of HRH <u>Charles Edward</u> George Albert of Great Britain and Ireland, Duke of Albany, Duke of Saxe-Coburg and Gotha and HH Princess <u>Victoria Adelheid</u> Helene Luise Marie Friederike of Schleswig-Holstein-Sonderburg-Glücksburg.

1. HRH Princess <u>Margaretha</u> Désirée Victoria of Sweden,[3] born October 31, 1934 at Haga. Married June 30, 1964 at Gärdslösa, Isle of Öland, <u>John</u> Kenneth Ambler, born June 6, 1924 at Dorking, Surrey, son of Captain Charles Ambler and <u>Louise</u> Gwendolen Cullen.
    1) <u>Sybilla</u> Louise Ambler, born April 14, 1965 at London
    2) <u>Charles</u> Edward Ambler, born July 14, 1966 at London
    3) <u>James</u> Patrick Ambler, born June 10, 1969 at Oxford

2. HRH Princess <u>Birgitta</u> Ingeborg Alice of Sweden, born January 19, 1937 at Haga. Married May 25 (civil) at Stockholm and May 30, 1961 (religious) at Sigmaringen, HSH Prince <u>Johann-Georg</u> Carl Leopold Eitel-Friedrich Meinrad Maria Hubertus Michael of Hohenzollern,[4] born January 31, 1932 at Sigmaringen, third son of HH <u>Friedrich</u> Viktor Pius Alexander Leopold Karl Theodore Ferdinand, Prince of

Hohenzollern and HRH Princess Margarete Karola Wilhelmine Viktoria Adelheid Albertine Petrusa Bertram Paula of Saxony.

1) HSH Prince Carl Christian Friedrich Johannes Meinrad Maria Hubertus Edmund of Hohenzollern, born April 5, 1962 at Munich

2) HSH Princess Désirée Margareta Victoria Louise Sybilla Catarina Maria of Hohenzollern, born November 27, 1963 at Munich

3) HSH Prince Hubertus Gustav Adolf Veit Georg Meinrad Maria Alexander of Hohenzollern, born June 10, 1966 at Munich

3. HRH Princess Désirée Elisabeth Sibylla of Sweden,[5] born June 2, 1938 at Haga. Married June 5, 1964 at Stockholm, Baron Nils-August Otto Carl Niclas Silfverschiöld, born May 31, 1934 at Koberg, Sweden, elder son of Baron Carl-Otto Nils Henning Silfverschiöld and Elsa Madelaine Bennich.

1) Baron Carl Otto Edmund Silfverschiöld, born March 22, 1965 at Göteborg

2) Baroness Christina-Louise Ewa Madelaine Silfverschiöld, born September 29, 1966 at Göteborg

3) Baroness Hélène Ingeborg Sibylla Silfverschiöld, born September 20, 1968 at Göteborg

4. HRH Princess Christina Louise Helena of Sweden,[6] born August 3, 1943 at Haga. Married June 15, 1974 at Stockholm, Tord Gösta Magnuson, born April 7, 1941 at Stockholm, second son of Tord Lennart Magnuson and Gerda Ingrid Klemming.

1) Carl Gustaf Victor Magnuson, born August 8, 1975 at Stockholm

2) Tord Oscar Frederik Magnuson, born June 20, 1977 at Stockholm

3) Victor Edmund Lennart Magnuson, born September 10, 1980 at Stockholm

5. HM CARL XVI GUSTAF (Folke Hubertus), KING OF SWEDEN. Succeeded on the death of his grandfather, King Gustaf VI Adolf, September 15, 1973. Born April 30, 1946 at Haga. Married June 19, 1976 at Stockholm, Silvia Renate Sommerlath, born December 23, 1943 at Heidelberg, (West) Germany, only daughter of Walther Sommerlath and Alice Soares de Toledo.

1) HRH Crown Princess Victoria Ingrid Alice Désirée of Sweden,[7] born July 14, 1977 at Stockholm

2) HRH Prince Carl Philip Edmund Bertil of Sweden,[8] Duke of Värmland, born May 13, 1979 at Stockholm

3) HRH Princess Madeleine Thérèse Amelie Josephine of Sweden, Duchess of Hälsingland and Gastrikland, born June 10, 1982 at Drottningholm, near Stockholm

A2 HRH Prince Sigvard Oscar Frederik of Sweden, Duke of Uppland, [9] born June 7, 1907 at Drottningholm. Married (1) March 8, 1934 at Caxton Hall, London (div. 1943) Erika Maria Regina Rosalie Patzek, born July 12, 1911 at Wilmersdorf, near Berlin, daughter of Anton Patzek and Marie Lala. (No Issue.) Married (2) October 26, 1943 at Copenhagen (div. 1961), Sonja Helene Robbert, born October 12, 1909 at Copenhagen, daughter of Robert Alexander Robbert[10] and Ebba Elisabeth Suenson.

1. Count Michael Alexander Sigvard Bernadotte af Wisborg, born August 21, 1944 at Copenhagen. Married February 6, 1976 at Stuttgart, Christine Diotima Elisabeth Wellhöfer,[11] born April 26, 1947 at Stuttgart, daughter of Ernst Wellhöfer and

Erna Kromer.

1) Countess <u>Kajsa</u> Michaela Sophia Bernadotte af Wisborg, born October 12, 1980 at Stuttgart

Sigvard married (3) July 30, 1961 at Stockholm, Gullen <u>Marianne</u> Lindberg,[12] born July 15, 1924 at Helsingborg, only daughter of Nils Gusatf <u>Helge</u> Lindberg and Thyra Dahlman.

A3 HRH Princess <u>Ingrid</u> Victoria Sofia Louise Margareta of Sweden, born March 28, 1910 at Stockholm. Married May 24, 1935 at Stockholm, HM (Christian) FREDERIK IX Franz Michael Carl Valdemar Georg), KING OF DENMARK, born March 11, 1899 at Sorgenfri; died January 14, 1972 at Copenhagen, elder son of HM CHRISTIAN IX (Carl Frederik Albert Alexander Vilhelm), KING OF DENMARK[13] and HH Duchess <u>Alexandrine</u> Auguste of Mecklenburg-Schwerin.[14]

1. HM MARGRETHE II (Alexandrine Thorhildur Ingrid), QUEEN OF DENMARK.[15] Succeeded to the throne on the death of her father, January 14, 1972. Born April 16, 1940 at Amalienborg Palace, Copenhagen. Married June 10, 1967 at Copenhagen, Count <u>Henri</u>-Marie-Jean-André de Laborde de Monpezat,[16] born June 11, 1934 at Talence, Girond, France, eldest son of Count André de Laborde de Monpezat and <u>Renée</u> Yvonne Doursenot.
    1) HRH <u>Frederik</u> André Henrik Christian, Crown Prince of Denmark, born May 26, 1968 at Copenhagen
    2) HRH Prince <u>Joachim</u> Holger Valdemar Christian of Denmark, born June 7, 1969 at Copenhagen

2. HRH Princess <u>Benedikte</u> Astrid Ingeborg Ingrid of Denmark, born April 29, 1944 at Amalienborg Palace, Copenhagen. Married February 3, 1968 at Fredensborg, Denmark, HH <u>Richard</u> Casimir Karl August Robert Konstantin, 6th Prince of Sayn-Wittgenstein-Berleburg,[17] born October 29, 1934 at Giessen, elder son of HSH <u>Gustav Albrecht</u> Alfred Franz Friedrich Otto Emil Ernst, 5th Prince of Sayn-Wittgenstein-Berleburg and Margareta Fouché d'Otrante.
    1) HH Hereditary Prince <u>Gustav</u> Frederik Philip Richard of Sayn-Wittgenstein-Berleburg, born January 12, 1969 at Frankfurt-am-Main
    2) HH Princess <u>Alexandra</u> Rosmarie Ingrid Benedikte of Sayn-Wittgenstein-Berleburg, born November 20, 1970 at Copenhagen
    3) HH Princess <u>Nathalie</u> Xenia Margareta Benedikte of Sayn-Wittgenstein-Berleburg, born May 2, 1975 at Copenhagen

3. HRH Princess <u>Anne-Marie</u> Dagmar Ingrid of Denmark, born August 30, 1946 at Amalienborg Palace, Copenhagen. Married September 18, 1964 at Athens, HM CONSTANTINE II, KING OF THE HELLENES,* born June 2, 1940 at Psychiko, only son of HM PAUL I, KING OF THE HELLENES and HRH Princess <u>Friederike</u> Luise Thyra Viktoria Margarete Sophie Olga Cecilie Isabelle Christa of Hanover. (For issue, see Chapter XII.)

A4 HRH Prince <u>Bertil</u> Gustaf Oscar Carl Eugen of Sweden, Duke of Halland, born February 28, 1912 at Stockholm. Married December 7, 1976 at Drottningholm, <u>Lilian</u>

May Davies,[18] born August 30, 1915 at Swansea, Wales, daughter of <u>William</u> John Davies and Gladys Curran.

A5 HRH Prince <u>Carl Johan</u> Arthur of Sweden, Duke of Dalecarlia,[19] born October 31, 1916 at Stockholm. Married February 19, 1946 at New York City, Elin <u>Kerstin</u> Margareta Wijmark,[20] born March 4, 1910 at Stockholm, third daughter of Oscar <u>Henning</u> Wijmark and <u>Elin</u> Mathilda Larsen.

B
HRH Prince <u>Arthur</u> Frederick Patrick Albert of Connaught, born January 13, 1883 at Windsor Castle; died September 12, 1938 at London. Married October 15, 1913 at the Chapel Royal, St. James's Palace, HH Princess <u>Alexandra</u> Victoria Alberta Edwina Louise, Duchess of Fife,* born May 17, 1891 at East Sheen Lodge, Richmond; died February 26, 1959 at London, elder daughter of <u>Alexander</u> William George Duff, 1st Duke of Fife and Earl of Macduff and HRH The Princess <u>Louise</u> Victoria Alexandra Dagmar of Great Britain and Ireland, Princess Royal.

B1 HH Prince <u>Alastair</u> Arthur of Connaught, 2nd and last Duke of Connaught and Strathearn, Earl of Sussex,[21] born August 9, 1914 at London; died April 26, 1943 while on active service at Ottawa, Canada.

C
HRH Princess Victoria <u>Patricia</u> Helena Elizabeth of Connaught,[22] born May 17, 1886 at Buckingham Palace; died January 12, 1974 at Ribsden Holt, Windlesham, Surrey. Married February 27, 1919 at Westminster Abbey, Admiral Honourable Sir <u>Alexander</u> Robert Maule Ramsay, born May 29, 1881 at London; died October 8, 1972 at Ribsden Holt, Windlesham, Surrey, third son of <u>John</u> William Ramsay, 13th Earl of Dalhousie and Lady <u>Ida</u> Louisa Bennet.

C1 <u>Alexander</u> Arthur Alfonso David Maule Ramsay of Mar, born December 21, 1919 at London. Married October 6, 1956 at Fraserburgh, Scotland, <u>Flora</u> Marjory Fraser, 20th Lady Saltoun,[23] born October 18, 1930 at Edinburgh, only daughter of <u>Alexander</u> Arthur Fraser, 19th Lord Saltoun and <u>Dorothy</u> Geraldine Welby.
1. Honourable <u>Katharine</u> Ingrid Mary Isobel Fraser,[24] born October 11, 1957 at Fraserburgh. Married May 3, 1980 at Fraserburgh, <u>Mark</u> Malise Nicolson, born September 24, 1954 at Calcutta, India, son of <u>Malise</u> Allen Nicolson and <u>Vivian</u> Bridget Riley.
    1) <u>Louise</u> Alexandra Patricia Nicolson, born September 2, 1984 at London

2. Honourable <u>Alice</u> Elizabeth Margaret Ramsay, born July 8, 1961 at Edinburgh

3. Honourable <u>Elizabeth</u> Alexandra Mary Ramsay, born April 15, 1963 at Inverness

ENDNOTES

1. When Crown Princess Margaret died suddenly following complications as a result of an ear infection, she was expecting her six child.
2. Until 1919, also bore the title of Princess of Great Britain and Ireland.
3. Now known as HRH Princess Margaretha, Mrs. Ambler. Following the Princess's marriage, her grandfather, King Gustav VI Adolf "asked his ambassador in London to inform the Foreign Office that Princess Margaretha remained a Royal member of the Swedish Royal Family."
4. Younger brother of HRH Friedrich Wilhelm, Prince of Hohenzollern, who is married to Princess Margarita of Leiningen, a descendant of Victoria.
5. Know known as Princess Désirée, Baroness Silfverschiöld without the qualification of Royal Highness or Highness.
6. Know known as Princess Christina, Mrs. Magnuson, without the qualification of Royal Highness or Highness.
7. According to the new Act of Succession, effective from January 1, 1980, the eldest child, regardless of sex is heir to the throne. Previously the succession was based on Salic Law, which excluded females.
8. Crown Prince of Sweden from May 13, 1979 until December 31, 1979.
9. Because of his marriage to a commoner, Prince Sigvard was required to renounce the style and title of Royal Highness Prince of Sweden and adopted the surname Bernadotte. He was created Count Bernadotte af Wisborg by HRH The Grand Duchess of Luxembourg, July 2, 1951.
10. Born Robert Alexander Christiensen. He changed his name to Robert Alexander Robbert by registration February 10, 1914.
11. Married (1) June 10, 1967 at Basel, Switzerland (div.), Mario Betti, born April 13, 1941 at Lucca, Italy.
12. Married (1) February 7, 1980 at Stockholm (div. 1960), Gabriel Antoine Chang, born June 24, 1919 at Beijing, China; died August 11, 1980 at Stockholm.
13. Succeeded his father, April 20, 1947, as King of Denmark, of the Wends and the Gothas, Duke of Schleswig, Holstein, Storman, Sithmarschen, Lauenberg and Oldenburg, and was the last Danish monarch to be so styled.
14. Elder sister of HH Duchess Cecilie of Mecklenburg-Schwerin who married Crown Prince Wilhelm of Germany.
15. Succeeded her father January 14, 1972. Until June 5, 1953 when the Salic Law was abolished and a new Act of Succession allowed for female succession, the heir to the Danish throne was King Frederik's younger brother, Prince Knud (1900-1976).
16. Created HRH Prince Henrik of Denmark, June 10, 1967.
17. Elder brother of HSH Princess Tatiana of Sayn-Wittgenstein-Berleburg, formerly wife of HRH Prince Moritz of Hesse. In Denmark, Prince Richard and his three children are styled HH, and not HSH. According to Queen Margrethe II's private secretary, "in the official documents drawn up at the marriage, Prince Richard was styled His Highness, and consequently, this style is being used in Denmark and includes here Prince Richard's three children as well."

18. Became HRH Princess Lilian of Sweden upon her marriage to Prince Bertil. Married (1) September 27, 1940 at Horsham, Sussex (div) Walter Ivan Sackville Craig, born February 22, 1912 at Edinburgh.

19. Because of his marriage to a commoner, Prince Carl Johan was required to renounce the style and title of Royal Highness, Prince of Sweden and adopt the surname of Bernadotte. He was created Count Bernadotte af Wisborg by HRH The Grand Duchess of Luxembourg, July 2, 1951. Count Carl Johan and and his wife have adopted two children:

    1. Monika Kristina Margaretha Bernadotte, born March 5, 1948 at Salzburg (adopted 1951).

    2. Christian Carl Henning Bernadotte, born December 3, 1949 at Stockholm (adopted 1950).

20. Married (1) June 29, 1935 at Stockholm (div. 1936), Axel Erik Johnson, born October 21, 1908 at Hanebo, Gävleborgs, Län; died Seotember 1, 1953 at Hanebo.

21. From 1917 until January 16, 1942 when he succeeded his grandfather as 2nd Duke of Connaught and Strathearn, HH Prince Alastair was styled as Earl of Macduff, taking the secondary title of his mother's Dukedom of Fife.

22. HRH Princess Patricia was authorized by Royal Warrant, February 25, 1919, to relinquish the style of Royal Highness and the title of Princess of Great Britain and Ireland and adopt the title of Lady Patricia with precedence before the Marchionesses of England.

23. Succeeded her father as Peeress in her own right, August 31, 1979.

24. Her use of the surname Fraser was officially recognized by Lord Lyon King of Arms, March 26, 1973.

CHAPTER XIX

THE DESCENDANTS OF PRINCE LEOPOLD
OF GREAT BRITAIN AND IRELAND, DUKE OF ALBANY

HRH Prince <u>Leopold</u> George Duncan Albert of Great Britain and Ireland. Created Duke of Albany, Earl of Clarence and Baron Arklow, May 24, 1881. Born April 7, 1853 at Buckingham Palace; died March 28, 1884 at Cannes.[1] Married April 27, 1882 at St. George's Chapel, Windsor Castle, HSH Princess <u>Helene</u> Friederike Auguste of Waldeck and Pyrmont, born February 17, 1861 at Arolsen; died September 1, 1922 at Hinterris, Tyrol, third daughter of HSH Georg Viktor, Prince of Waldeck and Pyrmont and HH Princess <u>Helene</u> Wilhelmine Henriette Pauline Marianne of Nassau.

A

HRH Princess <u>Alice</u> Mary Victoria Augusta Pauline of Albany,[2] born February 25, 1883 at Windsor Castle; died January 3, 1981 at Kensington Palace.[3] Married February 10, 1904 at St. George's Chapel, Windsor Castle, HSH Prince <u>Alexander</u> Augustus Frederick William Alfred George of Teck, 1st (and last) Earl of Athlone and Viscount Trematon,[4] Born April 14, 1874 at Kensington Palace; died January 16, 1957 at Kensington Palace, eldest son of HH Franz (<u>Francis</u>) Paul Karl Ludwig Alexander, 1st Prince and Duke of Teck[5] and HRH Princess <u>Mary Adelaide</u> Wilhelmine Elizabeth of Cambridge, Princess of Great Britain and Ireland.

A1 HSH Princess <u>May</u> Helen Emma of Teck,[6] born January 23, 1906 at Claremont House, Esher, Surrey. Married October 23, 1931 at Balcombe, Sussex, Colonel Sir Henry Abel Smith, born March 8, 1900 at London, second son of Francis Abel Smith and Madeleine St. Maur.
1. <u>Anne</u> Mary Sibylla Abel Smith, born July 28, 1932 at Kensington Palace. Married December 14, 1957 at St. George's Chapel, Windsor (div. 1981), <u>David</u> Ian Liddell-Grainger, born January 26, 1930 at London, only son of Captain <u>Henry</u> Hubert Liddell-Grainger and Lady <u>Muriel</u> Felicia Vere Bertie.
    1) <u>Ian</u> Richard Peregrine Liddell-Grainger, born February 23, 1959 at Edinburgh. Married October 31, 1985 at London, Jill Nesbit, born March 9, 1956 at Berwick-upon-Tweed, Northumberland, daughter of Ralph <u>Nicol</u> Nesbit and <u>Isabella</u> Chisholm Anderson.
        (1) <u>Peter</u> Richard Liddell-Grainger, born May 6, 1987 at Hexham, Northumberland
    2) <u>Charles</u> Montagu Liddell-Grainger, born July 23, 1960 at Edinburgh
    3) <u>Simon</u> Rupert Liddell-Grainger, born December 28, 1962 at Edinburgh. Married January 26, 1984 at Montreal, Quebec, Canada, <u>Romana</u> Maria Rogoshewska,[7] born September 17, 1945 at Hutturm, Bavaria, daughter of <u>Roman</u> Emmanuel Anton Rogoshewski and Marie Napadyj.

4) Alice Mary Liddell-Grainger, born March 3, 1965 at Edinburgh

5) Malcolm Henry Liddell-Grainger, born November 14, 1967 at Edinburgh

2. Richard Francis Abel Smith, born October 11, 1933 at Kensington Palace. Married April 28, 1960 at London, Marcia Kendrew, born March 27, 1940 at Fulmer, Buckinghamshire, only daughter of Major General Sir Douglas Anthony Kendrew and Norah Elizabeth Harvey.

1) Katharine Emma Abel Smith, born March 11, 1961 at Windsor. Married October 16, 1980 at London, Honourable Hubert Wentworth Beaumont, born April 13, 1956 at Hong Kong, elder son of Rev. Timothy Wentworth Beaumont, Baron Beaumont of Whitley and Mary Rose Wauchope.

(1) Amelia May Beaumont, born November 12, 1983 at London

(2) George Wentworth Beaumont, born August 24, 1985 at London

3. Elizabeth Alice Abel Smith, born September 5, 1936 at Kensington Palace. Married April 29, 1965 at London (div. 1974), Peter Ronald Wise, born December 29, 1929 at London, son of Captain Anthony Forster Wise and Eve Baillie.

1) Emma Charlotte Abel Wise, born September 1, 1973 at Sherborne, Dorset; died June 9, 1974 at Reading, Berkshire

A2 HSH Prince Rupert Alexander George Augustus of Teck,[8] born August 24, 1907 at Claremont House, Esher, Surrey; died April 15, 1928 at Bellevue-sur-Salone, France.

A3 HSH Prince Maurice Francis George of Teck, born March 29, 1910 at Claremont House, Esher, Surrey; died September 14, 1910 at Schloss Reinhardsbrunn.

B
HRH Prince Charles Edward George Albert of Albany, 2nd and last Duke of Albany, Earl of Clarence and Baron Arklow. Succeeded on the death of his paternal uncle Alfred (see Chapter XV) as Duke of Saxe-Coburg and Gotha.[9] Born July 19, 1884 at Claremont House, Esher, Surrey (posthumously); died March 6, 1954 at Coburg. Married October 11, 1905 at Coburg, HH Princess Victoria Adelheid Helena Luise Marie Friederike of Schleswig-Holstein-Sonderburg-Glücksburg,[10] born December 31, 1885 at Grünholz; died October 3, 1970 at Coburg, eldest daughter of HH Friedrich Ferdinand Georg Christian Karl Wilhelm, Duke of Schleswig-Holstein-Sonderburg-Glücksburg and HH Princess Viktoria Friederike Auguste Marie Caroline Mathilde of Schleswig-Holstein-Sonderburg-Augustenberg.

B1 HH Hereditary Prince Johann Leopold Wilhelm Albert Ferdinand Viktor of Saxe-Coburg and Gotha, Duke of Saxony, Prince of Great Britain and Ireland, born August 2, 1906 at Schloss Callenberg; died May 4, 1972 at Grein, Austria. Married (1) March 4, 1932 at Dresden (div. 1962), Baroness Feodora Maria Alma Margarete von der Horst,[11] born July 7, 1905 at Wolka, elder daughter of Baron Alfred Hermann Bernhard von der Horst and Elsa Gürtler.

1. Caroline Mathilde Adelheid Sibylla Marianne Erika Prinzessin von Sachsen-Coburg und Gotha, born April 5, 1933 at Hirschberg. Married December 5, 1953 at Mühlacker, Württemberg, Michael Adalbert Wilfried Nielson, born August 12, 1923 at Frankfurt-am-Main; died September 20, 1975 at Vienna, son of Friedrich Nielson and Anneliese Wacker.

1) Margarete Brigitte Nielson, born August 31, 1954 at Mühlacker, Württemberg
2) Renate Christine Nielson, born April 1, 1957 at Leverkusen-Wiesdorf. Married (1) July 26, 1978 at Dortmund-Innenstadt (div. 1981), Wolfgang Willi Reinhard Blechert,[12] born June 7, 1947 at Böhlen Krs., Borna, son of Willi August Blechert and Marta Minna Anna Allewohl. (No Issue.) Married (2) September 30, 1986 at Tokyo, Japan, Jörg Bracker, born September 24, 1955 at Lünen, Westphalia, son of Erwin Günther Bracker and Iris Helene Johanna Knauer.

2. Ernst-Leopold Eduard Wilhelm Josias Prinz von Sachsen-Coburg und Gotha, born January 14, 1935 at Hirschberg. Married (1) February 14, 1961 at Herrenberg, Württemberg (div. 1963), Ingeborg Henig,[13] born August 16. 1937 at Nordhausen, Harz, daughter of Richard Henig and Emmy Luise Duckwitz.
   1) Hubertus Richard Ernst Leopld Prinz von Sachsen-Coburg und Gotha, born December 8, 1961 at Herrenberg
   Ernst-Leopold married (2) May 29, 1963 at Regensberg, Gertraude Maria Monika Pfeiffer, born July 1, 1938 at Ströblitz, Krs. Cottbus, daughter of Hermann Horst Pfeiffer and Gertrud Marianne Jardin.
   2) Victoria Feodora Monika Prinzessin von Sachsen-Coburg und Gotha,[14] born September 7, 1963 at Regensberg
   3) Ernst-Josias Carl Eduard Hermann Leopold Prinz von Sachsen-Coburg and Gotha, born May 13, 1965 at Landshut
   4) Carl-Eduard Wilhelm Josias Prinz von Sachsen-Coburg und Gotha, born July 27, 1966 at Regensberg
   5) Friedrich-Ferdinand Georg Ernst Albert Prinz von Sachsen-Coburg und Gotha, born December 14, 1968 at Regensberg
   6) Alice-Sibylla Calma Beatrice Prinzessin von Sachsen-Coburg und Gotha, born August 6, 1974 at Regensberg

3. Peter Albert Friedrich Josias Prinz von Sachsen-Coburg und Gotha, born June 12, 1939 at Dresden. Married May 11, 1964 at Tegernsee, Roswitha Henriette Breuer, born September 11, 1945 at Wolnzach, Kreis Pfaffenhofen an-der-Ilm, daughter of Robert Breuer and Hedwig Harraschein.
   1) Peter Carl Eduard Alexander Prinz von Sachsen-Coburg und Gotha, born October 4, 1964 at Munich
   2) Malte Georg Albert Prinz von Sachsen-Coburg und Gotha, born October 6, 1966 at Ingolstadt

Prince Johann-Leopold married (2) May 3 (civil) and May 5, 1963 (religious) at Bad Reichenhall, Maria Theresia Elisabeth Reindl,[15] born March 13, 1908 at Bad Reich-enall, daughter of Max Reindl and Elisabeth Ortner. (No Issue.)

B2 HH Princess Sibylla Calma Marie Alice Bathildis Feodora of Saxe-Coburg and Gotha, Duchess of Saxony, Princess of Great Britain and Ireland, born January 18, 1908 at Schloss Friedenstein, Gotha; died November 28, 1972 at Stockholm. Married October 19 (civil) and October 20, 1932 (religious) at Coburg, HRH Hereditary Prince Gustaf Adolf Oscar Frederik Arthur Edmund of Sweden, Duke of Västerbotten,* born April 22, 1906 at Stockholm; died January 26, 1947 in an air accident at Kastrup, Denmark, eldest son of HM (Oscar Frederik Vilhelm Olaf) GUSTAF VI ADOLF, KING OF SWEDEN and HRH Princess <u>Margaret</u> Victoria Charlotte Augusta Norah of Connaught, Princess of Great Britain and Ireland. (For issue, see Chapter XVII.)

B3 HH Prince Dietmar <u>Hubertus</u> Friedrich Wilhelm Philipp of Saxe-Coburg and Gotha, Duke of Saxony, Prince of Great Britain and Ireland, born August 24, 1909 at Schloss Reinhardsbrunn; killed in action November 26, 1943 near Mosty, Roumania.

B4 HH Princess <u>Caroline Mathilde</u> Helene Ludwiga Beatrice of Saxe-Coburg and Gotha, Duchess of Saxony, Princess of Great Britain and Ireland,[16] born June 22, 1912 at Schloss Callenberg; died September 5, 1983 at Erlangen. Married (1) December 14, 1931 at Veste, Coburg (div. 1938), H Ill H Count <u>Friedrich</u> Wolfgang Otto of Castell-Rüdenhausen,[17] born June 27, 1906 at Berlin; killed June 11, 1940 in action over Portland, Dorset, elder son of H Ill H Count <u>Hugo</u> Friedrich Alfred of Castell-Rüdenhausen and H Ill H Countess <u>Clementine</u> Gabriele Justine of Solms-Sonnenwalde.
1. H Ill H Count <u>Bertram</u> Friedrich of Castell-Rüdenhausen, born July 12, 1932 at Golssen, Kreis Luckau. Married October 10, 1964 at Vienna, Countess <u>Felizitas</u> Anna Maria Elisabeth von Auersperg, born September 20, 1944 at Vienna, only daughter of Count <u>Hanno</u> Herward Maria Josef Leo von Auersperg and Klothilde Ryndziak.
    1) H Ill H Count <u>Dominik</u> Dimitrij Johannes Friedrich of Castell-Rüdenhausen, born July 20, 1965 at Vienna
    2) H Ill H Count <u>Michael</u> Alexis Wolfgang Friedrich of Castell-Rüdenhausen, born November 4, 1967 at Vienna

2. H Ill H Count <u>Conradin</u> Friedrich of Castell-Rüdenhausen, born October 10, 1933 at Berlin. Married July 6, 1961 at Helsinki, Finland, Märta Catharina Lönegren, born April 17, 1939 at Helsinki, daughter of Bjarne Lönegren and <u>Göta</u> Ingeborg Isakson.
    1) H Ill H Countess <u>Anne Charlotte</u> Catharina Victoria of Castell-Rüdenhausen, born April 7, 1962 at Helsinki.
    Anne-Charlotte has a natural son
    (1) <u>Henrik</u> Mikael Frederik zu Castell-Rüdenhausen, born December 23, 1982 at Ekenäs, Finland.
    Anne-Charlotte married July 4, 1986 at Ekenäs, Finland, <u>Martti</u> Kalevi Rappu, born October 26, 1963 at St. Karins, Finland, son of Valdemar Rappu and <u>Arja</u> Maila Inkeri Mustikkama.
    2) H Ill H Count <u>Carl-Eduard</u> Friedrich Hubertus of Castell-Rüdenhausen, born March 15, 1964 at Helsinki

3. H Ill H Countess <u>Victoria Adelheid</u> Clementine Louise of Castell-Rüdenhausen, born February 26, 1935 at Coburg. Married June 20, 1960 at the Queen's Chapel, St. James's Palace, John <u>Miles</u> Huntington-Whiteley, born July 18, 1929 at Fareham, Hampshire, youngest son of Captain Sir <u>Herbert</u> Maurice Huntington-Whiteley, 2nd Baronet and Lady <u>Pamela</u> Margaret Baldwin.[18]
    1) Alice <u>Louise</u> Esther Margot Huntington-Whiteley, born July 22, 1961 at London. Married February 1, 1985 at the Chapel Royal, St. James's Palace, Charles <u>Percy</u> Sewell, born December 22, 1958 at Banbury, Oxfordshire,

youngest son of Major <u>Geoffrey</u> Richard Michael Sewell and Joan Williams-Wynn.

2) <u>Beatrice</u> Irene Helen Victoria Huntington-Whiteley, born September 6, 1962 at London

3) <u>Leopold</u> Maurice Huntington-Whiteley, born July 15, 1965 at London

Princess Caroline-Mathilde married (2) June 22, 1938 at Berlin, Captain <u>Max</u> Otto Schnirring, born May 20, 1895 at Stuttgart-Unterturkheim; died July 7, 1944 in a flying accident at Straslund, son of <u>Karl</u> August Schnirring and Friederike Hummel.

4. <u>Calma</u> Barbara Schnirring, born November 18, 1938 at Valparaiso, Chile. Married (1) July 5, 1961 at Fremont, Ohio (div. 1973) <u>Richard</u> Darrell Berger,[19] born February 16, 1941 at Fremont, Ohio, son of Wesley Berger and <u>Marjory</u> Beulah Mason.

1) <u>Sascha</u> Nikolaus Hubertus Berger,[20] born September 20, 1960 at Munich. Married November 19, 1982 at Houston, Texas, <u>Bonita</u> Isabelle Oden,[21] born November 9, 1952 at Shreveport, Lousiana, daughter of <u>James</u> Olin Oden and <u>Argyle</u> Shirley Doyle.

(1) <u>Tristan</u> Lee Berger, born November 20, 1984 at Houston

(2) <u>Nicole</u> Calma Berger, born November 20, 1984 at Houston

2) <u>Richard</u> Darrel Berger, born July 3, 1962 at Fremont, Ohio. Married August 9, 1982 at Tacoma, Washington, <u>Gypsy</u> Dianna Wheeler,[22] born June 1, 1956 at High Point, North Carolina, daughter of <u>Donald</u> Eugene Wheeler and <u>Barbara</u> Ellen Nixon.

(1) <u>Richard</u> Jonathan Ross Wheeler, born August 31, 1984 at Honolulu, Hawaii

3) <u>Victor</u> Dean Berger, born September 28, 1963 at Groton, Massachusetts. Married August 15, 1986 at Columbia, South Carolina, <u>Sylvia</u> Diane McKinney, born April 16, 1955 at South Carolina, daughter of N.N. and N.N.

(1) Mary Katherine Berger, born June 11, 1985 at Columbia, South Carolina

4) <u>Samuel</u> Clinton Berger, born May 28, 1965 at Fort Knox, Kentucky

5) <u>Wesley</u> Martha Berger, born October 11, 1967 at Fort Hood, Texas

6) <u>David</u> Charles Berger, born September 25, 1968 at Fort Hood, Texas

Calma Schnirring married (2) May 15, 1976 at Lincolnton, North Carolina, James Cook, born August 5, 1940 at Robinsville, North Carolina, son of <u>James</u> Hamilton Cook and Alice Cooper.

5. <u>Dagmar</u> Sibylla Schnirring, born November 22, 1940 at Grosswusterwitz. Married February 26, 1964 at Munich, Heinrich Walz, born July 29, 1937 at Forchheim, son of Fritz Walz and Ottilie Kraus.

1) Maria <u>Valesca</u> Walz, born August 14, 1965 at Munich

2) Larissa Walz, born September 16, 1967 at Bamberg

6. Peter <u>Michael</u> Schnirring, born January 4, 1943 at Grosswusterwitz; died February 10, 1966 at Munich

Princess Caroline Mathilde married (3) December 21, 1946 at Coburg (div. 1947), <u>Karl</u> Otto Andrée, born February 10, 1912 at Düsseldorf, son of Karl Andrée and Maria Magdalena Katherina Müller. (No Issue.)

B5 HH Prince <u>Friedrich Josias</u> Carl Eduard Ernst Kirill Harald of Saxe-Coburg and Gotha, Duke of Saxony. Head of the Ducal House of Saxe-Coburg and Gotha.[23] born November 29, 1918 at Schloss Callenberg. Married (1) January 23, 1942 at Casel, N. Lusatia (div. 1946), H Ill H Countess <u>Victoria-Luise</u> Friederike Caroline Mathilde of Solms-Baruth, born March 13, 1921 at Casel, N. Lusatia, only daughter of H Ill H Count <u>Hans</u> Georg Eduard of Solms-Baruth and HH Princess Viktoria Irene Adelheid Auguste Alberta Feodora <u>Caroline-Mathilde</u> of Schleswig-Holstein-Sonderburg-Glücksburg.

1. HH Prince <u>Andreas</u> Michael Friedrich Hans Armin Siegfried Hubertus of Saxe-Coburg and Gotha, Duke of Saxony, born March 21, 1943 at Casel, N. Lusatia. Married June 18, 1971 at Hamburg, Carin Dabelstein, born July 16, 1946 at Hamburg, daughter of <u>Adolf</u> Wilhelm Martin Dabelstein and Irma Callsen.
   1) HH Princess <u>Stephanie</u> Sibylla of Saxe-Coburg and Gotha, Duchess of Saxony, born January 31, 1972 at Hamburg
   2) HH Prince <u>Hubertus</u> Michael of Saxe-Coburg and Gotha, Duke of Saxony, born September 16, 1975 at Hamburg
   3) HH Prince <u>Alexander</u> Philipp of Saxe-Coburg and Gotha, Duke of Saxony, born May 4, 1977 at Coburg

Prince Friedrich Josias married (2) February 14, 1948 at San Francisco, California (div. 1964), <u>Denyse</u> Henriette von Muralt,[24] born December 14, 1923 at Basel, Switzerland, daughter of <u>Gaston</u> Robert von Muralt and <u>Pierette</u> Gabrielle Maurice.

2. HH Princess Maria <u>Claudia</u> Sibylla of Saxe-Coburg and Gotha, Duchess of Saxony, born May 22, 1949 at San Francisco, California. Married March 17, 1971 at Berne, Switzerland, Gion Schäfer, born July 20, 1945 at Coire, Switzerland, son of <u>Géza</u> Johann Robert Schäfer and Silvia Stieger.
   1) Maria <u>Christina</u> Sibylla Schäfer, born June 23, 1972 at Berne, Switzerland
   2) <u>Gianetta</u> Antonia Schäfer, born February 18, 1974 at Chur, Switzerland

3. HH Princess <u>Beatrice</u> Charlotte of Saxe-Coburg and Gotha, Duchcess of Saxony, born July 15, 1951 at Berne. Married June 11 (civil) at Coburg and June 12, 1977 (religious) at Veste, Coburg, <u>Friedrich-Ernst</u> Georg Bernhard Prinz von Sachsen-Meiningen,[25] born January 21, 1935 at Meiningen, elder son of HH <u>Bernhard</u> Friedrich Julius Heinrich, Prince of Saxe-Meiningen, Duke of Saxony and Margot Grössler.
   1) Maria Alexandra (<u>Alix</u>) Elisabeth Beatrice Prinzessin von Sachsen-Meiningen, born July 5, 1978 at Heilbronn, West Germany
   2) Friedrich <u>Constantin</u> Prinz von Sachsen-Meiningen, born June 3, 1980 at Heilbronn, West Germany

4. HH Prince <u>Adrian</u> Vincens Edward of Saxe-Coburg and Gotha, Duke of Saxony, born October 18, 1955 at Coburg. Married October 20, 1984 at Berne, Switzerland, Lea Rinderknecht, born January 5, 1960 at Mülligen Aargau, Switzerland, daughter Martin Rinderknecht and Elsbeth Ulrich.
   1) Simon Prinz von Sachsen-Coburg und Gotha, born March 10, 1985 at Berne, Switzerland

Prince Friedrich-Josias married (3) October 30, 1964 at Hamburg, Katrin Anna Dorothea Bremme, born April 22, 1940 at Berlin, daughter of Dietrich Karl Bremme and Margarethe Spottke.

ENDNOTES

1. Prince Leopold suffered from hemophilia and died at Villa Nevada following a fall when he slipped and bumped his knee.
2. After 1917 styled as HRH Princess Alice, Countess of Athlone. Although her husband relinquished his German titles and was created Earl of Athlone, Princess Alice, a British princess in her own right, retained her rank.
3. Princess Alice lived longer than any other member of the British Royal Family and died age 97 years, 312 days. She surpassed HRH Princess Augusta of Cambridge, Grand Duchess of Mecklenburg-Strelitz, born July 19, 1822; died December 4, 1916. Princes Augusta was the elder daughter of HRH Prince Adolphus, Duke of Cambridge and Princess Augusta of Hesse-Cassel. She also was the elder sister of Princess Mary Adelaide, Duchess of Teck, who was the mother of Prince Alexander of Teck, later Earl of Athlone, and therefore, Princess Alice's mother-in-law.
4. Relinquished all German titles and adopted the surname Cambridge, July 14, 1917. Created Earl of Athlone and Viscount Trematon, July 16, 1917.
5. Prince of Teck in the Kingdom of Württemberg (1863) and Austrian Empire (1864) with the qualification of Serene Highness. Duke of Teck in the Kingdom of Württemberg (1871). Granted the qualification of Highness by Queen Victoria, July 11, 1887.
6. After July 16, 1917 styled as Lady May Cambridge.
7. Married (1) July 17, 1973 (div.) at Geneva, Philippe Guillaume Perrot. Romana Rogoshewska is a direct descendant of Tadeusz Kosciusko (1746-1817), the Polish patriot who aided the Americans during the American Revolution.
8. After July 16, 1917 styled as Rupert Cambridge, Viscount Trematon. He suffered from hemophilia and died fourteen days after an auto accident.
9. Reigned as Carl Eduard, Duke of Saxe-Coburg and Gotha from July 23, 1900, having succeeded his paternal uncle, Duke Alfred. During his minority, the Regency was exercised by HSH Ernst, Prince of Hohenlohe-Langenburg, who was married to Duke Alfred's third daughter, Alexandra. Duke Carl Eduard abdicated November 14, 1918. His British titles were struck from the Roll of Peers by Order in Council, March 28, 1919. Until this date, his children were also entitled to the title of Prince or Princess of Great Britain and Ireland.
10. Sister of Duke Friedrich of Schleswig-Holstein-Sonderburg-Glücksburg, who was married to Princess Marie Melita of Hohenlohe-Langenburg, a great granddaughter of Queen Victoria. Another sister, Alexandra Viktoria, was married to Prince August Wilhelm of Prussia, son of Kaiser Wilhelm II.
11. Married (1) November 8, 1924 at Königsberg (div. 1931), Baron Wolf Sigismund Pergler von Perglas, born May 16, 1900 at Bayreuth, Saxony.
12. Blechert remarried in 1982.
13. Ingeborg Henig has remarried.

14. Victoria Prinzessin von Sachsen Coburg und Gotha may have married sometime in early 1987 to Peter Schmidt. One source (C.E.D.R.E) lists the marriage as having taken place at Herrenberg, Württemberg, but the Standesamt in Herrenberg has no record of the marriage.

15. Married (1) March 7, 1934 at Munich (div, 1962), Werner Müller, born October 7, 1899 at Wiesbaden; died August 26, 1972 at Strub, near Berchtesgaden.

16. The _Genealogisches Handbuch des Adels Fürstlichen Häuser_ (1984 edition) lists a fourth marriage and divorce for Princess Caroline Mathilde (the entry is found under Castell-Rüdenhausen) to Günther Heinzmann. According to Princess Caroline Mathilde's brother, Prince Friedrich Josias of Saxe-Coburg and Gotha and three of her children, Victoria Adelheid Huntington-Whiteley, Calma Cook and Count Conrad zu Castell-Rüdenhausen, no marriage ever took place.

17. Married (2) April 26, 1939 at Rüdenhausen, H Ill H Countess _Elisabeth_ Clea Freda Amalie Irmgard Emma Marie Hedwig of Castell-Rüdenhausen, born August 24, 1914 at Rüdenhausen.

18. Daughter of the 1st Earl Baldwin of Bewdley (Stanley Baldwin, Prime Minister, 1923-24; 1924-9; 1935-7.)

19. He remarried sometime in the 1970s to Colleen N.

20. Most sources list September 22, 1961 at Coburg for the date and place of birth for Sascha Berger. According to Sascha, he was born at Munich on September 22, 1960.

21. Married (1) May 7, 1977 at Houston, Texas (div.), _Patrick_ Eugene Fowler, born March 12, 1951 at Houston.

22. Married (1) May 30, 1974 at Deep River, North Carolina (div.), _Raundle_ Lee Chandler, born October 1, 1953 at King, North Carolina.

23. Prince Friedrich Josias and Countess Viktoria-Luise are first cousins. Her mother, Princess Caroline Mathilde was the younger sister of Prince Friedrich Josias's mother, Viktoria Adelheid.

24. Married (2) December 8, 1983 at Flims Grison, Switzerland, _Werner_ Paul Leuch, born December 13, 1901 at Berne, Switzerland; died March 20, 1984 at Goa, India.

25. Married (1) March 3, 1962 at Schwieberdingen, Württemberg (div. 1973), Ehrengard von Massow, born October 25, 1933 at Straslund.

CHAPTER XX

THE DESCENDANTS OF PRINCESS BEATRICE OF GREAT BRITAIN AND IRELAND,
PRINCESS HENRY OF BATTENBERG

HRH Princess <u>Beatrice</u> Mary Victoria Feodore of Great Britain and Ireland, born April 14, 1857 at Buckingham Palace; died October 26, 1944 at Brantridge Park, Balcombe, Sussex. Married July 23, 1885 at Whippingham Church, Isle of Wight, HSH Prince <u>Henry</u> Maurice of Battenberg. Granted the qualification of Royal Highness, July 23, 1885 by Queen Victoria. Born October 5, 1858 at Milan; died January 20, 1896 on board HMS Blonde,[1] son of HGDH Prince <u>Alexander</u> Ludwig Georg Friedrich Emil of Hesse and By Rhine and Countess Julie von Hauke.[2]

A

HH Prince <u>Alexander</u> Albert of Battenberg,[3] 1st (and last) Marquess of Carisbrooke, Earl of Berkhamsted and Viscount Launceston. Born November 23, 1886 at Windsor Castle; died February 23, 1960 at London. Married July 19, 1917 at London, Lady <u>Irene</u> Frances Adza Denison, born July 4, 1890 at London; died July 16, 1956 at London, only daughter of William Francis Henry Denison, 2nd Earl of Londesborough and Lady <u>Grace</u> Augusta Fane.

A1 Lady <u>Iris</u> Victoria Beatrice Grace Mountbatten, born January 13, 1920 at London; died September 1, 1982 at Toronto, Ontario. Married (1) February 15, 1941 at Haywards Heath, Sussex (div. 1946), Captain <u>Hamilton</u> Joseph Keyes O'Malley,[4] born October 18, 1910 at Farnborough, Hampshire, elder son of Lieutenant-Colonel <u>Middleton</u> Joseph O'Malley Keyes and <u>Jane</u> Byrnes Malley. (No Issue)

Married (2) May 5, 1957 at Pound Ridge, New York (div. 1957), <u>Michael</u> Neely Bryan,[5] born August 9, 1916 at Byhalia, Mississippi; died August 20, 1972 at Glendale, California, son of James R. Bryan and Laura A. Neely.
1. <u>Robin</u> Alexander Bryan, born December 20, 1957 at New York City

Lady Iris married (3) December 11, 1965[6] at Toronto, Ontario, <u>William</u> Alexander Kemp,[7] born July 10, 1921 at Toronto, son of <u>Clarence</u> Arthur Kemp and <u>Helen</u> Janet Ballantyne. (No Issue.)

B

HRH Princess <u>Victoria Eugenie</u> Julia Ena of Battenberg,[8] born October 24, 1887 at Balmoral Castle; died April 15, 1969 at Lausanne. Married May 31, 1906 at Madrid, HM ALFONSO XIII (Leon Fernando Santiago Maria Isidro Pascual Antonio), KING OF SPAIN,[9] born May 17, 1886 at Madrid (posthumously); died February 28, 1941 at Rome, only son of HM ALFONSO XII (Francisco de Asis Fernando Pio Juan Maria de la Concepción Gregorio Pelayo), KING OF SPAIN and HI & RH Archduchess Marie <u>Christine</u> Désirée Henriette Felicitas Raineria of Austria.[10]

B1 HRH Infante Don <u>Alfonso</u> Pio Cristino Eduardo Francisco Guillermo Carlos Enrique Fernando Antonio Venancio of Spain, Prince of the Asturias, Count of Covadonga,[11] born Mary 10, 1907 at Madrid; died September 6, 1938 at Miami, Florida. Married (1) June 21, 1933 (civil) at Lausanne and at Ouchy, near Lausanne (religious) (div. 1937), Doña <u>Edelmira</u> Ignacia Adriana Sampedro y Robato, born March 5, 1906 at Sagua-la-Grande, Cuba, daughter of Don <u>Luciano</u> Pablo Sampedro y Ocejo and Doña Edelmira Robato y Turro. (No Issue.) Married (2) July 3, 1937 at Havana (div. 1937), <u>Marta</u> Esther Rocafort y Altuzarra,[12] born September 18, 1913 at Havana, Cuba; died ...., daughter of <u>Blas</u> Manuel Rocafort y González and Rogelia Altuzarra y Cabonell. (No Issue.)

B2 HRH Infante Don <u>Jaime</u> Luitpold Isabelino Enrique Alberto Alfonos Victor Acacio Pedro Maria of Spain, Duke of Segovia,[13] born June 23, 1908 at San Ildefonso; died March 20, 1975 at St. Gallen, Switzerland. Married (1) March 4, 1935 at Rome (div. 1947 and again in 1949), Vittoria Jeanne Joséphine Pierre Marie <u>Emanuela</u> de Dampierre,[14] born November 8, 1913 at Rome, elder daughter of Vicomte <u>Roger</u> Richard Charles Henri Etienne de Dampierre, 2nd Duke of San Lorenzo and Donna <u>Vittoria</u> Emilia Ipsycrathea Acricola Rusipoli dei Principi di Poggio Suasa.

1. HRH Prince Don <u>Alfonso</u> Jaime Marcelino Manuel Victor Maria de Borbón y de Dampierre, Duke of Cadiz,[15] born April 20, 1936 at Rome. Married March 8, 1972 at El Pardo, Madrid (div. 1983; annulled 1986), Doña Maria del <u>Carmen</u> Esperanza Alejandra de la Santíssima Trinidad Martinez-Bordiu y Franco,[16] born February 26, 1951 at Madrid, eldest daughter of Don <u>Cristóbal</u> Martinez y Bordiu, 10th Marqués de Villaverde and Doña Maria del Carmen Franco y Polo, 1st Duchess of Franco and a Grandee of Spain.[17]

    1) HRH Prince <u>Francisco</u> Alfonso Cristóbal Victor José Gonzalo Cecilio de Borbón y Martinez-Bordiu, born November 22, 1972 at Madrid; died February 7, 1984 at Pamplona, Spain as a result of a car accident.

    2) HRH Prince <u>Luis</u> Alfonso Gonzalo Victor Manual Marco de Borbón y Martinez-Bordiu, born April 25, 1974 at Madrid

2. HRH Prince Don <u>Gonzalo</u> Victor Alfonso José Bonifacio Antonio Maria de Borbón y de Dampierre, born June 5, 1937 at Rome. Married (1) January 28, 1983 at Puerto Vallarta, Mexico (marriage is not recognized in Spain), Doña Maria del <u>Carmen</u> Harto y Montealegre,[18] born ..., 1947 at Toledo, Spain, daughter of Rafael Harto and Felisa Montealegre. (No Issue.) Married (2) June 25 (civil) at Madrid and June 30, 1984 (religious) at Olmedo, Valladolid, Spain (legally separated, 1987), Doña Maria de las <u>Mercedes</u> Licer y Garcia, born October 14, 1963 at Valencia, Spain, elder daughter of Don Luis Licer and Doña Maria de las <u>Mercedes</u> Garcia. (No Issue.)

    Don Gonzalo has a natural daughter by <u>Sandra</u> Lee Landry:
    1) <u>Stephanie</u> Michelle de Borbon, born June 19, 1968 at Miami, Florida

The Duke of Segovia married (2) August 3, 1949 at Innsbruck, Austria, <u>Charlotte</u> Luise Auguste Tiedemann,[19] born January 2, 1919 at Königsberg, Prussia; died July 3, 1979 at Berlin, daughter of <u>Otto</u> Eugen Tiedemann and <u>Luise</u> Amalia Klein. (No Issue.)

B3 HRH Infanta Doña Beatriz Isabel Federica Alfonsa Eugenia Cristina Maria Teresa
    Bievenida Ladislàa of Spain, born June 22, 1909 at San Ildefonso. Married January
    14, 1935 at Rome, Don Alessandro Torlonia, 5th Prince of Civitella-Cesi, born
    December 7, 1911 at Rome; died May 12, 1986 at Rome, only son of Don Marco
    Torlonia, 4th Prince of Civitella-Cesi and Elsie Moore.
1. Donna Sandra Vittoria Torlonia dei Principi di Civitella-Cesi, born February 14,
    1936 at Rome. Married June 20, 1958 at Rome, Count Clemente Lequio de
    Assaba,[20] born December 9, 1925 at Paris; died June 28, 1971 at Trieste, only
    son of Nobile Franceso Lequio di Assaba and Maria Francesca Casciani.
    1) Count Alessandro Vittorio Eugenio Lequio di Assaba, born June 20, 1960 at
        Lausanne
    2) Nobile Desideria (Désirée) Elyse Francesca dei Conti Lequio di Assaba, born
        September 19, 1962 at Lausanne. Married September September 11, 1986 at
        the Palazzo Torlonia, Rome, Count Oddone Paulo Tournon, born June 2, 1957
        at Turin, eldest son of Count Giovanni Felice Tournon and Angela Bonelli.

2. Don Marco Alfonso Torlonia, 6th Prince of Civitella-Cesi, born July 2, 1937 at
    Rome. Married (1) September 15, 1960 at Piacenza, Donna Orsetta Caracciolo dei
    Duchi di Melito dei Principi di Castagneto, born March 17, 1940 at Rome; died
    March 10, 1968 at Rome, second daughter of Don Adolfo Caracciolo dei Dichi di
    Melito dei Principi de Castagneto and Donna Anna Visconti di Madrone dei Duchi
    Grazzano.
    1) Don Giovanni Torlonia de Principi di Civitella-Cesi, born April 17, 1962 at
        Rome

    Don Marco married (2) November 9, 1968 at Rome (div. 1985,) Philippa Catherine
    Blanche McDonald,[21] born June 3, 1942 at Sydney, Australia, daughter of John
    Linden McDonald and Honor Kingswill Kater.
    2) Donna Vittoria Eugenia Carolina Honor Paola Alexandra Maria Torlonia dei
        Principi di Civitella-Cesi, born May 8, 1971 at Rome.

    Don Marco married (3) November 11, 1985 at Rome, Blazena Anna Helena
    Svitaková, born October 16, 1940 at Prague, Czechoslovakia, daughter of Václav
    Jan Svitak and Maria Anna Zemanová.
    3) Donna Catarina Agnese Torlonia dei Principi di Civitella-Cesi, born June 14,
        1974 at Rome

3. Don Marino Riccardo Francesco Giuseppe Torlonia dei Principi di Civitella-Cesi,
    born December 13, 1939 at Rome.

4. Donna Olimpia Torlonia dei Principi di Civitella-Cesi, born December 27, 1943 at
    Rome. Married June 26, 1965 at Rome, Paul-Annick Weiller, born July 28, 1933 at
    Paris, son of Paul-Louis Weiller and Aliki Diplearakos.
    1) Aliki Beatrice Victoria Weiller, born March 23, 1967 at Neuilly-sur-Seine
    2) Sibella Sandra Weiller, born June 12, 1968 at Neuilly-sur-Seine
    3) Paul-Alexandre Weiller, born February 12, 1970 at Neuilly-sur-Seine; died
        April 10, 1975 at Paris

4) <u>Laura</u> Daphne Lavinia Weiller, born January 24, 1974 at Neuilly-sur-Seine; died March 5, 1980 at Paris

5) <u>Cosima</u> Marie Elisabeth Edmée Weiller, born January 18, 1984 at Neuilly-sur-Seine

6) <u>Domitilla</u> Louise Marie Weiller, born June 14, 1985 at Neuilly-sur-Seine

B4 A son, stillborn, May 21, 1910 at Madrid.

B5 HRH Infanta Doña <u>Maria Cristina</u> Teresa Alejandra Guadalupe Maria de la Concepción Victoria Eugenia of Spain, born December 12, 1911 at Madrid. Married June 10, 1940 at Rome, <u>Enrico</u> Eugenio Francesco Antonio Marone Cinzano, 1st Count Marone,[22] born March 15, 1895 at Turin; died October 23, 1968 at Geneva, Switzerland, son of Alberto Marone and Paola Cinzano.

1. Donna <u>Vittoria</u> Alfonsa Alberta Pilar Enrica Paola dei Conti Marone Cinzano, born March 5, 1941 at Turin. Married January 12, 1961 at Geneva, Don José Carlos Alvarez de Toledo y Gross, 8th Count of Villapaterna, born November 30, 1929 at Malaga, eldest son of Don <u>José</u> Ignacio Alvarez de Toledo y Mencos, 7th Count of Villapaterna and Julia Gross.

   1) Doña <u>Victoria</u> Eugenia Alvarez de Toledo y Marone, born October 8, 1961 at Malaga. Married September 29, 1982 at Madrid, Don Alfonso Codorniu y Aguilar, born April 24, 1954 at Madrid, son of Ricardo Codorniu y González-Villazon and Doña Cristina Aguilar y Ortiz.

      (1) Don Jaime Codorniu y Alvarez de Toledo, born February 15, 1985 at Madrid

      (2) Doña Ana Codorniu y Alvarez de Toledo, born January 24, 1987 at Madrid

   2) Don Francisco de Borja Alvarez de Toledo y Marone, born March 27, 1963 at Malaga

   3) Don <u>Marco</u> Alfonso Alvarez de Toledo y Marone, born January 23, 1965 at Malaga

   4) Don Gonzalo Alvarez de Toledo y Marone, born October 1, 1973 at Madrid

2. Donna <u>Giovanna</u> Paola Gabriella dei Conti Marone Cinzano, born January 31, 1943 at Lausanne. Married July 24, 1967 at San Martino de Zoagli-Rapallo, Italy, Don Jaime Galobart y Santrústegui,[23] born February 4, 1935 at Barcelona, son of Don Juan Galobart y Senchermés and Doña Maria Satrústegui y Meurvilla.

   1) Don <u>Alfonso</u> Alberto Galobart y Marone, born April 12, 1969 at Madrid

3. Donna <u>Maria Teresa</u> Beatrice dei Conti Marone Cinzano, born January 4, 1945 at Lausanne. Married April 22, 1967 at Geneva, Don José Maria Ruiz de Arana y Montalvo, 5th Marqués de Brenes, 13th Marqués de Castromonte, Grandee of Spain, born April 27, 1933 at Madrid, eldest son of Don <u>José</u> Javier Ruiz de Arana y Fontagud, Ossario de Morosco y Aguilera, 4th Marqués de Brenes, 12th Marqués de Castromonte, Grandee of Spain and Doña Maria del Carmen Montalvo y Orovio.

   1) Doña <u>Cristina</u> Carmen Margarita Ruiz de Arana y Marone, born March 24, 1968 at Madrid

   2) Doña <u>Isabel</u> Alfonsa Ruiz de Arana y Marone, born May 17, 1970 at Madrid

3) Doña <u>Inés</u> Carla Ruiz de Arana y Marone, born December 27, 1973 at Madrid

4. Donna Anna Alessandra (<u>Anna Sandra</u>) Paola Maria Tomassa dei Conti Marone Cinzano, born December 21, 1948 at Turin. Married (1) June 21, 1969 at Turin (div. 1985), Gian Carlo Stavro di Santarosa, born May 25, 1944 at Fribourg, Switzerland, son of Guido Stavro di Santarosa and Christiane Privat.
   1) <u>Astrid</u> Cristina Antonia Stavro di Santarosa, born April 24, 1972 at Trieste, Italy
   2) <u>Yara</u> Christiane Stavro di Santarosa, born June 29, 1974 at Trieste Donna Anna Sandra married (2) September or October , 1985 at ..., Don Fernando Schwartz y Girón,[24] born November 16, 1937 at Geneva, son of Don Juan Schwartz y Diaz-Flores and Doña Carmen Girón y Camino.

B6 HRH Infante Don <u>Juan</u> Carlos Teresa Silvestre Alfonso of Spain, Count of Barcelona,[25] born June 20, 1913 at San Ildefonso. Married October 12, 1935 at Rome, HRH Princess Maria de las <u>Mercedes</u> Cristina Januaria Isabel Luisa Carolina Victoria of the Two-Sicilies, Infanta of Spain,[26] born December 23, 1910 at Madrid, second daughter of HRH Prince <u>Carlo</u> Maria Francesco di Assisi Pasquale Fernando Antonio di Padova Francesco di Paola Alfonso Andrea Avelino Tancredi of the Two-Sicilies,[27] and HRH Princess <u>Louise</u>-Francoise-Marie-Laure of Orléans.
1. HRH Infanta Doña Maria del <u>Pilar</u> Alfonsa Juana Victoria Luisa Ignacia of Spain, Duchess of Badajoz, born July 30, 1936 at Cannes. Married May 5, 1967 at Lisbon Don Luis Gómez-Acebo y Duque de Estrada, Visconde de la Torre, born December 23, 1934 at Madrid, fourth son of Don Jaime Gómez-Acebo y Modet and Doña Isabel Duque de Estrada y Vereterra, 9th Marquesa de Deleitosa.
   1) Doña Maria de Fatima <u>Simoneta</u> Luisa Gómez-Acebo de y de Borbón, born October 28, 1968 at Madrid
   2) Don <u>Juan</u> Filiberto Nicolas Gómez-Acebo y de Borbón, born December 6, 1969 at Madrid
   3) Don <u>Bruno</u> Alejandro Gómez-Acebo y de Borbón, born June 15, 1971 at Madrid
   4) Don <u>Beltran</u> Luis Ataulfo Gómez-Acebo y de Borbón, born May 20, 1973 at Madrid
   5) Don <u>Fernando</u> Umberto Gómez-Acebo y de Borbón, born September 13, 1974 at Madrid

2. HM JUAN CARLOS I (Alfonso Victor Maria), KING OF SPAIN,[28] born January 5, 1938 at Rome. Married May 14, 1962 at Athens, HRH Princess Sophie of Greece and Denmark,* born November 2, 1938 at Psychiko, elder daughter of HM PAUL I, KING OF THE HELLENES and HRH Princess <u>Friederike</u> Luise Thyra Viktoria Margarete Sophie Olga Cecilie Isablle Christa of Hanover.
   1) HRH Infanta Doña <u>Elena</u> Maria Isabel Dominica de los Silos of Spain, born December 20, 1963 at Madrid
   2) HRH Infanta Doña <u>Cristina</u> Federica Victoria Antonia de la Santíssima Trinidad of Spain, born June 13, 1965 at Madrid
   3) HRH Infante Don <u>Felipe</u> Juan Pablo Alfonso of Spain, Prince of the Asturias, born January 30, 1968 at Madrid

3. HRH Infanta Doña <u>Margarita</u> Maria de la Victoria Esperanza Jaime Felicidad Perpetua of Spain, 2nd Duchess of Hernani,[29], born March 6, 1939 at Rome. Married October 12, 1972 at Estoril, Portugal Don Carloa Zurita y Delgado, 1st Duke of Soria and a Grandee of Spain, born October 9, 1943 at Antequera, Malaga, eldest son of Don Carlos Zurita y González-Vidalte and Doña Carmen Delgado y Fernandez de Santaella.

    1) Don <u>Alfonso</u> Juan Carlos Zurita y de Borbón, born August 9, 1973 at Madrid

    2) Doña <u>Maria</u> Sofia Emilia Carmen Zurita y de Borbón, born September 16, 1975 at Madrid

4. HRH Infante Don <u>Alfonso</u> Cristino Teresa Angel Francisco de Asis of Spain,[30] born October 3, 1941 at Rome; died March 29, 1956 at Estoril, Portugal.

B7 HRH Infante Don <u>Gonzalo</u> Manuel Maria Bernardo Narciso Alfonso Mauricio of Spain,[31] born October 24, 1914 at Madrid; died August 13, 1934 at Krumpendorf, Austria.

C

HH Prince <u>Leopold</u> Arthur Louis of Battenberg,[32] born May 21, 1889 at Windsor Castle; died April 23, 1922 at Kensington Palace.

D

HH Prince <u>Maurice</u> Victor Donald of Battenberg,[33] born October 3, 1891 at Balmoral Castle; killed in action, October 27, 1914 at Sonnebeek, near Mons, Belgium.

ENDNOTES

1. Prince Henry died on board HMS Blonde off the coast of Sierra Leone having contracted a fever while serving with the British expeditionary force in the Ashanti.
2. Created Countess of Battenberg with the qualification of Illustrious Highness by Grand Duke Ludwig IV of Hesse and By Rhine, and Princess of Battenberg with the qualification of Serene Highness, December 26, 1858 for herself and her children.
3. Relinquished the style and title of HH Prince of Battenberg and assumed the surname Mountbatten. Created Marquess of Carisbrooke, Earl of Berkhamstead and Viscount Launceston by King George V, July 18, 1917.
4. Granted the qualification of Royal Highness by her uncle, King Edward VII, April 3, 1906. After her conversion to the Roman Catholic faith, Ena took the additional names of Maria Cristina.
5. Alfonso XIII succeeded to the throne at birth. His father, Alfonso XII, had died on November 25, 1885. Alfonso XIII left Spain on April 14, 1931. He abdicated in favor of his third son, HRH Infanta Don Juan de Borbón y Battenberg (HRH The Count of Barcelona,) January 15, 1941.

6. Queen Regent of Spain from November 25, 1885 until May 7, 1902.

7. Married (2) January 25, 1947 at Richmond, Yorkshire (div. 1970), Eleonore Mary Winifred (<u>Sadie</u>) de Pentheny O'Malley, born May 9, 1922 at Dorchester, Dorset. Married (3) December, 1970 Betty Saunders.

8. Michael Bryan was married previous to his marriage to Lady Iris. Information concerning Bryan's name (Michael Neely Bryan) was provided by a number of sources including Lady Iris, several reference books on jazz, The New York Times, and his death certificate.

9. Lady Iris and William Kemp were separated after only two weeks of marriage, but they were never divorced. This fact was verified by Kemp himself who corrected a Canadian Press obituary on Lady Iris that stated they had been divorced.

10. Married (1) Helen Shields, who died in 1963.

11. After renouncing his rights of succession for himself and for his descendants on June 21, 1933, Alfonso took the title Count of Covadonga. He suffered from hemophilia and died as the result of a car accident.

12. Married (2) March 18, 1938 at Miami, Florida, E. H. Adkins. Married (3) Rodolfo Cabalero. Information concerning Marta Esther Rocafort's birth was obtained through diplomatic channels between the U.S.A. and Cuba -- two nations that do not have diplomatic relations. In the spring of 1985, I sent a letter of Cuba's Ambassador to the United Nations, asking for his assistance in locating the exact date and place for Marta's birth. Nine months later, I received a response from the Czechoslovak Socialist Republic Embassy in Washington D.C. (The Czechs handle Cuba's interests in the USA, while the Swiss Embassy handles U.S. interests in Cuba.) I was sent certified copies of Martha's birth certificate as well as her marriage license to the Count of Covadonga. Both documents were certified as authentic by Cuban officials and were stamped as official by the U.S. Vice Consul at the Swiss Embassy in Havana. The documents were then sent via diplomatic bag to the Czech Embassy in D.C., where the documents were then forwarded on to me. In 1985, I also located a cousin of Marta Rocafort, Manuel Rocafort, who lives in the Miami area. He told me that Marta was deceased, but could not provide a date or a place.

13. Renounced his rights of succession for himself and for his descendants, June 21, 1933. Assumed the title of Duke of Anjou, February 28, 1941.

14. Married (2) November 21, 1949 at Vienna, Antonio Sozzani, born July 12, 1918 at Milan.

15. Created Duke of Cadiz with the qualification of Royal Highness, November 22, 1972.

16. Married (2) December 11, 1984 at Reuil-Malmaison, France, Jean-Marie Rossi.

17. Daughter of General Francisco Franco y Bahamonde, who ruled Spain from 1939 until November 20, 1975 and Doña Maria de Carmen Polo y Vales.

18. Married (1) N. Bays.

19. Married (1) N. Buchler. Married (2) N. Hippler.

20. Married (1) Maria Ferrer.

21. Married (1) July 26, 1962 at London (div. 1968), Vicomte Luc de la Barre de Nanteuil, born September 21, 1925 at Lhommaizé, France.

22. Married (1) June 1929 at Paris, Doña Noemi de Alcosta y Garcia de Mansilla, born December 26, 1907 at Buenos Aires; died June 1929 at Paris.

23. Married (1) May 20, 1961 at Milagro, Navarre, Doña Soledad Sánchez-Marco y Mendizábal, died May 27, 1967 at Madrid.

24. Married (1) Sarah Ann Kimber McRobert (div.) In 1985, Schwartz was appointed as Spain's Ambassador to the Kingdom of the Netherlands. In a letter to me, Schwartz said his marriage to Donna Anna Sandra took place "early fall" in 1985, but would not provide the date or the place.

25. Following his brothers' renunciation of their rights, Infante Don Juan became Prince of the Asturias, June 21, 1933. Following his father's abdication, January 15, 1941, he became Head of the Royal House of Spain. He renounced all claims to the throne, May 14, 1977.

26. Eldest sister of Princess Maria de la Esperanza, who is the mother of Princess Maria da Gloria of Orléans and Branganca, the first wife of Crown Prince Alexander of Yugoslavia.

27. First married to HRH Infanta Doña Maria de las Mercedes of Spain, elder sister of King Alfonso XIII. The children of his second marriage to Princess Louise of Orléans were granted the titles of Infante and Infanta of Spain by Royal Decree, August 3, 1908.

28. The monarchy was restored November 22, 1975 following the death of General Franco. Juan Carlos had been designated heir, July 22, 1969.

29. Succeeded her kinsman, Don Manfredo de Borbón y Bernaldo de Quiros (1889-1979) as Duchess of Hernani.

30. Accidentally killed when a gun went off while playing with his elder brother.

31. He suffered from hemophilia and died following a car crash when a car in which he was a passenger, driven by his sister, Infanta Beatriz, swerved to avoid a cyclist and crashed into the all of Krumpendorf castle.

32. Relinquished the style and title of HH Prince of Battenberg, July 14, 1917 and assumed the surname Mountbatten, becoming known as Sir Leopold Mountbatten, G.C.V.O. On September 11, 1917, he was granted the title and precedence of the younger son of a Marquess by Royal Warrant, being styled as Lord Leopold Mountbatten. He suffered from hemophilia and died after a relapse, following an operation for a hip problem.

33. Prince Maurice suffered from hemophilia and died as a result of wounds received in action during the second battle of Ypres.

ACKNOWLEDGEMENTS

In compiling this work, I have received a tremendous amount of help from a great many people, the descendants themselves, various archives, records offices and libraries in the USA, Great Britain, and in Europe; and not least, from my family and friends and my happiest duty is to thank them all.

It is perhaps invidious to single out individuals, but I am especially indebted to His Majesty King Michael of Roumania, TSH The Prince and Princess of Hohenlohe-Langenburg, The Countess Mountbatten of Burma, HRH Princess Margaret of Hesse and By Rhine, HRH The Landgrave of Hesse, HH Prince Friedrich Josias of Saxe-Coburg and Gotha, and HRH Princess Georg Wilhelm of Hanover.

I also would like to thank the following people: Lady May Abel Smith; Mother Alexandra (Princess Ileana of Roumania); John Ambler, Herbert Appeltshauser; The Duke of Aosta; Brigadier General M.G. Arnaoutis, Private Secretary to HM The King of the Hellenes; the Margrave of Baden; Prince Ludwig of Baden; Dr. and Mrs. Victor von Baillou (Archduchess Alexandra of Austria); the Count of Barcelona; Mechtilde Bauscher; Luc de la Barre de Nanteuil; Lord Beaumont of Whitley; Richard and Gypsy Berger; Sascha and Bonita Berger; Count Michael Bernadotte af Wisborg; Count Sigvard Bernadotte af Wisborg; the late Joyce Beaumont; Holbrook Bonney; Paul Brandram; Richard Brandram; the late Duchess Viktoria Luise of Brunswick-Lüneburg; the Duke of Cadiz; Count Conrad zu Castell-Rüdenhausen; the Marqués of Castromonte; Princess Marie Louise of Bulgaria, Mrs. Chrobok; Calma Schnirring Cook; The Marquess and Marchioness of Douro; Marina Patterson Engel; Helene van Eyck; Thomas, Baron de Foran Saint Bar; Princess Astrid, Mrs. Ferner; the Duke of Fife; Dr. E .G. Franz, Hessisches Staatarchiv, Darmstadt; Juan Carlos and Désirée Gamarra; Anne Grainger; the Hon. Desmond Guinness; Stefan and Jerrine Habsburg-Lothringen; The Prince of Hanover; Princess Ernst August of Hanover; The Earl of Harewood; Princess Christina of Hesse; Lady Pamela Hicks; Prince Albrecht of Hohenlohe-Langenburg; The Prince of Hohenlohe-Öhringen; The Princess of Hohenzollern; Hereditary Prince Karl Friederich of Hohenzollern; Antonia Hohenzollern; Baroness Maria Magdalena von Holzhausen; J. Miles Huntington-Whiteley; Kira Harris Johnson; Helen Kemp; Viscountess Lascelles; Alexandra Lascelles; the Hon. Mr.and Mrs. James Lascelles; Frederika Lascelles; the Hon. Mr. and Mrs. Gerald Lascelles; the Hon. Mrs. Jeremy Lascelles; J. Robert Lee; Donna Sandra Lequio di Assaba; David Liddell-Grainger; Jill Nesbit Liddell-Grainger; Romana Rogoshewska Liddell-Grainger; Denyse von Muralt Leuch; Jason Lindsey; Princess Ragnhild, Mrs. Lorentzen; Hereditary Princess Aloys-Konstantin of Lowenstein-Wertheim-Rosenburg; the late Arnold McNaughton; Duchess Barbara of Mecklenburg; Tord Magnuson;

Infanta Maria Cristina of Spain, Countess Marone; the late Lady Iris Mountbatten; the late Earl Mountbatten of Burma; the Marchioness of Milford Haven; the Hon. Mrs. Mark Nicolson; Renate Nielson; Felicitas von Nostitz-Wallwitz; Prince Alvaro of Orléans-Borbon; Prince Alvaro-Jaime of Orléans-Borbon; Princess Gerarda of Orléans-Borbon; Dr. Friederich Oswald; Valerie Owen; Nelly and Jacques Parisot; Dohna Patterson Pearl; Christel Pratzat, Herzoglich Holstein-Glücksburgische Generalverwaltung; Prince Adalbert of Prussia; Prince Burchard of Prussia; Princess Donata-Viktoria of Prussia; Princess Friederich Wilhelm of Prussia; Prince Louis Ferdinand of Prussia; Princess Michael of Prussia; Prince Nicholas of Prussia; Prince Stephan-Alexander of Prussia; Prince Wilhelm-Karl of Prussia; Prince and Princess Wilhelm-Viktor of Prussia; Bernhard and Friederike von Reiche; Ingeborg Lorentzen Ribiero; Dr. Anton Ritthaler; Lord Romsey; Prince Wladimir of Russia; Dr. Karl Sablik, Institute für Geschichte der Medizin der Universität Wien; Prince Andreas of Saxe-Coburg and Gotha; Ernst-Leopold Prinz von Sachsen-Coburg und Gotha; Marianne prinzessin von Sachsen-Coburg und Gotha; the Countess of Scarborough; Prince Christoph of Schleswig-Holstein; Prince Friederich-Ferdinand of Schleswig-Holstein; the late Duke Peter of Schleswig-Holstein; Count Rudolf von Schönburg-Glauchau; Fernando Schwartz y Giron; Ileana Habsburg-Snyder; J.F. von Strantz, Generalverwaltung des Vormals Regierden Prussischen Königshauses; Elisabeth Tarras-Walberg, Press Secretary to the King and Queen of Sweden; Branko Terzic; Marion Thorpe; Sylvana Tomaselli, Infanta Beatriz, Princess Torlonia; Blazena Torlonia, Philippa Torlonia; Jean-Pierre Tytgat, Arenberg archivist; Donna Olimpia Weiller; Princess Friederich-Karl of Windisch-Graetz; Crown Prince Alexander of Yugoslavia; Prince Andrej of Yugoslavia; and Prince Tomislav of Yugoslavia.

I also would like to thank the staffs at the embassies and consultates of Australia; Denmark; Finland; France; the Federal Republic of Germany; the German Democratic Republic; Italy; Norway; Spain; Sweden; the United Kingdom; and the embassies of the United States of America in the German Democratic Republic and Greece; the Swiss Embassy in Cuba; the Cuban Mission to the United Nations; the British Information Service; the Danish Information Office; the Norwegian Information Service in the United States; the Private secretaries and press offices of Queen Elizabeth II; Queen Elizabeth, the Queen Mother; the Prince and Princess of Wales; the Duke and Duchess of Gloucester; the Duke and Duchess of Kent; Prince and Princess Michael of Kent; Princess Alexandra, the Hon. Mrs. Angus Ogilvy; Queen Margrethe II of Denmark; Princess Richard of Sayn-Wittgenstein-Berleburg; King Olav V of Norway; Crown Prince Harald and Crown Princess Sonja of Norway; King Juan Carlos II and Queen Sofia of Spain; King Carl XVI Gustaf and Queen Silvia of Sweden; and Prince Bertil and Princess Lilian of Sweden.

I cannot list all the libraries I used, but the staff of the Local History and Genealogy section of the New York Public Library should be singled out because of their help as well as the staff of the Dokumentation und Archiv section of the West German news agency, DPA; the New York office of the *Daily Telegraph* (London) and A. Springer Verlag, GMBH; the Departments of Health or Vital Records in California, Florida, Maryland, Massachusetts. New York; and Ohio; the General Register Office in London; various Standesmater in West Germany and the respective equivalents in France and Italy; *The Miami News; The Denver Post; The New York Times; The Washington Post; Hannoversche-Allgemeine Zeitung;* and *The Times, Daily Mail and Daily Express*, all London.

My thanks also are due to Elyse Fradkin; Ted Rosvall; the late Patrick Montague-Smith; Charles Kidd, editor of *Debrett's Peerage and Baronetage*; Karen Murdoch Kennedy; Paul Harten for a million things; Claudia Craig; G. Nicholas Tantzos; David Duff, for his support and friendship; Philip Ziegler; and to The Associated Press News Library, headed by Susan Pistilli; to Hal Buell for his patience and his permission to use Associated Press photographs is warmly appreciated; and a special thank you to AP's Communications Department for use of a wonderful machine called the word processor. Many thanks are also due to Log_On Computer Services.

But above all, my greatest debt is to Arthur Addington. A renowned genealogist in his own right, he has been steadfast in his support and encouragement since the book's inception. His help has extended to beyond the genealogy, and I am particularly grateful to him and to John Wimbles for their assistance with the text of this book. Without Mr. Addington's help, this book might still be only a dream.

Marlene A. Eilers
Little Ferry, New Jersey
United States of America

Addington, A.C.- THE ROYAL HOUSE OF SCOTLAND: THE DESCENDANTS OF KING JAMES VI OF
SCOTLAND, JAMES I OF ENGLAND. 3 vols. London: 1969, 1974 & 1976
Alice, Grand Duchess of Hesse and By Rhine - BIOGRAPHICAL SKETCH AND LETTERS. New
York; 1884
Almedingen, E.M. - AN UNBROKEN UNITY: A MEMOIR OF THE GRAND DUCHESS SERGE OF RUSSIA.
London: 1964.
Almanach de Gotha (1890-1944).
Argyll, Duke of - VRI: HER LIFE AND EMPIRE. London: 1901
Aronson, Theo - GRANDMAMMA OF EUROPE: THE CROWNED DESCENDANTS OF QUEEN VICTORIA. New
York: 1973.
          - FAMILY OF KINGS: THE DESCENDANTS OF CHRISTIAN IX OF DENMARK. London:
1976.
          - PRINCESS ALICE, COUNTESS OF ATHLONE. London: 1981
Ashton, Sir George - HRH THE DUKE OF CONNAUGHT AND STRATHEARN. London: 1929.
Athlone, HRH Princess Alice, Countess of - FOR MY GRANDCHILDREN. London: 1966.
Battiscombe, Georgina - QUEEN ALEXANDRA. London: 1969.
Bennett, Daphne - VICKY: PRINCESS ROYAL OF GREAT BRITAIN AND GERMAN EMPRESS. New York:
1971.
          - KING WITHOUT A CROWN: ALBERT PRINCE CONSORT OF ENGLAND. London:
1977.
          - QUEEN VICTORIA'S CHILDREN. London 1980.
Benson, E.F. - DAUGHTERS OF QUEEN VICTORIA. London: 1939.
Bergamini, John D. - THE TRAGIC DYNASTY: A HISTORY OF THE HOUSE OF ROMANOV. New York:
1969.
          - THE SPANISH BOURBONS. New York: 1974.
Brook-Shepherd, Gordon - UNCLE OF EUROPE. London: 1975.
Brunswick-Lüneburg, Duchess Viktoria Luise - THE KAISER'S DAUGHTER. New York: 1977.
Bryan III, J. Murphy and Charles, J.V. - THE WINDSOR STORY. New York:1979.
BURKE'S GUIDE TO THE ROYAL FAMILY. London: 1973
BURKE'S ROYAL FAMILIES OF THE WORLD. Volume 1. London: 1977.
CERCLE D'ETUDES DES DYNASTIES ROYAL EUROPEENES. Paris: 1980-1987.
Corti, Count Egon Caesar - THE ENGLISH EMPRESS. London: 1957.
Donaldson, Frances - EDWARD VIII. London: 1974.
Duff, David - THE LIFE OF PRINCESS LOUISE, DUCHESS OF ARGYLL. London: 1940.
          - THE SHY PRINCESS. London: 1958.
          - VICTORIA AND ALBERT. London: 1972.
          - HESSIAN TAPESTRY. London: 1979.
          - ALEXANDRA: PRINCESS AND QUEEN. London: 1981.
Elgklou, Lars - BERNADOTTE: OCH HISTORIER OM EN FAMILJ. Stockholm: 1978.
Elsberry, Terrence - MARIE OF ROUMANIA. London: 1973.
Epton, Nina - VICTORIA AND HER DAUGHTERS. London: 1971.
Fenyvesi, Charles - SPLENDOR IN EXILE. Washington D.C: 1979.
Fjellman, Margit - LOUISE MOUNTBATTEN: QUEEN OF SWEDEN. London: 1968.
Foran de Saint Bar, Baron Thomas - PORTRAIT D'UN ROI: PIERRE II DE YUGOSLAVIE. Paris:
1973.
Frankland, Noble - PRINCE HENRY, DUKE OF GLOUCESTER. London: 1980.
Fulford, Roger - DEAREST CHILD: LETTERS BETWEEN QUEEN VICTORIA AND THE PRINCESS ROYAL
          (1858-1861). London: 1964.
          - DEAREST MAMA (1861-1965). London: 1968.
          - YOUR DEAR LETTER (1865-1871). London: 1971.
          - DARLING CHILD (1871-1878). London: 1976.
          - BELOVED MAMA (1878-1885). London: 1981.
          - THE PRINCE CONSORT. London: 1949.
Genealogisches Handbuch des Adels, Der Fürstlichen Häuser. Band I-XIII. Limburg an der
Lahn: 1951-1987.
Germany, Wilhelm II, Emperor - MY MEMOIRS. London: 1922.
                    - MY EARLY LIFE. London: 1926.
Gloucester, HRH Princess Alice, Duchess of - THE MEMOIRS OF PRINCESS ALICE, DUCHESS OF
                    GLOUCESTER. London: 1983.
Gore, John - KING GEORGE V: A PERSONAL MEMOIR. London: 1941.
Graham, Evelyn - PRINCESS MARY, VISCOUNTESS LASCELLES. London: 1929.
Graham, Stephen - ALEXANDER OF YUGOSLAVIA. London: 1938.

Harewood, George, Earl of - THE TONGS AND THE BONES. London: 1981.
Hellenes, Queen Frederika - A MEASURE OF UNDERSTANDING. New York: 1971.
Holden, Anthony - CHARLES, PRINCE OF WALES. London: 1979.
Hough, Richard - THE MOUNTBATTENS. New York: 1975.
              - MOUNTBATTEN: HERO OF OUR TIME. London: 1980.
              - EDWINA, COUNTESS MOUNTBATTEN OF BURMA. New York: 1984
              - ADVICE TO A GRANDDAUGHTER: LETTERS BETWEEN QUEEN VICTORIA TO PRINCESS
              VICTORIA OF HESSE. New York: 1975.
Hourmouzios, Stelio - NO ORDINARY CROWN: A BIOGRAPHY OF KING PAUL OF THE HELLENES.
           London: 1972.
James, Robert Rhodes - ALBERT, PRINCE CONSORT. London: 1983.
Junor, Penny - DIANA, PRINCESS OF WALES. New York: 1983.
King, Stella - PRINCESS MARINA: HER LIFE AND TIMES. London: 1969.
Kurth, Peter - ANASTASIA: THE RIDDLE OF MRS. ANDERSON. Boston: 1983.
Lee, Arthur Gould - THE ROYAL HOUSE OF GREECE. London: 1948.
              - CROWN AGAINST SICKLE: THE STORY OF KING MICHAEL OF ROUMANIA:
              London: 1950.
              - HELEN, QUEEN MOTHER OF ROUMANIA. London: 1956.
              - THE EMPRESS FREDERICK WRITES TO SOPHIE. London: 1955.
Longford, Elizabeth - QUEEN VICTORIA: BORN TO SUCCEED. New York: 1964
McNaughton, Arnold - THE BOOK OF KINGS. London: 1973.
Magnus, Sir Philip - KING EDWARD THE SEVENTH. London: 1964.
Marie Louise, Princess - MY MEMORIES OF SIX REIGNS. London: 1956.
Massie, Robert K. - NICHOLAS AND ALEXANDRA. New York: 1967.
Moats, Alice-Leone - LUPESCU. New York: 1955.
icolson, Harald - KING GEORGE VI: HIS LIFE AND REIGN. London: 1952.
Noel, Gerard - PRINCESS ALICE: QUEEN VICTORIA'S FORGOTTEN DAUGHTER. London: 1974.
          - ENA - SPAIN'S ENGLISH QUEEN. London: 1984.
Pakula, Hannah - THE LAST ROMANTIC. New York: 1984.
Pool, James & Pool, Suzanne - WHO FINANCED HITLER. New York: 1978.
Ponsonby, Sir Frederick (editor) - THE LETTERS OF THE EMPRESS FREDERICK. London :
             1929.
Pope-Hennessy, James - QUEEN MARY. New York: 1960.
von Preussen, Prinz Friedrich Wilhelm - DAS HAUS HOHENZOLLERN 1918-1945. Munich: 1986.
von Preussen, Prinz Louis Ferdinand - THE REBEL PRINCE. New York: 1952.
                          - IN STROM DER GESICHTE. Munich: 1983.
von Preussen, Prinz Michael - EIN PREUSSENPRINZ ZU SEIN. Munich: 1986.
Rose, Kenneth - KING GEORGE V. London: 1983.
Roumania, Princess Ileana - I LIVE AGAIN. New York: 1952.
Roumania, Queen Marie - THE STORY OF MY LIFE. 3 volumes. New York and London: 1934-5.
Russia, Grand Duke Cyril - MY LIFE IN RUSSIA'S SERVICE. London: 1939.
Ruvigny, Marquis of - THE TITLED NOBILITY OF EUROPE. London: 1914.
St. Aubyn. Giles - EDWARD VII: PRINCE AND KING. London: 1979.
Sinclair, Andrew - ROYAL WEB. New York: 1982.
Sulzberger, C.L. - FALL OF EAGLES. New York: 1976.
Summers, Anthony & Magnold, Tom - THE FILE ON THE TSAR. New York: 1976.
Thornton, Michael - ROYAL FEUD. London: 1985.
Tjerneld, Staffan - 'DARLING DAISY' EN BOK OM KRONPRINSESSAN MARGARETA AV SVERIGE.
             Stockholm: 1981.
van der Kiste, John - FREDERICK III. Gloucester: 1981.
                - QUEEN VICTORIA'S CHILDREN. Gloucester: 1986.
van der Kiste John & Jordaan, Bee - DEAREST AFFIE; ALFRED, DUKE OF EDINBURGH, QUEEN
VICTORIA'S SECOND SON. London: 1984.
Warwick, Christopher - PRINCESS MARGARET. London: 1983.
Weintraub, Stanley - QUEEN VICTORIA. New York: 1987.
Wheeler-Bennett, John W. - KING GEORGE V; HIS LIFE AND REIGN. London: 1958.
Whittle, Tyler - THE LAST KAISER. London: 1977.
Windsor, Duchess of - THE HEART HAS ITS REASONS. London: 1956.
Windsor, HRH Duke of - A KING'S STORY. New York: 1951.
Woodham-Smith, Cecil - QUEEN VICTORIA: FROM HER BIRTH TO THE DEATH OF THE PRINCE
             CONSORT. New York: 1972.
Yugoslavia, Queen Alexandra - FOR A KING'S LOVE. London: 1956.
                - PRINCE PHILIP. New York: 1959.
Yugoslavia, King Peter - A KING'S HERITAGE. London: 1955.
Ziegler, Philip - MOUNTBATTEN. New York: 1985.

Princess Alexander of Teck (Princess Alice, Countess of Athlone), with two of her children, May and Rupert (Author's collection.)